George Timothy Hudson, born 11 February 19
Manchester, should, by all the rules of inheritan
and unblemished life as a cotton merchant: mi
respected.

Instead he became cricketer (for Lancashire and Surrey second cleven,
leading DJ in Hollywood, rock and roll promoter, discoverer of The Moody
Blues, launcher (in California) of Flower Power, Los Angeles property
owner, builder, renovator, innovator and restaurateur, the intended spouse
of Dean Martin's daughter, husband of four, lover of many, Ian Botham's
friend and business adviser, owner of a Cheshire mansion and of a private
adjoining cricket pitch: a man constantly effervescent with plans and
projects.

He has been both penniless and rich, not once, but several times. He has
suffered the slings of outrageous fortune but invariably volleyed them back.

Men invariably do not take to him easily; women have been known to
take to him too easily. He has the raffish air of a latter-day Errol Flynn (in
whose house he once lived).

His cotton merchant stepfather told him not to run with too fast a
crowd. Hudson ran with the fastest. His stepfather said a man should
appear in newspapers only three times in his life: when he was born, when
he married and when he died. Hudson has figured in headlines all his life.

He is the black sheep who ended up richer than the white, flew the skull
and cross-bones flag at his Cheshire home together with that of the
Republic of California, entertains a stream of diverse visitors, and goes back
to California (where he has two homes) with his New Yorker wife, Maxi,
when the weather turns cold. A Californian showbiz agent described him
'Hollywood's untold legend', thus missing the chance of telling it. Now,
Hudson has written his own book From The Beatles to Botham to show
how the legend unfolds.

*Many of those who come to my door are clear-headed on arrival, but confused upon exit –
particularly those who have to write about my life.*

*Nothing connects, you see. My life seems logical enough to me in its progression from
Lancashire textiles to cricket, to rock and roll, to DJ, to property, back to DJ, to real estate,
back to cricket, back to textiles, back to Lancashire (the club) and Cheshire (the county),
taking in along the way four wives, cannabis, LSD, mescaline, a couple of homes in California
and a couple of homes in Britain. It is totally baffling to everyone else.*

*To compound the confusion, I have been young tycoon, sartorial Beatle, Errol Flynn, honest
craftsman, squire, poet, hippie, lover and guru. Compressed in the fashion of newspapers this
makes little sense; it is as if they write about a dozen different people. And since they are
confused, viewers and readers are also confused. I hope I am now dispelling the mystery with
some success.*

Tim Hudson

This book is dedicated to my wives,
lovers and friends, but above all
to Maxi – the one who made it happen.

FROM THE BEATLES TO BOTHAM

and all the b...s... in between

Tim Hudson

Foreword by John Bellany, A.R.A.

G2 entertainment

RETRO CLASSICS
is a collection of facsimile reproductions
of popular bestsellers from the 1980s and 1990s

From The Beatles to Botham was first published in hardback in 1990
by Lennard Books Ltd

Re-issued in 2014 as a Retro Classic
by G2 Entertainment

Copyright © Timothy Hudson 1990

ISBN 978-1-78281-096-4

Designed by Pocknell & Co
Jacket Illustration by Peter Sutton
Cover design by Pocknell & Co

Printed and bound by Lightning Source

CONTENTS

for TIM HUDSON

MAN of JOY

best wishes

John

MORNING, MR TIMOTHY

—

Around the year 1959 a curious ritual was to be observed at Prestbury railway station in Cheshire, that area of the county known to newspapers then, and now, however erroneously, as 'the stockbroker belt of Manchester'.

Henry B. Hudson, my stepfather, and I would be off to our work at the cotton firm of Richard Hudson and Sons Ltd in the city's Newton Street. I was 19, fresh out of public school. I always walked three paces behind, and invariably referred to him as 'Sir'.

'Morning, Mr Hudson [this to my stepfather]. Those geraniums were marvellous at the show. I don't think you should have taken second place.'

I to my third-class compartment to read Swanton in the *Daily Telegraph*, he to his first-class compartment to read the *Daily Mail*.

At the office – 'Morning, Mr Henry. Morning, Mr Timothy.' 'Morning, Beckers.' Desks with stools all the way along. Big invoice books. Scratchy dip pens. Deference, pride, service, quality and arrogance all had a home here. 'Thank you for your letter of the 3rd inst … We [never I] thank you for your business. Yours faithfully, Henry B. Hudson.'

For him, I was to send out countless invoices in countless brown manilla envelopes, the envelopes embossed in small type with the name of the firm. Our forte was shirtings, interlinings and bra fabrics. Scratch, scratch, dip, dip, and home to that merchant-class house with

1940 | 1941 | 1942 | 1943 | 1944

1940

THE BEGINNING OF THE BRAVE NEW WORLD

THE FABULOUS FORTIES

MUSIC

When You Wish Upon A Star . . . Pinocchio.
Beat Me Daddy Eight to the Bar . . . Andrews Sisters.
We'll Meet Again . . . Vera Lynn.
Fantasia . . . I still play the soundtrack.
Sinatra joined the Benny Goodman Orchestra.

MOVIES

Castle on the Hudson . . . John Garfield (died, too much booze and drugs).
Best movie . . . Rebecca with James Stewart.
Grapes of Wrath . . . Henry Fonda.

EVENTS

Germany invades Denmark.

1941

SONGS

American Patrol . . . Glenn Miller.
The White Cliffs of Dover . . . Vera Lynn.
Silent Night . . . Bing Crosby.
Lili Marlene . . . Marlene Dietrich.

MOVIES

How Green Was My Valley.
High Sierra.
The Sea Wolf.
Sgt York.

EVENTS

Hello Pearl Harbor and the Japanese . . . Good Morning.
Joe Dimaggio . . . Where Are You . . . Superman.
Joe Louis . . . The Brown Bomber . . . Bang Bang, Shot You Right Down.

1942

SONGS

Chattanooga Choo Choo . . . Glenn Miller.
Yi Yi Yi Yi (I Like You Very Much) . . . Carmen Miranda.

MOVIES

Casablanca.
They Died With Their Boots On . . . Errol Flynn.
Yankee Doodle Dandy.
Mrs Miniver . . . Greer Garson . . . She always reminded me of my Aunt Molly . . . even when I met the great lady.

1943

SONGS

Coming In On A Wing And A Prayer . . . Anne Shelton.
People Will Say We're In Love . . . Oklahoma . . . The first original cast album.
Besame Mucho.
Jingle Bells . . . Andrews Sisters . . . Bing Crosby.
Pistol Packin' Mama.

MOVIES

For Whom The Bell Tolls.
The Outlaw . . . the bra 38DD . . . the wire job . . . the first sexy picture I remember.

EVENTS

Don't forget the Blonde Bombshell herself . . . the one inside all the American guys' lockers . . . Betty Grable.

1944

SONGS

Swinging On A Star . . . Bing Crosby.
Begin The Beguine . . . You'll Never Know . . . Dick Haymes . . . didn't he marry Rita Hayworth?
Into Each Life Some Rain Must Fall . . . Ella . . . the lady . . . weren't The Inkspots in here somewhere?

MOVIES

Arsenic And Old Lace.
To Have And To Have Not.

its conservatory, lawn at the front, swishing drive, and two and a half acres of garden.

We were neither snobs nor aristocrats, but my stepfather had the impeccable dress and the withdrawn looks of a man to the manor born. He was the archetypal boss's son and I do not think he ever did a day's real work in his life. He did not have A Job. He had A Station. At the office he read the *Mail*, *Express* and *Times* and had his coffee, looked at this or that, then lunched at the Queen's Hotel in the city centre close by. Returning, he would make a couple of bets, and catch the train home at twenty-past four.

He never made a business trip. He refused to sell because it would have offended his dignity to think of himself as a salesman. His shirts were superbly tailored as befitted someone of reputation in the shirting business; he wore gold cuff-links; the suit was a fit companion for the shirt; his shoes were highly polished; and he had enjoyed The Regiment (Cavalry) in wartime because he spent a great deal of it playing polo in Poona and eating well without having the indignity of seeing action.

He never beat me, although he was stern in the home. There was an arrogance about him. When he drank with friends in the pub on Friday nights and returned, loud in voice, and a little unsteady, I found him not entirely to my liking. He was yellow socks and Parker pens, old school tie and white Jaguar, a man who invariably said, 'No', and he was all that I am not. He was to leave me out of his will.

This, then, was the life that had been charted for me and if my stepfather's plans had persisted, it would have gone to its entirely managed, and entirely predictable end.

Did he ever – I wonder – have any inkling that I had been known to my schoolfriends as Hudders, or as Hampton Hartley Hooter Hudson (Hampton for the pecker, hooter for the nose, Hartley for heaven knows what)? Could he ever have conceived the strange things that had already happened to me as a result of assignations planned or accidental with ladies much older than myself? Did he know that, far from dreaming of occupying his office chair, and taking his place for lunch at the Queen's Hotel, I had, when asked at school my intentions for my future, replied: 'Gentleman cricket player'?

Could he, in the ledger columns of his mind, have seen me as

principal disc jockey in Hollywood? As a Los Angeles property
developer? As a contemporary and close observer of both The Beatles
and Rolling Stones? As creator and part-owner of a restaurant on Sunset
Strip? As the intended husband of Dean Martin's daughter or the actual
husband of four women? As discoverer of The Moody Blues or the
author of Flower Power? As a penniless adventurer? As a millionaire?
As manager of Ian Botham? As contender for the chairmanship of
Lancashire County Cricket Club – that club which, at one time, gave me
space as a second-eleven player? As a player of stock markets? As a
purveyor of dreams?

Could he see me, after a quarter of a century in California,
returning to buy the mansion so close to the Cheshire home of my
youth; the mansion in which I now live for the warmer parts of the
year, with its own cricket field and tennis court and outdoor swimming
pool – against all his predictions and expectations?

I think not. Nor would he have conceived my two homes in
California. Such imaginings had no place in the first-class compartment
of a gentleman aware of his place in a reliable and largely unchanging
environment and satisfied with his lot. I was the rebel, the renegade, the
adventurer who, by common consent, would do no good. And he was
none of these.

For the time being it was enough that the pens were scratching and
that the manilla envelopes were making their regular progression to the
outside world where the name of Richard Hudson and Sons Ltd had
earned its respect. The business had been started by the family in 1827.

At school, I excelled at sport. I do not think I ever sounded
Lancastrian. My mother was determined that I would have the best, and
appear to be the best.

She would take a C & A label from my jacket and substitute a
Kendal Milne (the Harrods of the North) label (a fact of life which now
embarrasses her and amuses me). Through Henry Hudson she had lifted
herself from the poorer side of town and carried out the wish of her
dead flying-officer husband. 'My son,' he had said, 'will go to public
school.' I wanted to be somebody. I suppose my mother had instilled in
me the idea that I had to be. When I got my colours for soccer at prep
school I had taken the first step. A boy who got his colours felt wanted

and successful. For the first time in life, I had been rewarded for my own effort.

I have always been highly conscious of style and colour in clothes and surroundings. I was to adopt, as my symbol, a flower with petals of black, yellow, red and green and these colours were to dominate the decoration of my homes and other possessions.

I wore pyjama tops as shirts at the age of eight because they had vivid colours: blues, reds, yellows. I wore bright yellow or turquoise socks, and short shorts. The socks were rolled over my ankles. I had long, tanned legs.

Earlier in life than most, I developed an abiding love for women which has remained with me. Sailing the *Queen Elizabeth* on the great Atlantic crossing of '48 with my mother, I had my first erotic experience. I had teamed up with two girls aged 18 or 19 and remember one of them raising her foot to a bunk. Her skirt fell back. She was big, strong, healthily English, and her appearance suggested the sharp thwack of hockey-sticks but she was attractive. I could not believe that this thigh, so revealed, was so big compared with me. Climbers scale mountains Because They Are There. I had much the same attitude towards thighs. A friend's sister took me to an air-raid shelter and, again, it is the memory of a large thigh that remains. Sex, I was discovering, is not what matters. What matters are the incidents surrounding it. She wore, I remember, pink knickers.

I played the role of prep schoolboy to perfection. 'Goodbye father. Thank you for a marvellous Christmas. Yes, I will write twice a week, mother...' as the train pulled out of Victoria Station in Manchester bound for the Cumbrian coast and halting frequently.

It was on a train, at the age of 13, that curiosity about women got the better of me. I was travelling in one of those carriages with four seats at each side and with pictures of Llandudno and Rhyl framed above them, all faded. English railway coaches of the period were built as if for sustained siege. They had strong leather straps on the windows which could be operated by strong people sound in wind and limb. They were self-contained and corridors had no part of their function.

If you stuck your head out of the window you got an eye full of

1945 | 1946 | 1947 | 1948 | 1949

1945

SONGS

Accent The Positive.
The Trolley Song.
Don't Fence Me In.
There Goes That Song Again.
You Always Hurt the One You Love.
We'll Gather Lilacs.
Money Is the Root of All Evil.

MOVIES

The Lost Weekend ... Ray Milland.
Objective Burma ... Errol ... where are you ... England needs you.
God is my Co-pilot.

1946

SONGS

Give Me Five Minutes More.
Let It Snow.
I'm Always Chasing Rainbows.
McNamara's Band.
Let Bygones Be Bygones.
The Coffee Song.
Cement Mixer (putty putty).

MOVIES

The Big Sleep.
The Best Years of Our Lives ... Jimmy Stewart.
My Darling Clementine.
Citizen Kane ... Orson Welles ... the Renaissance man of his time.

1947

SONGS

Open the Door Richard ... Louis Jordan ... the first Rock and Roll singer.
Dance Ballerina Dance.
Alexander's Ragtime Band.

MOVIES

Duel in the Sun.
Kiss of Death.

EVENTS

Babe Ruth retired ... (Maxi told me that).

1948

SONGS

Buttons and Bows ... Dinah Shore.
Mañana ... Edmundo Ros.
All I Want For Christmas Is My Two Front Teeth.
La Vie En Rose.

MOVIES

Red Shoes.
Key Largo.
The Treasure of Sierra Madre.
Red River.
Hamlet.
Johnny Belinda ... Jane Wyman won an Oscar for that one ... isn't she Reagan's ex-?

1949

SONGS

Rudolph The Red Nosed Reindeer.
Riders in the Sky.
'A' You're Adorable.
I've Got a Lovely Bunch of Coconuts.
Dem Bones ... that was Rock and Roll to me.

MOVIES

South Pacific ... the musical ... My Mom saw it at the Opera House.
All the King's Men.

grit. They huffed and puffed and ran to the precise time of a turnip watch kept in the well-polished black serge of an official waistcoat.

I was wearing my maroon school blazer, and heading for Seascale Preparatory School. My companion was a stranger, a lady with a tartan rug covering her legs. My hand went under the rug and under the dress, and it was no sudden impulse. No words were spoken and I had no invitation beyond that of inaction on her part. She did not stop me. She continued to read her book. I slowly moved my hand to her thigh and satisfied my curiosity at leisure (the journey took five and a half hours). She rewarded me with a sandwich for lunch.

I was centre-forward for the school soccer team. Kids would be vicious and rude to each other and a boy – with my background – became better than them because he said: 'I'm going to kick hell out of you when I get you out there.' It worked well. I was co-ordinated and tough. I scored five goals against one team and three against another. I had a little letter F to stitch on my pocket to denote football and C for cricket, but nothing to denote conquests in trains, which I now rated a rewarding sport in my private curriculum.

After Seascale came Strathallan, a public school in Scotland. I enjoyed Strathallan and Scotland and was in the first eleven cricket squad for five years, so I literally never had a hard time.

It was the first time I realised that males got jealous of each other. I was in the first squad at 14, the first summer I came from prep school and went straight into senior colts. I did not have very long to be a child. The headmaster said, 'Hudson, I hear you are good with your hands (a tribute to my prowess behind the stumps rather than with ladies). How would you like to keep wicket?' I said, 'Yes', on the principle that one never argues with headmasters, and so, at 15, I was keeping wicket for the first team which meant that I was in a classroom with the lower fourth, playing cricket with the upper sixth and wearing the school colours. My friends were saying, 'We don't want to hang about with you.' There, I observed hurtful and unaccustomed jealousy. I cruised through school although it became obvious that I was the opportunist and sportsman rather than an academic. I ended with two O-levels and unbounded faith in my future. My concept was to work for the family firm and spend the summer playing for Lancashire. There

15

were still amateurs and professionals. My hero, Jack Ikin, walked tallest in my imagination.

And enter the family firm I did, at 18, just out of boarding school.

'Morning, Mr Henry. Morning, Mr Timothy.' I was working on the mail desk sending out invoices and going to Salford Technical College at night to study business administration and textile design. I was top in my first term but all I wanted to do was sell. There were advantages to that. I wanted the office car. I had it at week-ends occasionally, but not often. There was one company car, a big Austin with lots of chrome, but when I persuaded them to let me loose on the outside world they sent me on a train with two brown suitcases containing samples of sheets and pillow-cases.

I went to Bradford. I had a starched collar. I visited a wholesaler.

'Vot do you vant, boy? Nineteen-forty-seven was the last time one of you people came in.'

I got my first order: 12 pairs of sheets, assorted colours. My prices were probably higher than other people's and I will never forget that first sale. I had free lunches, on expenses. That was exciting: better than sitting in an office. Lancashire County Cricket Club did not send for me. I played for Prestbury, had my fair share of fifties, and in winter I played rugby. I was an all-round Jock working for daddy.

But life was not without incident. I had a party at the family home remembered by people to this day. My mother and father had gone away and I invited hookers, strippers, débutantes, equestrian ladies, and this strange cocktail produced 200 to 250 cars. The police arrived and I said: 'I can't do anything about it.' One guest was a frightfully-frightfully sort of chap, brushed-back hair, very clipped, Guards or something; and there was a famous stripper with huge mammaries upon which she wore tassels. Every adventurous businessman in Manchester had sneaked off at lunch-time to see her exercise her professional talents. I retain this vision of him erect, reserved, impeccable, eyeballs popping at these enormous breasts. All this outside the front door of this very English house, this fine Prestbury home in 'the stockbroker belt' of Manchester in Cheshire. She was wearing a black cocktail dress with no top. It was like the Queen observing Marilyn Monroe for the first time. Mahomet had met his mountain, discovering a facet of life he found barely credible.

I went to Liverpool to see people from Great Universal Stores and called at a café named The Jackaranda in a back street where there was rock and roll at lunch-time. Espresso coffee. Downstairs, a cellar. I was wearing a striped shirt with stiff, starched, white cut-away collar, old school tie, cuff-links, dark suit, waistcoat and black brogue shoes. The place was full of people in black leather. They had greasy hair and were art students. A guy next to me had so many rings on his fingers I lost count and he said, 'Hello – will you buy me a coffee? I play drums for Rory Storm and the Hurricanes. My name is Ringo Starr. See those fellows over there? The Beatles. They're good friends of mine.' Of course I would buy him a coffee. I was on expenses. It was September,1959. I was to go back a few times after that.

When my stepfather decided to visit Sweden I went with him and we took the boat from Harwich to the Hook of Holland. As we were getting off we saw a dirty old van and the lads in it said, 'Hey, it's the fellow from Manchester. How are you?' The Beatles were on their way to the top. They were talking about amps and in those days I did not know what an amp was.

Our paths were to cross again in life, but in the meantime my stepfather said, 'Who are these disreputable people?'

Two worlds had collided in mutual incomprehension. I was to make them both my own.

EARLY TIMES

—

I remember going to New Brighton with my mother and my Aunt Kate who was very influential in my mother's life and mine. She was a spiritualist. They took me to this restaurant and I kept saying, 'Where's the ocean?' I thought the ocean was upstairs. I had never seen it ... I must have been three. We got home, we were living with my aunt at the time, in Whalley Range and there was a telegram behind the door and it stated that my father, Thomas Brumwell, had been killed in action during a Bomber Command raid over Belgium. They were preparing for D Day. I don't really remember him as a father ... once he hoisted me above his shoulders with his uniform on. I remember the wings on his jacket.

He used to send my mother records and on these records he would say, 'We are going to live in America. When the war is over we are going to go to America. I am going to get an airline company or something. I'm going to fly aeroplanes in America...' He kept mentioning America because the RAF pilots during the war were trained in Canada. I have taken a slagging sometimes in the papers where mean people have stated that I am not a Hudson ... that my mother married a Hudson. I laugh at that because, if anything, the Brumwells were much more established, gentlemen farmers from Grantham, than the Hudsons. My grandfather was an Alderman. He was head of the parish council. He lived to be a hundred and one. He was a gentleman farmer. He must have been very wealthy because he had a train, a real small-gauge railway, going around his estate. I remember getting on that train and being taken for this trip around the estate.

My father, Thomas Brumwell, was captain of the cricket team at Lincoln School and later he trained as an accountant. He didn't like that. I don't think he got on too well with his mother and he ran away from home and joined Manchester police force. He joined because, I think, he knew he would be able to play soccer or cricket. He was in the force for seven years. Apparently, in Bootle Street in Manchester, there is a war memorial with my father's name on it.

My dad didn't have to join up, because police were exempt from national service, but he wanted to be a flier. After his demise, I remember several things between the ages of five and eight. Twice I went to America. I went on the *Queen Mary, The Aquitania.* I think my mother had a short-lived romance with a Canadian flier ... or was he a movie star?

My mother had known Henry Broughton Hudson before she knew my father. My mother always tells me stories about how, when she was sixteen and Henry was thirty-two, he would take her to Manchester races and he would turn up in his white Jaguar, with the big headlights, with his golf clubs in the back seat and his yellow socks ... his suede shoes. The funny thing is that my aunt used to tell me that Henry Hudson was really my father and I got really confused with this one. My aunt told me this when I went to stay with her in Montreal. My aunt, I was later to find out, had a few nervous breakdowns and had been known to play her own 'theatre of the mind'. I still think that Thomas Brumwell was my father. One only has to look at the pictures of him and you will see it.

But my aunt told me this famous story of how Thomas Brumwell came in to see the midwife and the fact is that my mother had known Henry Hudson in 1938–39. There was obviously a lot of discussion between Thomas Brumwell, Henry Hudson and my mother at that time ... but my mother married Thomas Brumwell about three months before I was born, I think. The ironical part was that Henry Hudson told me that I was born in the Collar House at Prestbury.

Squadron Leader Thomas Brumwell was killed in action with Bomber Command pulling the gliders for the D-day landings in 1944.

On my trips to America, I remember New York ... Madison

19

1950 | 1951 | 1952 | 1953 | 1954

SINGERS

Sinatra
Johnny Ray
Guy Mitchell . . .
Just opening up
the decade.
Johnny Mathis
. . . Names of the
time.
Pat Boone
Fats Domino
Doris Day
Frankie Laine
David Whitfield
. . . Cara Mia
Mine.
Frankie Vaughan
. . . Green Door.

MOVIES

Panic in the
Streets.
All About Eve.
Asphalt Jungle.
Broken Arrow.
Annie Get Your
Gun . . . The
Palace.
Elizabeth Taylor
. . . marries the
Hilton
Sunset Boulevard.

Churchill re-
elected . . . do
you remember it?
The preparatory
school, the public
school and the
varsity produce
the kind of fellow
who is a scarcity
. . . where does
he learn to ask a
chorus girl to
dine . . . where
does he learn to
spot the girl who
does?
This was one of
a collection of my
Dad's 78s from a
cupboard that
had been there
since before the
war . . . that I
found one
Sunday
afternoon.
Another song I
recall was Take
Your Hands Off
My Nylons.

MOVIES

Streetcar Named
Desire . . .
Brando.
Singing In The
Rain.

Doris Day . . . the
all-American girl
next door.
Alma Cogan . . .
Eve Boswell . . .
Dinah Shore.
Elvis . . . where
are you?
I was a fan of
Frankie Laine . . .
The Midnight
Gambler . . . Cool
Water.
Wasn't there
something about
Laramie recorded
by Jimmy Young?

MOVIES

African Queen
. . . Bogart . . .
Hepburn . . .
wonderful.
High Noon . . .
Gary Cooper.

Marilyn Monroe
. . . Jane Russell
. . . Gentlemen
Prefer Blondes.
Vat 69 . . .
quality tells.
Julius Caesar . . .
Brando again.
Quo Vadis.
Shane . . .
remember Alan
Ladd.
Maltesers . . .
have a Capstan
. . . they are
made to make
friends . . . Ponds'
and Cadbury's
commercials.
Liquorice and
Blackcurrant and
Spearmint were
my favorite
sweets.

MOVIES

On the
Waterfront . . .
Brando Brando
Brando . . . Eva
Marie Saint.
Animal Farm.
A Star Is Born.
Dial M For
Murder.
Hondo . . . John
Wayne.

1955

1956

1957

1958

1959

Where were you in '55???

MUSIC

Bill Haley . . . Rock Around The Clock.
Chuck Berry . . . Maybelline.
Bo Diddley . . . Bo Diddley.

HAPPENINGS

Alan Freed coined the term Rock and Roll.
Jive and Be-bop dancing.
Sex symbols . . . Brigitte Bardot . . . Marilyn Monroe.
Kerouac and Ginsberg were the writers.

MOVIES

Blackboard Jungle . . .
The Wild One . . . B.R.A.N.D.O.
Rebel Without a Cause . . . James Dean.

FASHION

Teddy Boys.
Brothel creepers.
Blue suede shoes.
Motor cycle jackets and tight jeans.

MUSIC

Elvis . . . Heartbreak Hotel.
Gene Vincent . . . Be-Bop-a-Lula.
Bill Haley . . . See You Later Alligator.
Little Richard . . . Long Tall Sally.
Platters . . . The Great Pretender.

MOVIES

Love Me Tender . . . Elvis.
Jailhouse Rock . . . Elvis.
The Girl Can't Help It . . . Gene Vincent.

All Shook Up . . . Elvis.
Wake Up Little Susie . . . Everly Brothers.
Whole Lotta Shakin' Goin' On . . . Jerry Lee Lewis.
Peggy Sue . . . Buddy Holly.

MOVIES

High School Confidential.
And God Created Woman . . . Brigitte Bardot.

HAPPENINGS

I left school.
Captain of cricket.
Flunked nearly all my O-levels except two, English Lit and History.
Stereo comes on the popular market for the first time.

MUSIC

Bird Dog . . . Everly Brothers.
At the Hop . . . Danny and the Juniors.
Sweet Little Sixteen . . . Chuck Berry.
Peggy Sue . . . The Everly Brothers.
Fever . . . Peggy Lee.
Chantilly Lace . . . Big Bopper.
Rebel Rouser . . . Duane Eddy.

MOVIES

Black Orpheus . . . (Brazilian film) . . . sexy . . . hot.

Started working for the good old family business.
Good morning, Mr Henry.
Good morning, Mr Tim.

MUSIC

Till I Kissed Ya . . . Everly Brothers.
Mack the Knife . . . Bobby Darin.
Deck of Cards . . . Wink Martindale . . . (I worked with him on KFWB in '65).
Venus . . . Frankie (Beach Blanket Bingo) Avalon.

MOVIES

Room at the Top . . . Lawrence Harvey . . . sexy North of England, man . . . Simone Signoret . . . a real black bra French madame . . . 2 buttons undone . . . the earth-coloured silk blouse.

TV

Dragnet . . . with my Man Friday.

21

Square Garden, Empire State Building. The snow, I had a parka. Then, for a very short time, I was sent to a boarding school in Harrogate. I enjoyed it, I remember, I think it was like an orphanage for children whose parents had been killed in the war. I went there for a short time, then I was rushed onto one of those American trips, then I came back. In the meantime my mother had pensions from the RAF and from the Manchester Police and I was sent to APS, Altrincham Preparatory School. I went there for about two or three years. At this same time, my mother, being a widow, was given one of the new flats on Flotsall Road, Wythenshaw. We were the first people ever to move into this new flat ... it was upstairs, I don't remember the number. I remember having a really nice time there.

I remember my friends. We used to play cricket against the posts. We used to go and start fires at the school they were building at the back. We used to molest girls together. The usual things that kids do. I remember running across the bridge to the other side, to the sweet shop near the Co-op. We would buy a quarter of sweets, they were rationed at that time and we used to have to wait until the first day of the month to get our sweet coupons. I remember the fair. My mother was working at a doctor's. I only remember two schoolfriends from that era. One was David Morrison, the well-known real-estate agent, now deep-sea fisherman, and also a doctor called George Burns, good hockey player and not bad at rugby either.

So I did all the normal things that a seven-year-old would do. I had that little maroon blazer, maroon cap with APS on it in white lettering. A satchel. I had terrible trouble reading. I couldn't read. I was good at looking at pictures but I couldn't get into this reading trip.

Just around this time, 1947, Henry Hudson started coming round to our little flat in Wythenshaw. He came in a Triumph Roadster. Again, golf clubs in the back, yellow socks, suede shoes and a dickie seat. And the next thing I knew mother and Henry Hudson were getting married and my sister, Barbara, was born. My name was changed to George Timothy Hudson. I was rushed off to live in Macclesfield Road, Hazel Grove. Opposite the Five Ways pub. I was sent to the Junior school in Hazel Grove. Marbles, conkers ... all those kind of things ... the smelly toilets, the whole thing. But that was

only for a short time, and I was whisked off to Seascale Preparatory
School on the coast of Cumberland. I was nine. Off I went to boarding
school for three glorious years. My parents moved to a big house in
Prestbury, Cheshire. By this time I was well and truly Timothy
Hudson. I was playing centre-forward for the school soccer team. I was
in the cricket team. I remember taking five wickets for eleven runs
against Harecourt, our local rivals.

My academic grades were not that good enough for me to go to
Sedburgh, so my headmaster, Mr Burnett of Seascale, decided that I
should go to Strathallan. He knew I would fit in there.

So began my trip. I filled in a form when I left Strathallan that
asked what I wanted to do. I said that I wanted to work for the family
cotton business during the winter and play as an amateur for Lancashire
and hopefully go on to captain that team. I still believe that those
dreams would have been fulfilled if, due to certain circumstances, my
happy family had not broken up.

So, a war-widow's little boy went from a council flat in
Wythenshaw ... to Hollywood, where he achieved the highest you can
achieve because everybody in the entertainment industry dreams of
working there. And, I suppose, living at Birtles Old Hall was the plinth
of what is called the abode of everybody's dream.

But success is not to hold onto something. It is to taste it, and to
achieve. It is not to be married to the most beautiful women in the
world. It is to have known the most beautiful women in the world.
Within my temperament ... it is the challenge that matters. The
impossible dream. Which I achieved. I have nothing to hide. The reason
I fight the establishment, as we call them, is that they are not really
interested in people, they are only interested in themselves. I am more
interested in the people. The system needs revamping ... totally.

I KNOW THESE GUYS

—

Until the age of 19 I had played the role of public schoolboy but now there were sweeter mysteries to be explored. I had sneaked into a Continental cinema in Manchester during the school holidays and decided that the woman I really wanted to seduce or be seduced by was Martine Carol. It was my fantasy. I knew housewives and mothers in Prestbury and had hidden in a few cupboards in my time. There were many bored housewives when I was growing up and it was marvellous fun. A dozen red roses next day. A card. I asked my mother later whether she knew about these escapades and she said: 'Of course.'

My real fascination was with the French way of life. Two of my four wives have been very French (one was Swiss-German but had lived in Paris for much of her life). And it found its first physical form with Arlette. Arlette was a doctor's *au pair*.

In the summer of 1960 I had moved into a flat in Manchester's Rusholme and a whole new world was revealed. My parents had decided to get divorced. I had sided with both and was getting nowhere.

Arlette was the sweetness beyond this pain. She was 26, a gymnast, and she did not need to wear clothes. They did not do her justice. She should never have worn them at all. Those she did wear were simple and beautiful and she was my first real love. I was fit, rugby-fit, cricket-fit, popular with girls. For the first time in my life I was able to walk on the wild side.

1960

Scored over two thousand runs for Prestbury C.C. Won the batting prize.

SONGS

Cathy's Clown . . . Everly Brothers.

The Twist . . . Chubby Checker.
Only the Lonely . . . Roy Orbison.
Alley-oop . . . Hollywood Argyles.

TV

Have Gun Will Travel.

I discovered chorus girls and I had never before in my life met one.
I recall one with red-rouged face, aged 26 or 27, with two kids; bright
red hair. For her, it was tough going. She was one of many. There was
a rawness, a vibrancy, about these girls that appealed to me. I bedded
them all, top to bottom, with enthusiasm.

I discovered clubs. There was one called Guys and Dolls and a
cafe-bar named The Mogambo. I was Alain Delon at the time: I had the
hair-do and the anorak. I was one of the restless people who changed
character in a week according to whether I had read another book or
seen another film.

I walked into that club in a tweed suit, wearing suede shoes, and
stood in a corner for what seemed like hours. Five German *au pairs* were
sitting together. There was a pocket-sized dance floor. I must have
drunk half a dozen Cokes and I had entered Dante's *Inferno*. The public
school was gone. The old school tie could have been wrapped around
the nearest toilet and left for good. One German girl asked me to dance
and my confidence soared. I must subsequently have gone to bed with
every German girl at that table. I think I went to bed with every
nationality in Europe that summer. I had five different girls in one day.
That was my feat. I had a new toy and never realised I could use it so
much.

Meanwhile, in the summer of 1960 I scored so many runs for
Prestbury that I lost count. I was invited to join Lancashire County
Cricket Club as an amateur. I felt it was an honour. The family business
thought so. The business agreed to pay me £10 a week during the
summer. Lancashire were to pay me expenses and they were pretty
good. I was charging so much for this, so much for that – probably
another £10 a week – and I was making more than the club's legendary
Harry Pilling.

So there I was: cricket every day for Lancashire second eleven,
astounding my friends in my imagination when I went back to play
village cricket, and not exactly setting the world aflame. I think my
highest score was 38 not out against Staffordshire. By that time Jack
Ikin had retired and was captaining Staffordshire. I hit him for a huge
six – over his head and into the practice area. I remember thinking: I
have hit my hero out of the ground.

I kept wicket very well and also played as a batsman, but always thought I was unfairly treated. I was the gentleman. I was told that no amateur had kept wicket for Lancashire since the 1920s. The professionals did not like to bowl to an amateur keeping wicket. They had the feeling that he might drop a catch after tea if he were not playing for money.

I probably took the best catch I remember off Peter Lever, while playing against a Bermuda eleven at Old Trafford. The ball was heading high over the head of first slip but I somehow retrieved it. One of the watching members of the cricketing hierarchy complained to Lancashire that Hudson was not being given his proper chance.

At the end of summer, I decided to work in London; to try to get away from the seat of the family business in Manchester although I continued to work for the family firm. Stan Worthington, who was then coach at Lancashire, told me at the end of the season that, as I was going to London, he would arrange for me to be given a trial by Arthur McIntyre, the coach at Surrey County Cricket Club. I got myself a flat on the Chelsea embankment, sharing kitchen and bathroom. Television's Julian Pettifer had a room there; so did Ned Sherrin. I was in good company.

And into my life walked Alfie.

Autumn, 1961. I had a little red Mini; I was 21; and Alfie was to be my mentor. He was street-wise and he was shrewd. He knew the ropes of London and had one of the other rooms. He had one pin-striped suit, one pair of jeans, and he was the close companion of a lady-in-waiting to the Queen. Alfie had style. Alfie had confidence. Alfie knew it all and could do it all. Alfie had no money. Alfie said: 'Look, I know everybody in London. You've got your little car. I'll teach you the ropes. First thing you have to do is learn how to dance.'

He got me a long mirror for my room so that I could practise. He said, 'You've got to get into jazz. Miles Davis, Erroll Garner, Zoot Sims.' He took me to the New Establishment Club, downstairs. Lenny Bruce was upstairs doing his act. I saw Lenny Bruce so many times I

1961

Joined the
Lancashire CCC
staff for the
season.

MUSIC

Runaway . . . Del
Shannon.
Stand By Me . . .
Benny King.

Rubber Ball . . .
Bobby Vee.
Poetry in Motion
. . . Johnny
Tillotson.

HAPPENINGS

Surfing becomes
a fad.
Marijuana begins
to gain
popularity.
More Twist . . .
more Elvis.

could not believe it. One day I went to the bar and sat next to Liz Taylor and Richard Burton. The French wife of one of the biggest industrialists in England took me to her penthouse and reappeared wearing black silk underwear. I was so scared I must have made love in ten seconds. I expected her husband to crash through the door. 'Why so nervous?' she said. 'Where is your husband?' I replied. 'Oh,' she said, 'we have an understanding.' My growing-up was taking place.

I repaired my first deficiency with her many times. She is probably still opening the village fête.

Alfie had a little tailor in the East End and I had myself this black silk number made: narrow lapels, tight pair of hipsters, black Pinet boots, gingham shirt and a pink shirt from John Michael, black knitted tie. I smoked my first marijuana. You could walk down the King's Road and smoke a joint and nobody would even look at you. The Café des Artistes, the Kenya Coffee House, Peter Rachman, Mandy Rice Davies, the Nash brothers, the Krays all swam into my vision. I met everybody. Patti Boyd, George Harrison's wife, would arrive at the coffee house in a little white short bolero. I went to the cinema with her and she was a friend I did not even want to touch. I respected her as a very young and beautiful girl.

I flowed with life and did not want to get out of anything. I took a shine to Mandy Rice Davies at the time. I could not be seen going out of the Kenya Coffee House with her because Rachman was there. I remember walking one way while she walked the other. She drove round to my flat and I discovered that she wore knickers that cost £50. I had never seen anybody in silk knickers.

It was the time of Chubby Checker and Bobby Daren, Ronnie Scott's and the Flamingo. Georgie Fame was a big name. Rhythm and blues were starting to soar. Michael Caine was around. Terence Stamp was unknown. Chris Stamp was just hanging out three years before The Who.

In the summer of 1962 I was the beatnik cricketer of the coffee house in the King's Road. I was asked to keep wicket in the first game of the season for Surrey against the combined clubs of Surrey. I had been to a deb party that had gone on all night, had no sleep, and drove at

6.30 in the morning to The Oval, where I kept wicket. First ball, four byes. I was motionless. I did not even see it. I kept wicket all day. It was an arduous business and not very rewarding. But I went on to score 79, and as I walked into the pavilion, Peter May was sitting there with Boris Karloff, a strange communion for the time but one that matched the circumstances.

I had kept wicket like an ass and established myself as a batsman. I was in the position at Surrey that had existed in Lancashire, where the first team did not consider me, and the second team preferred to play me as a batsman rather than let me keep wicket. I made 40-odd against Warwickshire seconds, 50-odd against the Navy, and had quite a good season.

1962

Moved to Chelsea ... SW3.

MUSIC

Breaking Up Is Hard To Do ... Neil Sedaka. Twist and Shout ... Isley Brothers ... later The Beatles' big hit.

The Beatles begin ... Love Me Do ... Oct. 62.

HAPPENINGS

Locomotion ... The Mashed Potato ... dance craze. The Ad Lib club. Georgie Fame at the Flamingo club. The Crazy E.

Towards the end of summer, my mother gave me some money – two or three hundred pounds – and the possession of it unsettled me. I wanted to explore the South of France. I had never been there. I was confused about who and what I was. I knew someone who lived in Marseilles – one of the *au pair* girls from Manchester – and went to her house. Her father was something very grand, and I was the casual lad on the doorstep. She suggested I go to Cassis. I stayed in Cassis for two or three weeks and returned to England. My father's firm complained about my going for an extra week's holiday and the rot was in: I had felt it coming.

I told my mother I was going to live in France. I was off to the Sorbonne. There was a big party for me in Chelsea and on 1 January 1963, I departed. I had met people who said I could stay with them. God! I thought, I'm young and I have to get away. I lived for three months in Paris. I had no money. I cleaned Mini cars and that was the only employment I could find. I got a work card. Then a man who offered me a job reneged because I could not speak French well enough.

I hid away in a room at the top of a house. There was only cold water. I had packed loads of clothes which I never wore because I had no work. I was stranded. The family I lived with were becoming irritated by my being there but they did not want to throw me out.

They fed me three times a day. I either stayed in my room or walked. If I walked I was cold. For the first time in my life I did not meet anybody who could change the pattern of my existence. Nothing happened.

One day I had been out for dinner at the home of a girl friend and was returning on the Métro when I heard a woman speaking English. I was incredibly relieved. The suburb I lived in was French, French, French, and although I was learning the language well, hearing English was my liberation. Within four stops on the Métro I had told her my problems. I was broke – how did I get a job? Her husband was a diver in the South of France. She named a bar there – 'Walk in and tell them you are English and that you want a job on a boat as a deck hand cum steward.' I thumbed my way south, found the bar, spoke to the woman who ran it, and got a job from an Englishman.

So there I was, straightening out his boat, the sun on my back, shirt off, shorts on, earning 100 new francs a week, and my mind exploded: here were pink shorts, suntans and beautiful ladies. I became deck hand cum steward on several yachts.

We used to go off to little islands. And on one of these I found my great romance of the summer. I was walking on the beach, nobody in sight for miles, and into view came two people who appeared to be mother and son. I sat some distance from them and heard the boy speaking German. The mother was very attractive, mid-thirties, bronzed, with the German-Prussian look they try to capture in movies but rarely do. I talked with them. She was aloof. But she said, 'Would you like to play golf?' I did. I was the archetypal English gentleman again, picking balls from the holes for her. When we got to the last hole, she said: 'Would you like to escort me to a reception at the hotel this evening?' I said I would be delighted. I was the deck hand serving the food to people and there they were having coffee and liqueurs on the after deck, and this gorgeous Lancia open sports car with this matching Prussian woman arrived and I ran off to meet her. Again, the perfect English gentleman. The dance was at the country club attached to the golf club and that is where she was staying. My behaviour was frightfully English. When I later tried to kiss her, she smacked my face; no tap but a hard blow. Then she drove me somewhere on the

29

mountainside and we made love with a passion that exploded my mind. It was a battle. I was totally engrossed. She followed me to Cannes. I followed her to Munich. She followed me to London. Such was my summer romance.

Back in England, my mother said: 'What are you going to do now?' I was 23; I had no degree, and the future was blank. I applied for a job with the Prestige company and was interviewed at an hotel in East Lancashire. They had offices in London. I went out for dinner with an executive, knew the right fork to use, and got an offer: they would train me, send me to gain experience in their factories, and contemplated the possibility of my going to Harvard Business School.

The salary was good. I got a car. My mother was excited at my new, acceptably conventional, prospects, and I was back living in Chelsea.

Alfie, by this time, had married the daughter of an American film producer and was living in a flat by Buckingham Palace – an achievement which raised my eyebrows because I was still the naïve boy from the North. One evening, Alfie said: 'You are from near Liverpool, yes? Why don't you go up North and find another Beatles?' Back from France, I had found my sister – ten years younger than me – crazy about the group. Their first album was out. I had said, 'I know these guys.' She had said, 'Come off it.'

At that stage in my career with Prestige I was going on business training courses, market research things. I would go into a shop pretending I did not work for anybody and find out what was, or was not, selling. I went to East Lancashire, to one of the factories, and walked around in a white coat.

I had the London look. Someone came to me and said, 'We've got a group.' I said, 'Why are you talking to me?' He said, 'You are from EMI, aren't you?' He thought I was a record scout.

1963

Spent the year in Paris and the South of France.

MUSIC

Surf City . . . Ian and Dean. Heatwave . . . Martha and the Vandellas. The Crystals.

Little Red Rooster . . . Sam Cooke (later to be shot in a seedy L.A. motel).

HAPPENINGS

Beatles begin their rise in England. Kennedy assassinated in Nov.

I'm the Greatest . . . quote . . .

Cassius Clay. Bossa Nova . . . dance.

MOVIES

Dr No . . . the first James Bond film (Ursula Andress coming out of the ocean in that white bathing suit).

The group was the Ryan Brothers, or Ryan Express – something like that; they were friends of The Four Pennies, whose leader came from Blackburn. I made arrangements to meet their representative and waited for him outside the tube station at Sloane Square. He never turned up. About six months later they had a hit.

I went to Birmingham on a market research course and one night visited a club called The Moathouse. A group was singing *Bye Bye Birdie* and I was blown out by the music. Here were five members of five different groups and this was the first ten days of their performing as The Moody Blues. I said: 'I want to manage you. I am going to take you to London and make you stars.' I told Alfie. Alfie went to see them. Alfie made the mistake – from my point of view – of bringing in two sharp boys from the music business: Tony Sekunda and Alex Murray.

Here was my hero and my friend, the idol I thought knew it all, and he seemed to make fatal errors. He owned a company with a partner named Mickey Byrne and they had rights to The Beatles' name. They were making money all over the place. That business folded quite quickly but in the meantime Alfie convinced his associates to get behind The Moody Blues. So I think the money that went into renting The Moody Blues a flat – up above Kensington High Street – and buying new instruments came from Beatles money. Alfie, in the meantime, moved to Harley Street.

From being discoverer of The Moody Blues I was reduced to fan club secretary. I was given a contract promising me ten per cent of the net. Ten per cent of net in rock and roll is ten per cent of nothing.

The first record we cut for The Moody Blues was *Lose Your Money but Don't Lose Your Mind*. Our office boy at the time was Denny Cordell, who later was to produce Procul Harem's *A Whiter Shade of Pale*. Everybody slept in the office and that era still fascinates me. You can take the boy out of Prestbury but you cannot take Prestbury out of the boy.

The first plan we came up with was having homing-pigeons in boxes sent to the press. If you accepted the invitations to a conference the pigeons flew back. That was for the first Moody Blues party. We staged a party outside the Tower of London and got arrested.

Patti Boyd introduced met to Alan Freeman, the disc jockey. I went to his house in Maida Vale and the three of us went to see The Moody Blues perform their very first night at the Marquee Club in London. They were then booked into the Ad Lib Club. We popped a little upper, mother's little help (a Benny), into their beers as insurance and they did a marvellous show.

Everybody was living on petty cash. I remember the partners telling me I did not know enough about the business: it was probably better if I went and got a job with an agent.

In the meantime I had discovered Herman and the Hermits in Manchester through my friend, Charlie Silverman, later their manager. He said: 'Can you help my group in London?' The same two people Alfie had brought in went to the Grosvenor for tea with Charlie and this buck-toothed group leader, Peter Noone, and they walked through the men's room and kitchen, leaving behind the bill.

It would be a gross understatement to say that I was disillusioned as secretary of the fan club. The boys Alfie brought in got rid of me. I remember I could not afford a taxi. I had five pounds in the world and no job. I was the impresario with ten per cent of nothing walking down the road towards Victoria Station from Warwick Square and all I could think was: what am I going to tell my mother? I went back to my bedsitter above an antique shop on World's End corner and for a while I cleaned houses for Jewish families in North London for 2s 6d an hour, the hardest money I have ever earned. In my experience, cleaning toilet seats is not the world's best occupation: it may well be the worst.

A friend had contraceptive machines in pubs around London. I thought I might fill the machines for a while. But they were grotty

---

1964

In Oct. I went to Canada . . . started my radio career in Montreal.

MUSIC

Can't Buy Me Love . . . Beatles. Please Please Me. Pretty Woman . . . Roy Orbison. My Guy . . . Mary Wells. Little Children . . . Billy J. Kramer. Glad All Over . . . Dave Clark Five.

Baby Love . . . The Supremes. You Really Got Me . . . Kinks.

HAPPENINGS

Harold Wilson became Prime Minister. Beatles are on the Ed Sullivan TV show in USA. Johnson is President of USA . . . L.B.J. Vietnam War.

TV

Had to be . . . Top of the Pops . . .

with Cathy McGowan . . . I remember The Moody Blues getting on the show for the first time.

FASHION

Topless bathing suits.

MOVIES

Hard Day's Night . . . Beatles.

Remember those
Fairisle sweaters?

Those were the
days . . . aged 2.

Henry Broughton
Hudson.

My dad, 'Biggles'.

My mother was
considered the
most beautiful
woman in
Manchester.

Lord Tim. Aged 4.

The Behan clan in
Manchester, circa
1934.

It's me. L.T.,
Captain, 1st XI,
Strathallan, 1958.

STANDING (left to right): I. J. Willcox, B. D. C. Watts, H. Galt, D. C. Duncan,
W. M. S. Buchanan, C. P. Roselle, P. G. Wallace.
SEATING (left to right): A. W. Beattie, M. S. Jamieson, G. T. Hudson (Capt.).

Seascale
Preparatory
School, circa 1950.

CRICKET
CAPTAINS

1954 R.S.EASON	1970 A.D.G.DUNCAN
1955 J.G.CLARK	1971 A.B.WALKER
1956 J.G.CLARK	1972 J.H.R.PARKER
1957 W.R.GALBRAITH	
1958 G.T.HUDSON	
1959 I.J.WILLCOX	
1960 J.C.S.RANKIN	
1961 T.R.TAYLOR	
1962 A.J.HARVEY-WALKER	
1963 A.J.HARVEY-WALKER	
1964 D.N.STRACHAN	
1965 A.J.SLOAN	
1966 W.B.MELVILLE	
1967 C.J.W.MAUGHLINE	
1968 C.W.BALFOUR	
1969 S.S.ERIKSEN	

They wrote my
name on a wall at
Strathallan.

Lancashire Second
XI, Scarborough,
1961. Harry
Pilling, Colin
Hilton, Ken
Howard. Notice
the blazer.

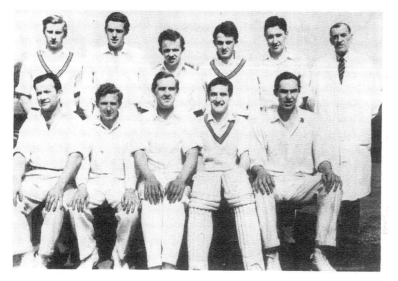

Prestbury CC, 1960. The best village side in town!

The Lancashire boys, 1961. L.T. somewhere among the famous.

First picture ever of The Moody Blues.

Still an all-time Top Ten favourite.

machines in awful places not so far removed from the johns of Jewish ladies and that was not my idea of gainful employment either.

The only person I knew well was Vic Lewis, the impresario. I had played showbiz cricket for his team. He offered me £5 a week to work for him. How was I going to live on that?

I learned about nepotism. You had to be related to somebody to break into that business. Chelsea was starting to come alive. I went to Brighton for a week-end and Radio Caroline came on for the very first time. Friends of mine were involved and they asked me whether I would like to be a DJ for £15 a week. And I said: '£15 a week to live on a boat?' I did not think of luxury liners. I thought of the *Titanic* and the British coming out with guns and warships.

People like John Michael, Mary Quant, Kikki Byrne, Ossie Clarke were coming to life and the mini-look of England was becoming a style. The Beatle haircut was a French style, Prince Valiant, brushed so that it flopped. It was also an English prep school look. There were Pierre Cardin jackets, Tom Jones shoes and Chelsea boots – which were really old Pinet boots. Carnaby Street lived.

The Ad Lib Club was the place to be seen. P.J. Proby, The Animals, The Kinks ... Tom Jones would never have had his chance if it had not been for Proby ripping his pants. An instant replacement was required and he stepped right in with one of the greatest rock and roll records of that time: *It's Not Unusual*. The art form of rock and roll writing is to encapsulate a song and its message in two and a half minutes. That song was the moment.

You could go to a club in the West End and somebody would always buy you a drink provided you looked right. It was hardly my solution.

A lady who owned a boat I worked on in the South of France was a countess who had a habit of appearing at 5.30 in the morning when I was scrubbing decks. She had beautiful white silk négligées and was in her middle years, strongly attractive, with a château in Belgium. She said: 'If you ever want to come over and continue your studies and things, call.' She would probably have offered me a job as a butler or whatever and I thought: I'll call her. Forget the rock business. I'm wasting my time with only two O-levels, at 24 years of age. I called and spoke to someone who may have been her butler and he said she was on a yacht or something, so another alleyway was blocked.

One night, at Alfie's flat in Harley Street, I met James Coburn, the film actor. He said, 'You sound like The Beatles, man. You even look like The Beatles. You should be a disc jockey in America. We haven't got a British DJ there.' Also there was B. Mitchell Reed, the head honcho from WMCA – 'Good evening world, this is your leader ... the Beamer (BMR), the man on the velvet couch' – he sat on Coburn's left while Pete Kameron, Mr Rock and Roll, smiled through his glasses.

I went to the American Embassy and told an immigration officer I would like to do precisely that. His face had a dazed expression. He had never come across such an ambition before. 'Do you realise', he said, 'that it is a profession to be a disc jockey, young man? They start at 14 or 15 cleaning out radio stations. There is no way an Englishman will ever be a disc jockey in the United States of America.' I said, 'Thank you very much', and walked out. At the other side of Grosvenor Square was the Canadian Embassy. I had no appointment. Equally, I had nothing to lose by walking in. At the back of my mind was the thought that I had an aunt in Canada.

There, the immigration officer said, 'We *need* young men like you in Canada. It is a land of golden opportunity. We will even pay your air fare. When would you like to leave?'

Within ten days I was on an Air Canada plane. I still remember the maple leaf on the fuselage. I had the equivalent of 27 dollars. I had phoned my aunt to say I was coming. I must have owed something like £50 to the owner of my bedsitter in London and I left behind me a Peter Scott signed painting. It had been given to me by a relative and was the only treasure I had. Everything else I had was gone: locked away with friends in Chelsea or shipped home. That was the dearest rent bill of my life.

I'M GOING TO BE A DJ, JUST LIKE YOU

—

It was getting dark as I flew into Montreal and the darkness matched my thoughts: no money, no job, a bed at the home of an aunt I had not seen for fifteen years. I presented my dilemma to an Italian steward. He said: 'What do you want to do?' I thought I might work in public relations and be respectable middle-class again. I had already realised that Canada welcomed someone with my background: Strathallan School, cotton merchant father. I looked like The Beatles, with floppy black hair. The steward advised going to the ski resorts. 'Knock on the back door where the kitchens are and just start talking English. They will snap you up.' So I had another choice if I failed.

It was October and cold as the plane landed in Montreal. Along came a long, blue Chevvy station wagon and out popped one, two, three little cousins. I had never met any of them. Then came Uncle George.

Uncle George was a great man, a sergeant-major all his adult life who was to drop dead the week he retired. He never did a wrong thing to anybody and was probably the finest man I ever met. He and his wife, Auntie Pat, my mother's sister and the same aunt who was to tell me those stories about my mother and Hudson, changed my life. She had been a wartime Land Army girl and I had gone to the wedding at around five years of age.

I walked into their house in Montreal – a beautiful wooden building, with thick pile carpets – and found such heat! I had never before been in a house that had warmth like it. The radio was on. I had not even unpacked when:

'Radio CFCF Montreal ... My name is Boxer.' Here was a DJ whose spiel was that The Beatles were the greatest and The Rolling Stones less than worthy. 'They'll never be as big as The Beatles.' I said: 'That is the biggest load of rubbish I have ever heard.' The Rolling Stones had been named in London as No. 1 group in England. My twelve-year-old cousin said, 'You can speak to this man. Right now.' It seemed incredible, if not impossible. Who, in England, would have been able to speak to a DJ in 1964?

He dialled the number:

'Hello, Dave Boxer, CFCF Montreal. Can I help you?' I said, 'Excuse me...' He said, 'Don't spell it. Get it out.' I said, 'My name is Timothy Hudson and I have just arrived from London and I would like to correct you on one point of your show.'

'Why, what is it?'

'You just said The Beatles were the greatest and The Stones were inferior. You are wrong, sir. They were voted No. 1 two weeks ago in London.' Silence. Then, 'Come on my show tomorrow night and talk about rock and roll and London in general.'

'I'd be honoured. Thank you.'

'Don't be honoured. Meet me at 11 o'clock tomorrow morning at the radio station.'

Next morning, my uncle drove me to the station. In the cafeteria was a record promoter, another guy, and the DJ. The DJ said, 'In the show tonight, we'll just talk.'

I was the first English character they had seen with long hair. This is the moment in history when I stepped on this iceberg, man, and they did not realise it.

I knew it, I knew it. I had found my moment after all the frustrations and hopes of Chelsea. I saw the people looking at me. I realised I was truly different. I had been different in England. Here, the difference was even more marked. Young Canadians were light years from the scene I knew in London, and it was a scene they all envied. I knew The Beatles. 'Wow! You know The Beatles!' I was talking about The Moody Blues the whole time. They had never heard of The Moody

Blues. I felt I was taking the show over. The switchboard indicators were going bananas. Nine o'clock the DJ came off the air, thankfully I suspect, and I said, 'Thank you very much. Very kind of you.'

Next day to an employment agency. I say I want to work in public relations. My uncle thought I should not sit around. He and my aunt were not rich. I had to get work and make money. Winter was coming on. He was a working man and he liked action. So I got an appointment with Alcoa, the big aluminum company, and had a meeting with the boss. We talked, and finally he said, 'Yep, I like you. I am prepared to pay you $8,000 a year.' It was a million dollars to me at that time. I walked out with new confidence but then...

The phone rang in my aunt's house. It was the producer of the biggest television show out of Montreal. Would Mr Hudson like to be on the show as guest this coming Saturday?

I went on in black silk suit, black Pinet boots, pink John Michael fly-fronted shirt, black knitted tie, hair fluffed up in best Beatles style, and wearing my French silver bracelet. I sat on a stool in front of 200 screaming kids ... It was a heady combination: an aphrodisiac in itself.

As I came off the DJ who had given me a break only four days before was standing in the wings. He looked at me closely and said, 'What are you going to do now?' I said, 'I am going to be a DJ, just like you.' He said, 'That is impossible. It takes ten years to get to Montreal. You are going to have to start somewhere in a little town.' I had no intention of going to any little town. The prize was too close. The fruit was ripe.

I waited around for about three days. By this time I knew I was back at the wheel. I was the smart cookie, was I not? A survivor. Not the kid who arrived from London. I knew people. There were very few people who were anybody in London at that time whom I did not know. My address, for four years, had literally been Chelsea.

I thought the reaction to the TV show would make the radio station realise that they should sign me up. But the phone remained silent. My uncle said, 'There is another rock and roll station in town.' We drove in the Chevvy to this downtown, beautiful building. Receptionist bleached blonde, cigarette dangling from red lips, long red fingernails, horn-rimmed glasses, black tight sweater.

'CKGM, Radio Montreal. Can I help yeeew? Yes, young man, what can I do for you?' And I said, 'Is it possible to see the general manager?' 'Sorry, young man, absolutely impossible without an appointment.'

I said I would write. I was suddenly despondent. As I walked back past these art deco plate-glass windows – 'Hey, young man, are you the Englishman on television the other night?' 'Yes, madam.' 'Hold on a moment...' She went away, returned, then: 'Would you come this way?' Down a corridor to an office. 'Could you wait here, please?' And she locked the door. She locked that damned door and I thought: Wow! This is on!

Some twenty minutes later I was ushered into a ballroom-sized office, chairs all along the back with many people sitting in them, and up there, like God on high, on a plinth as it were, was general manager and vice-president Mr Don Wall.

'What's your name, young man? Did you have any nicknames at school?'

Sitting next to me is this blonde secretary with the seamed stockings and patent leather shoes, tight skirt, and she is flashing her legs and her kneecaps are driving me insane. She has the reddest, most beautiful and longest fingernails and her bleached hair is combed back and she has these bee-oo-tiful glasses that American actresses used to wear, upswept, and she's looking down at me and all I can dream of is giving her one. Or two. This is the boss's secretary.

I said, 'Well, I was called Beau Brummell at school. And I was called Lord Tim, after the cricket-playing Ted Dexter.' So they said, 'Mmm, Lord Tim, Lord Timothy – sounds good...'

'Get a cashmere overcoat, three-quarter length, bowler, rolled umbrella, leather gloves, and walk around Montreal looking as English as you can. I'll pay you $75 a week for a one-hour show, Saturday, six to seven. You don't have to come in more than one day a week.'

So he was basically saying I could do another job as well. I went to work every single day at that station. My uncle was living twenty miles out of Montreal. I went on the bus. The very first day, I twisted my ankle in the snow. The weather was so cold. I was in agony. I met everybody at the radio station, every promotion man. I started choosing music for the station. I called for records from England. Anyone could call me. I remember getting Marianne Faithfull on the phone. Dusty Springfield. George Harrison. Patti Boyd. The Animals. Mick Jagger. The show was a smash. I never took the job at Alcoa.

Within three weeks, I was on every night for three hours in a two-man show: my partner put on the records; I was there to talk. He read news and commercials. I was doing hops every Saturday night – $100 here, $200 there, coming home and throwing $1,000 on the table. I moved into town – an apartment above the radio station in this high-rise building. It had a swimming pool at the top, shops and bars downstairs. I had never experienced so many women in all my life. I could not believe this.

Agents would fly from Toronto with groups and the girls among them would somehow end up in my bed. There were dentists' young daughters with hard Swedish bodies; mothers offering their girls. It was crazy.

I got the station to bring The Rolling Stones into town and it was the first time they had appeared in Canada. They went on to their North American tour of '65. I had been on the air for about three months and I felt there was one DJ I was knocking hell out of by now: the one on the other station.

Then along comes Mr Don Wall, the head of the station, and he says, 'You are booked on a flight to London – 6.30 tomorrow morning. We would like you to interview The Beatles.' He had called my bluff. I had no idea where I was going to stay. I just got on the plane and called Alfie in London. Alfie had it all worked out.

Within hours, I called all the big English rock stars in the middle of the night for interviews. I had read every single word of every available rock publication. I was a walking encyclopaedia of the British invasion. I had been playing records that were not even released in America.

Friday night, I am back with the interviews – The Beatles, The Rolling Stones, The Zombies, The Yardbirds, The Kinks, The Who, Adam Faith, Sandie Shaw, Del Shannon, Freddie and the Dreamers, P.J. Proby, Chuck Berry, Jimmy Savile, The Moody Blues. The DJ who had given me my start in Montreal has announced over the air that

come Saturday he will interview The Beatles in London. I am back in
Montreal before he has even left for London.

'Hello, hookers and honeys, models and mannequins; hello fifteen-
year-old ice-hockey fans, this is Lord Tim and this is Radio Montreal
CKGM ... The Beatles.'

In five weeks on the station I am voted No. 1 disc jockey. There
are two night clubs on the ground floor of my apartment building. 'Any
woman you want, man, just let us know.' Belly dancers, topless dancers,
jazz dancers, cigarette girls, the whole Who's Who of Montreal's magic
book. I have them all. If I pop my little purple heart, I am not so
nervous or insecure. The whole of the British invasion is on that pill. I
never go out into the Montreal winter unless a taxi comes to the door.

I get away with dialogue that other people could not get away
with. After Christmas, I am in an amazing situation. I have reached a
peak and yet am about to be toppled. The station decides to go middle
of the road. Nat King Cole instead of Beatles. They decide there is not
enough money in the youth market and want the middle audience. They
are right in one sense. The middle-aged group buy a lot more products.
The kids are really upset. There are placards outside the station. And
5,000 letters saying: 'We want Lord Tim'.

A letter from CKGM's Don Wall recommending me to another
station boss etches in the circumstances of the time:

> Tim came to us six months ago from London, where he was
> involved in the entertainment business for nearly five years.
>
> At CKGM he was part of a two-man teenage show from 6 to
> 9 pm as well as doing marvellous things in our Public Relations
> department and assisting in our music department ... doing music
> lists, dealing with record people and the like.
>
> Tim and Bob (my partner in the show) did the swingingest
> teenage show I have ever heard and in this short time, Lord
> Timothy became one of Montreal's best-known personalities. He
> was in constant demand for record hops and it kept him awfully
> busy trying to keep up with his fan mail.
>
> During the show, teenagers were allowed to phone in to speak
> to Lord Tim and the lines were always busy. They loved him. He

made two trips to London for us and got interviews with all the top English groups and is on a personal-enough basis with most of them to be able to telephone long-distance from time to time and speak to them on the show.

We found it necessary to change our 'up until now' pop sound to a more adult image with a lot of talk shows and a much more sophisticated music format. The only area we did not change was in this 6 to 9 period.

However, due to the obvious listening trends in this market, we decided about a month ago that we would have to go completely 'adult' and cut out the pop sound completely.

It was with sincere regret that we realised that there was no longer any place for Tim at CKGM. These past few weeks, mind you, we've had quite a bit of reaction ... some picketing, signs saying, 'We want Lord Tim', etc.

Over and above his popularity with our listeners ... he is undoubtedly one of the most enthusiastic, co-operative people I have ever met. Everything he does, he does extremely well ... and as a person he is a real gentleman.

I, along with every member of our staff, wish him every success in his future endeavours ... We are all going to miss him very much.

In the meantime, there was an indirect approach to the other rock station, the one my rival served. They decided not to answer. The attitude seemed to be: why create a monster? Let it fade ... I approached a French radio station. I did, after all, speak the language.

At the time I was sharing an office with Bob (Johnson), who chose all the records and wrote up shows for DJs. He contacted the *Gavin Sheet*, which collated material for rock and roll radio.

They got information from all over America and shipped it out every week. It would name a station that liked a new Beatle record; that kind of thing: a business trade paper. A week later an item appeared in the sheet that Lord Tim in Montreal was looking for entry into the American market. That was about all it said. It gave a phone number.

In the meantime, I was saying to myself, I can always take a

Greyhound bus. I've got money. I brought The Stones to town. I could see America, have a good time. I was still doing my show. Then:

'Hello, can I speak to Lord Tim, please?' 'Lord Tim speaking.' 'My name is Lee Bartell, president of MacFadden-Bartell. I have 28 publications, including *Photoplay*, six radio stations and three television stations from New York to Puerto Rico, from San Francisco to San Diego – where would you like to work?'

Then he says: 'How about San Diego?' I think: Where's that? Mexico? No, California. He says, 'Fly down tomorrow. Here is my address. I expect to see you in New York around midday. I will pay for the plane.'

1965

Toured America with The Beatles.

MUSIC

Downtown . . . Pet Clark . . . she was pretty . . . I kinda liked her. Satisfaction . . . The Stones. The Letter . . . Andrew Loog Oldham. My Girl . . .

Temptations. Mr Tambourine Man . . . The Byrds. Go Now . . . Moody Blues and Denny Laine. Eve of Destruction . . . Barry McGuire . . . the first record I ever played in California, in San Diego.

MOVIES

Goldfinger . . . James Bond.

Help . . . Beatles. Doctor Zhivago.

HAPPENINGS

Hollywood will eat you alive, says Lee Bartell. The Watts Riots happen the week I arrive in Tinseltown . . . 64 people lose their lives. Malcolm X assassinated.

Next morning, there I am with my little black silk suit, black tie, black shoes, and I walk down Madison Avenue and into this giant building. Up, up, up in the elevator and he says:

'Sit down. I want you in San Diego, one-year contract, $200 a week, all your expenses. I will put you in an hotel penthouse. I will buy you a sports car. I have influence and will get you a green work card. Have no fear. I can organise that.' All ding, ding, ding.

It felt so good to be young.

To run so freely with the wind. To smile a smile of smiles. To laugh with love and life. Now I'm running down that street in time. I see a man no longer a boy in the windows of my mind . . .

Within three weeks I was in San Diego, penthouse apartment, pink hotel. He bought me a green MGB sports car. He bought me a black cashmere blazer (because the kids had ripped my blazer when I visited a high school). He used to drive around San Diego in this huge Cadillac convertible, bright red. I did my show in a five-storey building dominated by plate glass. The audience in the street could watch me working.

'Hello, Southern California, this is Lord Tim on Radio KCBQ ...
50,000 watts of super power ... Sunshine, happiness, laughter and love,
beach blanket, Bingo city ... How do you pronounce that word – La
Jolla?'

The first record I ever played on that station was *Eve of Destruction*
by Barry Maguire. 'Something's happening, but I don't know what...'
It fairly reflected all I felt at that time.

I had never read a commercial before. I could not even read some
of the place names, which were Mexican. The programme director,
having discovered that I did not know how to run the board (the
electronic set-up for programming) stayed up all night teaching me. I
was first to play *Satisfaction* by The Rolling Stones. I got a beautiful flat
right down on the beach.

There was a swimming pool outside my door and, as in Montreal,
there were many beautiful ladies around. Young girls, old girls.

Everybody in town knew me. I was getting good. I felt hot and
fast and the formula was working. The Beach Boys came by. Denny
Cordell called me from London and said, 'One day I am going to be as
successful as you.' He sent me a record of *A Whiter Shade of Pale*.

The radio owner said, 'The Beatles are coming to tour America.
Why don't you write to your friends and get invited?' I had never
thought of that. So I wrote, and got a letter back from The Beatles'
press man, Tony Barrow: Seven disc jockeys are being invited. You are
one.

New York City, The Warwick Hotel. It is impossible to get in or
out. Four characters arrive in a limo pretending to be The Beatles and
almost get killed. First thing Ringo Starr says to me is, 'You wouldn't
step across the street to talk to me if I wasn't one of The Beatles.'
Hardly true since I had bought him a coffee when no one knew him.
John Lennon is wearing mirror-reflective sunglasses so that when I talk
with him all I can see is myself. This is a moment in the history of
mankind and I am in a room of the hotel with them. I see them all come
through to pay their homage: Bob Dylan, Paul Anka.

No one could judge what any of The Beatles would be like next
day. Their moods changed constantly and I was privileged to see many
sides of them. I was freaked out. I could not believe what was going on.

43

Shea Stadium, and the biggest crowd ever for a rock concert: 64,000 screaming kids. I had never been to a football stadium before. Brian Epstein talking a million miles a minute. John Lennon with a sore throat. Ringo asks me for an upper. The Rolling Stones arrive to watch The Beatles perform from a dugout. Mick Jagger says, 'We'll never be as big as that.'

The old Bentley ride with The Ronettes, Andrew Loog Oldham, The Stones, myself, others ... We were driving down Broadway, twelve of us in that Bentley. Andrew was sitting at the bottom and somebody dropped a roach and it burned right through his pants...

I went back to New York on the yacht owned by Allen Klein. We all had dinner in a restaurant behind a greengrocer's. Tiny Tim was singing guest of honour at the top of the table ... 'Tip-toe through the tu-lips...' Chicago ... and The Beatles had to hire extra security guards. They were told: 'If you don't pay, you don't play.' For the first time, Paul and John, Art Unger, publisher of a teenage magazine, and I talked about LSD – what it was, or what we thought it was.

Minneapolis, St Paul, the vice squad raiding our hotel. Blonde, healthy girls running up and down the hall, knickers in their hands. Someone bursting into my room with a badge and a girl behind me screaming, 'I-WANT-JOHN.' That story never got out of Minneapolis.

I was on a plane for three weeks, up and down, in and out of hotels and everywhere we went was total chaos. Toronto, Atlanta, San Francisco, San Diego, Houston, Hollywood. I was wasted. Too many pills. Too many nights without sleep. Too much travel. And I was getting hooked. The white rabbit. One pill gets you higher; one pill gets you down...

It was as if all creation was compressing itself into one frantic and ecstatic moment, the unreachable and unrepeatable peak, and I was experiencing it at the very core.

THE JOCK ON THE ROCK AT
6 O'CLOCK IN THE CITY OF ANGELS

—

I arrived in Hollywood on this Beatles tour and the other DJs were saying: 'Something is going to happen to you here.' The grapevine was reaching them but not me. I said, 'What are you talking about?' 'You'll see,' they said. 'They are going to offer you a job here.'

Of all the places to be, this was it. The mid-Sixties tour put a generation of kids in aspic so that anything they did afterwards had to be seen in relation to that time. The Beatles were a cult of unimaginable proportions to any generation that did not witness its progression. They had been seen by 70 million people when they appeared on the *Ed Sullivan Show*. From February to May (in 1964) they launched four singles to No. 1 – *I Want to Hold Your Hand, She Loves You, Can't Buy Me Love*, and *Love Me Do*.

They brought polish and artistry to the trade of rock and roll which, previously, tended to raise eyebrows for the wrong reasons. They had the authority and they had the indefinable magic. The Stones, who were to follow in the next big wave, were raw, less restrained, more aggressive, and enormously successful. But nothing challenged the four lads from Liverpool. Their influence began with the teenies and spread to their parents. They were more than music: they were a lifestyle. Anyone rejecting this lifestyle was forfeiting his place in the new order.

Vicars referred to them in their pulpits. Psychiatrists and

philosophers gave them deep thought. Serious musicians were called upon to give their verdicts. Aaron Copland was to say in 1968 that when people wanted to record the mood of the Sixties they would play Beatles music. It was to prove an accurate conclusion.

To be English and in America was to bask in the glow of this phenomenon. A man could be swept along with the tide, upwards, ever upwards. Providence and my own restless spirit had put me in the right place at the right time and with all the right qualifications in a revolution encompassing fashion, lifestyle, thought itself. There was not a child in the English-speaking world who went into class and spelt beetle with two 'ee's.

Which rising showbusiness man can resist tinseltown with all its inbred suggestion of sin and money and parties peopled by the substance behind the shadows of one's home-town cinema screen?

Here, with The Beatles at the sharp edge, was the great decade of the Beach Boys and Surf music, Motown sound, San Francisco sound, Woodstock, Batman, *Beverly Hillbillies, Lolita, Sound of Music, Bonnie and Clyde, Space Odyssey, Easy Rider,* James Bond, spaghetti Westerns, long hair and hippies, the Twist and discotheques, skateboards and Barbie dolls, Tom Wolfe, and the New Journalism, Marshall McLuhan and pop poet Rod McKuen, Tolkien and *Mad* magazine: a decade so powerful that many of those involved in it did not move on into the Seventies, but remained mentally motionless in the one short stretch of time.

Becoming a part of this seemed a wild fantasy. There was no reason for me to suppose that anyone was going to offer me a job. The one I had was proving rewarding enough. I was 24 or 25; these DJs with me on The Beatles tour were mostly in their mid-thirties and at the summit of their profession.

But they were right in their forecast. I had hardly settled down in the hotel before I was contacted by a Beverly Hills agency named Seymour Heller and Associates, who managed Liberace and Frankie Laine. One of their team had been on a promotional tour and had gone by Montreal at the time when I had my radio show there, and had reported back that I was worthy of their interest and attention.

That very first afternoon in Hollywood a Seymour Heller associate called and took me to an apartment building off Sunset Strip. I walked into this flat and a girl appeared – high heels, black gear, suspenders; and he just said: 'Enjoy it.'

I am told, 'There are three rock stations in Los Angeles, KRLA in Pasadena, KFWB in Hollywood – these competing with each other – and KHJ, a new station just turned to rock and coming up on the rails.'

So they take me out to KRLA. Money is being talked and I am trying not to look too excited. Maybe $22,000 a year.

I am getting $200 a week at my San Diego station with a one-year contract that had run only six months. I feel I am being rushed, but no matter . . .

I am whisked to KHJ, and there Bill Drake, big guru behind the station, is offering $14,000 and promising to make me 'the biggest disc jockey America has ever seen'. Head swimming, the imagination reeling, the possibilities endless . . .

Then to KFWB on Hollywood Boulevard, the old Warner Brothers radio station. The guy who picked me up in London – Beamer, B. Mitchell Reed – and who had been sitting next to James Coburn when Coburn said I should go to America, had called his office and said: 'Got to get Lord Tim.' I was offered $100,000 a year and Beamer lost his slot. I had six to nine evening time and he had six to nine mornings. It was a twist of fate that, in later life, did not do me any good.

I got sued. There was the question of the unfulfilled contract. I went back to San Diego, met Lee Bartell, and he begged me to stay. He said, 'I'll give you your own radio show across the country. We'll get a television show. I will' – and here I thought was the ultimate in Jewish magnanimity – 'introduce you to my daughter.' He says, 'You've been talking about these great blue jeans in London. I'll set up a boutique. But go to Hollywood now and they will eat you alive. When they have finished with you they will spit you out. San Diego is beautiful. You are happy with me.'

He was right on all counts. But what was the sum of the parts against the totality of Hollywood? KFWB were offering a year's contract. The last thing I did for San Diego was to take The Beatles there for a show.

In Hollywood, I rented a house overlooking the whole of it: big, round bed, giant long balcony. I was interviewing and taking out to dinner people such as Michael Caine, Petula Clark.

Buddy Greco came by first day I was on the air. And I was still being sued, I think for $350,000 (an action that was to be dropped). Dean Martin was to say to me, 'Well, once you're above a hundred grand, you're a superstar.'

A picture appears five days running, full page, in the *Los Angeles Times*: 'Lord Tim, America's first British disc jockey.' I feel like phoning the American Embassy in London to remind a certain immigration official that I have Arrived against all his predictions to the contrary.

'Hello, Hollywood. This is Lord Tim, the jock on the rock at six o'clock in the city of angels. This is KFWB America ... Lord Tim, magic man inside your mind, inside your little radio. Pull me close inside; tell me you care. Pull me inside your living soul. Reach me, touch me, tell me you really care. Deeper, deeper, thrust your lust and feel me there. Tell me, help me, break me, make me ... Give me no choice in the end. Reach me, pull me, lull me with your voice. I am inside your radio. Reach inside and open me up. I have nothing to hide. Thrust your lust inside my radio. It is your words that keep me open and alive ... deeper, deeper inside your radio.'

During a three-hour show I smoke two packs of Marlborough and drink six bottles of Coke. I get a phone call – 'Have a girl friend. She'd love to meet you. She is centrefold of *Playboy* this month.'

'Call you back tomorrow.'

She lived in a stucco apartment and opened the door in full *Playboy* outfit, which does not overtax the textile industry half so much as it taxes a man's mind. Fantasies are coming alive every hour on the hour.

Call-girls would come up to my house with a bottle of champagne after work. There were several young starlets. These were people of the night.

I had all I wanted and the pace was both testing and exhilarating. The doctor was prescribing Benzedrine for my nerves.

Around Christmas time I was in a club used by big groups of the time. I was dancing, having a marvellous time. Then a guy wanted to punch me because I had long hair – long, that is, compared with American style. American males were still in the Beach Boys' cut, looking vaguely (as in Montreal) like young versions of their fathers, and long hair was an affront to their masculinity.

A tall, good-looking blond surfer pushed him aside and introduced himself: 'I am Eddie Garner.' He was under contract to American International Pictures and made beach movies. 'I have enjoyed your radio show. Maybe you would like a drink.' I would. He introduced me to various ladies he knew. I think Bob Dylan and Donovan were there. He said, 'Would you like to meet Claudia?' as if I should know who she was. This was Dean Martin's daughter.

I fell completely and madly in love with that girl that night. She drove me to the beach and I was so entranced I did not even want to make love to her. It was enough to be able to admire her and be close.

I became a visitor to her home. At 5 am in the morning I found myself playing billiards and Dean Martin appeared in dressing gown looking suggestively at his watch. Billiards – at five in the morning? His look said it all, and he was charming. What would any natural father do in the circumstances? He did not throw me out. He joined in the game.

Here was a scene, surely, where nothing could go wrong. The Supremes, Marvin Gaye, Martha and the Vandellas, Stevie Wonder, Donovan, The Rolling Stones... 'Come aboard the silver starship and fly with me to the skies ... I'll dress you in silks and satins, ermine and gold ... I'll tell you, darling, you will never grow old...' I caress that microphone like a lover. I am on a roller-coaster and I know it. I have an accountant, a lawyer, an answering service, a press agent, a sports car, a maid, a growing reputation, a wide audience, and from being three steps behind father, I am a whole Continent ahead. Hollywood, against all prediction, is not chewing me up or spitting me out. It is holding me in a warm and satisfying embrace.

I was popping my little pill at three o'clock each day and I was in splendid form by the time I went on air. To close friends, I was The Walking Benny, 'Get off of My Cloud', 'Nineteenth Nervous Breakdown...'

I ambled down to the radio station at 5 pm and read all the papers, I absorbed everything in sight, filled myself up. I could play anything I wanted to. I took sexuality and thrust it in people's faces. Nobody has done it this way before. I play Nancy Sinatra's *These Boots Are Made for Walking* ten times in a row. I knew every celebrity in the business but I

49

had no friends in radio management. None. They represented the Establishment. I represented the kids in the streets. I was not available for meetings. I always chose my own hits.

After my show, I might wander down to a restaurant called Martoni's, have my dinner, amble down Sunset Strip ... to The Trip ... I'd see The Temptations, Smokie, The Supremes ... there would be stars everywhere, just hanging out, very laid-back and Californian.

Dean Martin, at that time, was a bigger star than Sinatra. He had his own giant TV show and his name dominated Hollywood. I had a lot to learn. I was fascinated by the way the self-created 'royalty' lived. From beach-blanket girls, I was suddenly translated into the Polo Lounge, golf at Bel Air Country Club, Palm Springs for the week-end, The Daisy and La Scala for dinner.

I would go to the Martin house and see Lucille Ball or Debbie Reynolds or Tony Curtis. I was playing tennis there with people such as Jimmy Connors. Dean Martin had a young son whose best friend was Desi Arnaz, Lucille Ball's son. They all played tennis on the court in front of the living room. I had never been in awe of anybody, but I was in awe now.

I learned curious things about how a man's roots can reach out to him when, to all outward appearances, he has outgrown them. Dean Martin said that the biggest thing in his life was to walk into his house at any time of the day or night, open up a giant refrigerator and find it packed with food. That was his form of wealth: the ice box permanently full. He would watch TV endlessly. He would play golf. I never had a wrong word from the man.

I probably proposed to Claudia Martin two months after meeting her and to this day I find my relationship with her curious. She made me introverted and turned me back into a public schoolboy again. I was shy, withdrawn, a little awkward in the company of her father's friends. The brashness, the extrovert aggressions were muted to a disturbing degree. I could be extrovert on radio with my groupies and snoopies and little teeny-boppers but when I got into Beverly Hills I was a changed man. I did not help my own cause. I did not take advantage.

Perhaps it was something to do with Northern character: the roots reaching out to me as they did to Dean Martin and his ice box. There is a class of Northerner who will die for his country without once having set eyes on the people who control his destiny; who will come from poverty, risk his all, and go back to poverty without questioning the reasons for doing so. There is a class of Northerner who will say sorry if someone stands on his foot; whose only show of strength comes when he invades London with a mob of soccer supporters and wades in a fountain. He feels his disadvantage like a pain and will not acknowledge it to a soul. But it shows in every action.

I was never quite so affected because public school erases most of these things; but I was not totally unaffected.

So I did not quite know what to say to these people. What *do* you say to a table that includes Richard Harris, Frank Sinatra, Pancho Gonzales, Janet Leigh? I knew Nancy Sinatra very well and was invited to her 21st birthday party in Hillcrest Country Club. I would meet her on many occasions at the Daisy Club and she said the rumour was that I was marrying Claudia for her father's money. It was totally untrue. I was in love to the point where I had created an imaginary pedestal for a girl who had obsessed me.

I did an interview with ABC Television and the questioner said wasn't it fantastic to be marrying the daughter of the most famous entertainer in Hollywood?

'Well,' I said, 'maybe one day he will have a very famous son-in-law.'

In retrospect, I feel it was the wrong answer. Right or wrong, it reflected an English sense of humour. The words just fell out of my mouth. I felt, too, that I had enemies in the camp. Terry Melcher, Doris Day's son, had been engaged to Claudia before me and the rumour was around that he was not too fond of me. For my part I regarded him as a spoilt and rich Beverly Hills kid. I did not particularly like the set he moved in. I did not like their attitude towards others. They were élitist, arrogant, and they paraded their superiority. There is a myth abroad that America is the equal society. It is no more equal than Chelsea is equal to the East End. Every society has its chinless wonders. Every society has exploiters and exploited.

In Beverly Hills there were mobs who would destroy restaurants, turn over tables, as if it were their right; as if position and money gave

51

them that right. I was never a lover of anybody who did not respect the rights of others.

I hung around with Peter Fonda before he made *Easy Rider* (the story of two motor-cycling hippies travelling America)· a quiet, kind sort of boy. Many a night I would go into The Daisy – Hollywood's Annabelle's – with him and Dino Martin, Desi Arnaz ... six or seven movie stars' sons and daughters.

I was scheduled to marry Claudia at Dean Martin's house. I was in bed the night before the intended ceremony in the big sleep. The phone rang. Claudia was in tears – 'My father wants us to postpone the wedding. He is going away filming and maybe we should wait until he gets back.'

'No!' I said. It could not happen. But it did ... I was not banned from the Martin house. We did not stop going out with each other for a long time. My whole life was for her. I started to play my radio show for her. The airwaves were my way of talking to the world: colour, dreams, clouds running by. I was conducting my own symphony. She went off with her father to make the movie and when she returned the feeling was not mutual any more. This fine, placid California girl who did not want to be a singer or movie star; who was well balanced and who just wanted to be a happy person went out of my life for ever. And at the radio station I was about to be labelled: Rebel.

SCREWED AND SHAFTED

———

In California at this time, the drug culture was taking over. I saw it go from booze to marijuana to LSD to cocaine and whereas, once, if you smoked a joint other people would walk out of the room, everybody was smoking. It was not confined to a class. It encompassed street kids and intellectuals. The rich had the better-quality stuff. The leading pop groups had access to the best quality of all.

In music, California was beginning to come alive. We had had the British invasion of '64 and '65 and after that came the '66 West Coast sound. There were groups made to order in studios – manufactured, as it were, for the market place – and there was the organic music, creative, emerging spontaneously from the roots of the people's shifting consciousness. Raw music. That was the music I liked.

The real creativeness came from people at street level. They were the true innovators. During the spring of '66, when I was on radio, they started to let their hair grow long. They began to smoke marijuana. They started to have their own music, their own stage. At Pandora's Box, a night club on Sunset Strip, there was so much commotion involving youngsters that the police and people who owned restaurants nearby decided they would have to get rid of them, and there was a class war: one that could be interpreted as the haves against the have-nots; a revolution of a kind which sent its reverberations a long, long way in distance and in men's minds.

I always felt that in the area of Pandora we lost the children of yesterday. The authorities passed a law that kids could not stand still on Sunset Strip.

They had to keep on moving. If they stopped they would be arrested. The Seeds' first hit record was: *You're Pushing Too Hard You're Pushing On Me*. That was the anthem of a generation: the generation that lost on the fields of Pandora.

Buffalo Springfield came along with *Something's Happening But You Don't Know What*. Music Machine produced a song called *Talk, Talk*, and there was *Break on Through to the Other Side* from The Doors.

I was part of the battle. I reported this revolution on the radio station as it occurred. Sal Mineo and Elliot Mintz were phoning, telling me what was happening, and this went straight on air. The station did not like this. I was starting to get the image of the revolutionary. I wanted change. I dropped my English look. I was wearing jeans and went to work in bare feet.

Sal Mineo, the actor, was living with me (he was in *Rebel Without a Cause*) and I travelled to the radio station in his Bentley, a big Doberman in the back. The rules said people were not allowed in the booths where DJs worked. I would bring a beach bunny, who would sit there and watch – 'Hi Mary!'

I was the one kicking sand in their faces and I was asking for trouble. But I was totally in tune with what was happening in the streets, where it mattered.

I was voted No. 1 DJ. On the periphery, I was a voice in *The Jungle Book*, a voice in *The Aristocats*. I tested for the part in *Camelot* that David Hemmings got. They were talking of me doing a sort of young Johnny Carson-type TV show and instead they brought in David Frost.

In truth, I had gone radical.

After Claudia Martin and I broke up I still went to The Daisy. By this time I was dating everybody. One night I was picked up by Jayne Mansfield. She had a beautiful Mercedes and took my friend, Eddie Garner, and myself back to her house. She left us only to reappear in a white silk négligée, and I thought: 'My God!'

Then some man came in, his hand stuck inside his jacket where

1966

MUSIC

California Dreaming . . . Mamas and Papas.
These Boots Are Made for Walking . . . Nancy Sinatra.
Paint It Black . . . The Stones.

Good Vibrations . . . Beach Boys.
Bus Stop . . . Hollies.
Rainy Day Woman . . . Dylan.
River Deep . . . Ike and Tina Turner . . . my favourite record of all time.

MOVIES

Alice's Restaurant.

people of his kind keep a gun, and he said, 'You two guys had better move if you know what's good for you.' It was like being in a bad movie without benefit of script. But we needed no director to say that the best course of action was to get the hell out and get out fast.

We went back to Dean Martin's house and he said, 'You deserved what you got.' By his reasoning, we were in someone else's (the boy friend's) patch, and that was sufficient justification for the events of the night. But, we said, we nearly got shot! And he said, 'Yes, but you deserved it. You take the risk, don't you? You go in knowing she more than likely has a boy friend there. He's not going to be too pleased.'

I got to know Melissa Montgomery, Dinah Shore's daughter. At various times, according to mood and circumstances, I imagined myself in love with Geraldine Chaplin (Charlie's daughter), Nancy Sinatra and Melissa. I was living in a pretty fast world.

At one stage I had received an invitation to dinner from Rosalind Russell and Irene Dunne, the queens of Hollywood who had helped make Messrs Niven and Flynn years before. I did not even reply. At that time I did not know about the Hollywood code of ethics which divides peoples into A, B and C categories. Even now I am a little hazy. But as I understand it, the A guest is invited to dinner, the B guest to dessert, and the C guest to drinks afterwards, with slight variations on this stark definition.

Now why was I an A guest out of the blue? I suspect from what was said at the time that it was something to do with the formation of The Monkees, a group which had an enormous success at the time with one English member (coincidentally, from Manchester).

They were America's first made-for-TV rock band and their drummer, Mickey Dolenz, summed up the aim precisely: 'We're advertisers. We're selling a product. We're selling Monkees. It's gotta be that way.'

There was something enormously cynical about the whole business: four wholesome people reached out of nowhere, Beatle clones carving out their own slice of a rich cake at the instigation of smart businessmen.

The idea for The Monkees had originated in the minds of TV producer Boby Rafelson and Bert Schneider, son of the president of Columbia Pictures. They were seeking spontaneity in the individual members they were recruiting and they advertised in *Daily Variety* ('MADNESS! AUDITIONS!') for the group they eventually put together.

They had the finest writers and the finest recording studios – and for three-chord songs you don't have to be that good. I will never know whether I was destined to be a Monkee. And I will never know why I was invited to dinner by two representatives of the Hollywood establishment I did not even know.

Meanwhile, I continued to be a rebel with a cause (that of representing the people who listened to me in their thousands) against the massed forces of commercial advantage, and since the latter always win, they won.

In a letter dated 2 June 1966, I had the following warning from my radio station signed by one William J. Wheatley:

LORD TIM HUDSON. Tim: An expression you used last night in performing a live commerical for Kodak, coupled with the use of certain words in a *Teen Topics* program with Lou Christie, lead me to believe that you are entirely too flip with the station, the management of the station, your audience, and our license.

Specifically: on the Kodak commercial, the expression 'and all that crap' came out during the course of the commercial. On the *Teen Topics* show, words such as 'shafted' and 'screwed' were both used. Because this show was pre-recorded, we did not permit these tasteless words to get on the air. However, the Kodak commercial was being performed live and as such could not be edited.

The Kodak commercial came less than two weeks after you were cautioned about use of words in bad taste while performing for this station. I simply will not put up with this kind of nonsense. Mr Bernard (another executive) is out of the office today, and when he returns tomorrow I will discuss both incidents with him, and then I will talk again with you.

The record I played after that was *Rainy Day Women (Everybody Must Get Stoned)*, by Bob Dylan. To this day I deny I ever said 'and all that crap'. They never played me the tape. I never saw a reproduction

of it. The words 'screwed' and 'shafted' were regular colloquialisms and
I did not feel they were foul words. I believe the station had problems.
At any rate, Westinghouse bought it. The word went around that they
were going to change the format to all-talk. That rumour was confirmed
by events. They are all-talk twenty years later: news all the time.

I spent five minutes reading a poem about groupies and got fined
50 dollars. I believed the radio was mine. I was not concerned with
what was No. 1 or No. 20 in LA: I was concerned with my music,
what I chose. And all the time I was digging my own grave.

I did not like prissy records. I did not play Tijuana Brass or
Herman's Hermits. I liked macho records, something with a sexual feel.
My style reflected the mood: unshaven, T-shirts, lots of Speed. I was up
all the time. I could not make love. I could not do anything except my
show. I was a wreck.

My days with the station were ending. They were not going to
renew my contract. I had been offered jobs all over America – Houston,
Cleveland, Dallas, St Louis. The man who offered me $14,000 on KHJ
in Hollywood had a slot for me in San Francisco – and I did not want to
go. I was rich. I was going to stay in Los Angeles and feel sorry for
myself. I bought an E-type.

Now I was going to promote.

One day I parked my car on Clark Street up above the Whisky A-
Go Go on Sunset Strip and as I walked a fellow came up behind me –
large, black beard, long hair, and he said, 'Are you Lord Tim? Sky
Saxon would like to see you.'"Sky Saxon was leader of The Seeds. This
was fortuitous. As I became more anti-establishment I decided the time
had come to have my own group so big that they would give me back
my radio station. I could feel the violence of youth in the free form of
Sky Saxon's music: a repetition of message and thought similar to that of
The Sex Pistols years later. I was feeling used, abused, thrown away by
the Establishment. I had come to hate the control of the American way
of life and I saw violence in others that would break that control.

I found Sky Saxon lying on a mattress in a dark room in the back
streets of Hollywood. There were three padlocks on the door. A Pretty
Things album lay on the carpet. He looked like a rock and roll star:

57

long, greasy hair, rings on his fingers, chains around his neck, purple jacket. Here was my vehicle to the future and my head filled with visions of what might be.

We decided next night to recreate childhood memories, to turn the Seeds' violence and express peace, love, understanding. Since the group was already named, we decided that what had to come from a seed was a flower. We had to have a message upon which to hang our hats and this seemed most logical: seeds to flower. Flower Children. Flower Power. Flower Music. That is where the name for a movement began, in a house at Laurel Canyon in Hollywood, the home of a professor who was down in Mexico. I took out two press agents to dinner and said I was going to change the sound of music. Rock and roll was dead; now for the Flower Generation. Sky Saxon and myself wanted people to remember what it was like to be a child before they entered the adult traps of family, mortgages, taxes, death.

The record written was called *March of the Flower Children* and that was the opening cut to The Seeds' record named *Future*. I would buy hundreds of dollars-worth of flowers and throw them to the people. We sent flower rings to disc jockeys. We sent flowers to everybody. Bigger names were to follow but they were pretenders to the Flower throne of Sky Saxon. When everyone took up the theme and the words Flower Power were echoing across the country we knew we had set the ball rolling in a way that would never be stopped.

In the nature of such things we were denied our originality. Others laid claim to the start of the movement. But those are the facts, and there is no doubt in my mind that Saxon and I created the name for the mood that swept the world.

We started to dim the lights off and on during performances. We started to use smoke, and have TV sets on stage. The dress we conceived was that of Rudolph Valentino. Some of the biggest producers in the country offered to help produce a record Sky was writing, arranging, producing, singing, everything. All he had to do was wait for that circle of chance to turn slightly; but he was in too much of a hurry and he burned himself out.

Sky began to demand ridiculous things beyond normal expectation. Many of the things he asked in his musical progression came to pass within the next decade. The fear in those days was that if you did not have a hit record in the charts once a month, people would forget you. That theory was always suspect. It does not exist any more.

We went to New York too soon and it was not a success. The Seeds were not invited to the Monterey festival. We were very hurt by that. We had records in the national charts but played the wrong locations.

We were stoned out of our minds most days and nights. At the same time we were protesting that Flower Power was clean and nothing whatever to do with narcotics. In truth, it was to do with marijuana and LSD. The song I always think of is: *Mr Farmer, Won't You Plant Your Seeds?* That was a Sky Saxon song on stage. Flower Power was to blow itself away. Saxon and myself were spectators in the grandstand.

The underground did find its stage in Woodstock and the Chicago Convention, but Saxon went on to two wives, five kids and Hawaii – a James Dean character who never quite came through although he is still revered as an underground musician.

THE BEAT(EN) GENERATION

—

There were two sides to life in the Los Angeles of the Sixties, and they were connected. One side was represented by people expanding the consciousness, exploring the mind and so on. The other side put its emphasis on not becoming sheep and following society's old ways. Many were not interested in becoming wealthy businessmen and living lives that they considered had no meaning. There was a feeling, almost anti-social in a way, but not in the sense of wanting to harm other people.

Young people just wanted to be different. There was obviously dissatisfaction. These people could see it in their parents and in society and they were searching for something through this new kind of life: music, dancing, drugs, taking part in universal love.

The psychedelics made people blissful. The effect was similar to the ease supposedly coming from meditation: everything beautiful, sparkling, joyful, loving. Alcohol dulled the senses whereas psychedelics sharpened them. It was a sensual pleasure, too. It felt good. Enjoying the music, the rock groups, was great fun, like a big party which went on for years.

The Beat Generation, according to one of its foremost interpreters, the late Jack Kerouac (who invented that description), was aiming for a state of beatitude.

It was a generaton in revolt, rootless, attempting to destroy established concepts in what many considered to be an alarming fashion. It had (according to its critics) lost pride and patriotism. It stood for poetry, communes, indiscipline, drugs, booze, and it had no way to go but backward to some primitive, tribal area where decent standards of life would totally vanish.

It was too much to expect that the movement could achieve any more than it did. It is not that people mature into a different line of thought. They acquire things. They have to guard those things. They insure against this and that.

They become fearful. They have regular payments to make. The idealism of youth crumbles.

But here, for a short moment in time, was a mass movement which swept the Western world, bringing in its wake a shift towards Eastern philosophies among those who survived its moods.

The movement took muted forms. It splintered. Many within it were fakes anyway: they adopted the dress and habits because it was fashionable. Others more durable went on to seek their truths in Europe, particularly Greece; then in India, particularly Nepal, where monks, the gentle exiles of the Tibetan revolution, were spreading their Buddhist beliefs and principles, many of which echoed the principles of the Flower Generation.

The fact that the movement did not produce a lasting answer in no way proved that there was no question. The restless search for something better comes with each generation. In the case of the Beat Generation, the mood was enough to shake to its core every established mood and method of living.

In most cases, the young knew what they wanted to discard without knowing exactly what they wished to adopt. The new era was to be one of peace and freedom and co-operation without materialistic aims, but there was no clear way of achieving it.

So the search became bizarre, involving a union of simpler lifestyles allied to the use of drugs. It could not sustain itself. There was everything to make it appear but nothing to ensure its survival.

So much of the Beat Generation – the Flower Generation – was absorbed into more conventional society, having learned whatever lesson there was to learn. The poets, the dreamers, the purveyors of the simple life drifted back to the complicated life where old and discarded values reasserted themselves.

They became the forerunners of the yuppies of the Eighties.

What had India to offer? Hinduism, Yoga, Buddhism, Ashrams;
the roots of wisdom stretching down from beyond Christianity. The
seed had been scattered and some had taken root. Meaning had now
been found – not merely a Californian meaning springing spontaneously
from a generation, but something deeper and abiding that had affected
all generations down through known history.

A few who survived Flower Power with their principles intact
found their peace with exiled Tibetan Buddhist monks. And what were
they teaching? That material wealth, far from increasing satisfaction,
decreases it. That within the space of one or more lives man can escape
the cycle of death and rebirth. That death can be like a pleasant journey
back home. That knowledge must come from the heart. That each
person is not only responsible for his own confusion and suffering but
for his release as well.

Some remnants of the Sixties revolution degenerated and took
harder drugs. Some began to steal from each other. In the original
movement, hardly anyone took heroin. It was considered too extreme.
At any rate the hippie movement virtually vanished.

A survivor of the movement – one who went on to become a
Buddhist nun – described her Los Angeles of the Sixties thus:

> One of the high points was the love-in where everyone was on
> a warm, friendly basis. You would look into a stranger's eyes and
> he would smile back at you. It was a peaceful, warm feeling.
> Thousands of people would be in one mood and no one seemed to
> have negative vibrations. The energy was very strong and uplifting.
> You felt very safe. People were looking for something spiritual and
> it sort of spread. Even if you went to one of these gatherings not
> feeling particularly happy, by the time you left, you were beaming.
> You shared everything. It was one big family.

The effects of Flower Power were as strong in Europe as they were
in California because the problems of society were not confined to any
one time or place.

A university graduate from Kent, who went on to become a monk,
described it in this way:

The Flower Power movement in California was good. It seems to me that, after the war, people just seemed to settle down and start to make the same mistakes again. It seemed that our parents were just getting entrenched in accumulating material wealth at the expense of others and creating the conditions for the same old thing to happen again.

It wasn't the outbreak of brotherly love and sharing and caring that one would expect to result from such a war. I think there was tremendous disillusionment among the sons and daughters of the wartime heroes. They could see the nuclear holocaust coming. The next war would be the last one. They could see no earthly reason to assume that it would not happen. They also, I think, saw the worthlessness of just accumulating material wealth as a basis for one's existence. Initially, it was a reaction against that.

The role of drugs, particularly LSD, was twofold. In some senses it was just an anaesthetic to ease the pain of having to live in a society so corrupt and essenceless. Some people just wanted to block themselves out, drop out. And there were those who wanted to use the drugs to develop a new awareness, a new way of looking at the world. They wished to transform the environment so that there was a new set of relationships involving sharing and caring.

There was a recognition that the only way this planet is going to survive is through people coming together for the solution of their common problems. That is what was good about the movement: it offered a realistic alternative.

I do not think the movement fizzled out. I think it transformed. For me, it transformed. For every Flower Power community of the Sixties there are spiritual communities. It has transformed much more into an inner thing. We are realising that you can not transform the outside world until you can transform yourself. In the first place, it was just a kick. But one thing was clear to a lot of my generation: what we had been offered, we did not want.

When Sir George Trevelyan, one-time teacher at Prince Charles's old school, Gordonstoun, later director of the Wrekin Trust, talked at a monastery devoted to Tibetan Buddhism in the Lake District, he said:

> What we are watching is the running down of a culture based
> on getting for self; on greed. Energies which vitalised the old
> society are being withdrawn. But there is no dying without
> renewal. That is the nature of every form of spirit from the higher,
> eternal world taking form to operate in the density of earth...
>
> Living in an apocalyptic age is not necessarily comfortable,
> but it is assuredly exciting. We are in the position of a Fifth
> Column, an underground movement, in an occupied country in
> which we have heard the invasion signalled. There never was such
> a generation in which to be alive. I congratulate you young ones on
> having chosen to incarnate at this stage. When you come to your
> full powers, you are going to carry this tremendous entry into a
> new civilisation, a New Jerusalem. We know it is coming. The
> parallel with war is very close. Operation Redemption is going to
> be launched in this generation. It starts an operation which will
> spread over a thousand years of the Aquarian Age. And there was
> never such an age to be alive...

Redemption, seeking, dispensing with the old, bringing in the new:
I felt the moods and the surges at the very core of the movement for
which, with Sky Saxon, I claim to have invented a name.

This movement affected me daily in a thousand ways. I felt the
power of the streets although I was conventionally employed, making
money, furthering my career. I had sympathy for it. I honoured the
young people in the streets who had the courage to be different from
their parents. Their mood matched my own experience: that a man is
what he wishes to be. I could have been the Manchester man of textiles
for ever, but there was too much to know, too much to experience, too
much to achieve beyond Manchester, beyond England, for me to ignore
the possibilities.

Those who controlled me in radio represented the old order of
things. They were Authority and Rigidity and Commercialism. So I had
the fruits of their authority and their money while openly rejecting
whatever it was they claimed to represent. While others who acquired

Welcome to
America, Lord Tim.

My first great pay
day in North
America,
Montreal, spring
'65.

I can still hear
John Lennon
saying, 'Yes, yes,
yes . . . YES . . .
Lord Tim,
ANYTHING!' I did
tend to be a bit
aggressive.

Black silk suit,
knitted tie,
gingham shirt,
Tom Jones shoes
. . . Hello America.

Lord Tim of
Liverpool. Sorry,
Scousers, you
know how the US
publicity machine
works.

CKGM CLUB 980

GOES HOPPIN' WITH

LORD TIM & BOB GILLIES

at Victoria Hall, Westmount

"FRIDAY, MARCH 26"

Capitol Recording Star
ADAM FAITH and

Allied Recording Star
SANDIE SHAW

* CHUCK DARNELL and the Excels.
* ADAM FAITH appears in Montreal following a Nation Wide tour to North America.
* SANDIE SHAW for the FIRST appearance in North America following a BAN in the UNITED STATES.
  "Girl — Don't Come" — On come — welcome to Montreal

Radio Montreal welcomes Adam and Sandy, 1964.

L.T. with the late John Lennon.

Seven DJs were invited to tour America in 1965 and I was lucky to be one of them.

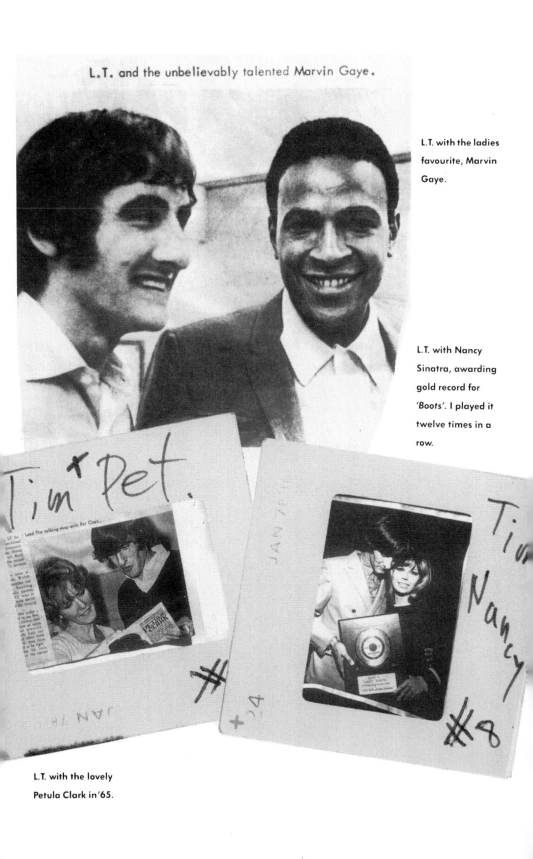

L.T. and the unbelievably talented Marvin Gaye.

L.T. with the ladies favourite, Marvin Gaye.

L.T. with Nancy Sinatra, awarding gold record for 'Boots'. I played it twelve times in a row.

L.T. with the lovely Petula Clark in '65.

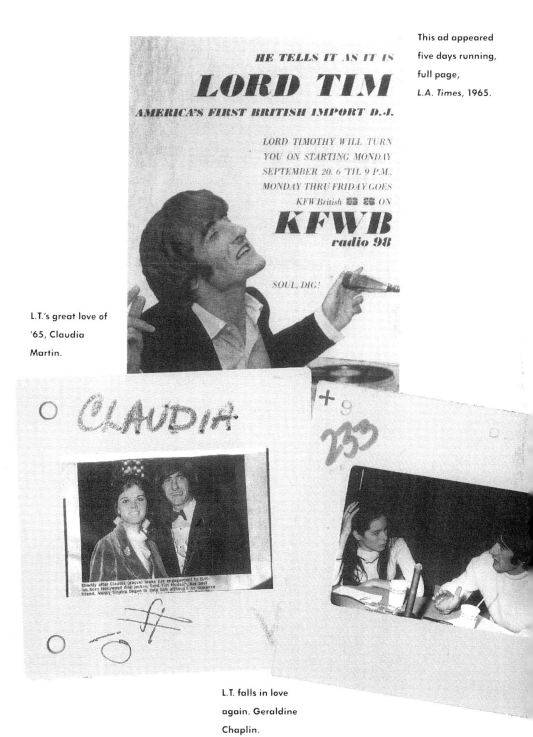

HE TELLS IT AS IT IS

LORD TIM

AMERICA'S FIRST BRITISH IMPORT D.J.

LORD TIMOTHY WILL TURN
YOU ON STARTING MONDAY
SEPTEMBER 20. 6 'TIL 9 P.M.,
MONDAY THRU FRIDAY GOES
KFWBritish 🇬🇧 🇬🇧 ON

KFWB
radio 98

SOUL, DIG!

This ad appeared
five days running,
full page,
L.A. Times, 1965.

L.T.'s great love of
'65, Claudia
Martin.

CLAUDIA

Shortly after Claudia (above) broke her engagement to British born Hollywood disc jockey, Lord Tim Hudson, her best
friend, Nancy Sinatra began to date him although no romance

L.T. falls in love
again. Geraldine
Chaplin.

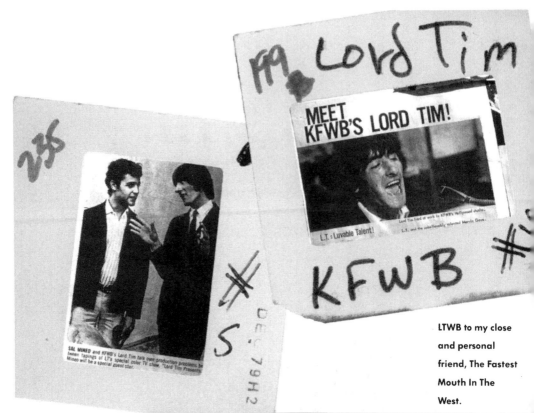

MEET KFWB'S LORD TIM!

L.T. : Luvable Talent!

Lord Tim hard at work in KFWB's Hollywood studios.

L.T. and the unbelievably talented Merula Gore.

Lord Tim

KFWB #1

SAL MINEO and KFWB's Lord Tim talk over production problems between tapings of LT's special color TV show, "Lord Tim Presents." Mineo will be a special guest star.

LTWB to my close and personal friend, The Fastest Mouth In The West.

My room-mate in the Hollywood hills . . . Sal Mineo. I remember meeting the young Don Johnson and Elliot Mintz through him.

The Dave Clark Five . . . '65.

DE 79H2

Tim + Mick

And just look at
those eyes.

.T. and Bobby Vee
. . look at *that*
airstyle.

Forget about L.T.
and Mick Jagger.
Here's B. Mitchell
Reed, the greatest
voice ever on rock
and roll radio . . .
my mentor.

Ektachrome
SLIDE

Mr Soul himself.
James Brown.

Tim James B

INTERVIEW

14

L.T. with Derek Taylor and Terry Melcher. *Definitely the enemy.*

Tim John Seb.
BX ₱

INTERVIEWS '19

I was told by the publicity department that I had the most famous line in *Jungle Book*. 'He has legs like a stork, he has.' That's me with the big beak.

John Sebastian – Lovin' Spoonful.

money took on the fetters of the society that controls money I retained a hold, however precarious, on both camps.

The lessons of Pandora's Box remain with me. Here was a catalyst where a man had to take sides, and I took the side of rebellion – reflecting it in what I said on radio against my better interests.

There was, for me, another catalyst in which I might – if chance had not determined otherwise – have had an unfortunate role.

At the stage in my life where the Hollywood radio station let me go – the era of being unshaven, taking lots of Speed – Terry Melcher, Doris Day's son, this man I never particularly liked, rented a house and asked whether I wished to share it with him.

Why not? It was a nice house. And that is the house where the Manson murders took place. I did not move in because the landlord objected to my doing so. (DJs had an undeserved reputation for being involved with under-age girls.) Melcher himself had moved out before the bizarre events that took place there.

Charles Manson, born 1934, spent his first term in reformatory at the age of nine. He drifted to San Francisco in 1967 and had spent most of his life in jail, mostly for offences such as car theft and credit-card frauds. He was a guitarist and father figure to girl hippies – the Manson ménage. By 1968 he was trying to move into the pop business. His 'family' of around 30 lived on a ranch. Roman Polanski, the film man, and his actress wife, Sharon Tate, moved into this Benedict Canyon home that Melcher had occupied.

Polanski went to London. Sharon Tate had a couple of friends in. They had taken LSD. Manson's people arrived. All three were killed. My belief is that they were after Melcher. He had proposed a record deal with Manson and had not followed it up. The house had become a symbol to Manson and his followers.

The world saw this event as a bizarre, drug-crazed episode. I saw it rather differently. I saw it as reflecting something of the outrage of the streets against the forces of capital and the establishment. I saw it as an extension of Pandora's Box.

There was a form of society in Los Angeles at the time that was totally unsavoury: rich kids picking up girls from the wrong end of town, taking them home, plying them with liquor or drugs, humiliating

them sexually, then returning them to their boy friends much the worse
for wear.

I remember a woman calling to some rich kids: 'I'll tell Charlie over
you.' Charlie was Manson.

I looked hippie myself at the time and, after Manson, people would
regard anyone so dressed in a guarded way. They were afraid because,
like me, they read into the Manson events connotations which went far
beyond one house and three people and a particularly gruesome set of
murders.

I could not then, or now, condone what Manson did. But I can
understand something of the mood that caused him to go to that house.

It was rich versus poor. It was privilege versus deprivation. It was
haves against have-nots. It appeared to mirror the arrogance of class
against the classless.

If the poor steal from the rich, the rich certainly steal from the
poor. They steal ideas from the poor. They mould the ideas and make
them commercial. The next rebel pop group to come along, however
fresh, however revolutionary, will have been absorbed within a few
years, as if it never existed. Today's rampaging lead singer, bellowing on
about the injustices of the age, idolised by thousands of street people
because he suddenly represents their motivations and hopes, is seduced
by money so that he sends his children to public school and no longer
represents anyone except himself.

There is no lure in life like respectability. And once a man acquires
real money – as The Beatles did, as The Rolling Stones did – he
acquires isolation. He can no longer pursue his real purpose. He is
surrounded by contracts, media, guards who will isolate him from those
who adore him. He lives in houses which are secure against the outer
world. He spends his life trying to protect what he has acquired. He has
achieved his own prison walls, created by his own efforts and by his
own hands. He becomes a tax exile.

So, in a sense, we are all victims either of success or failure. I have
had both nothing and everything. I have been poor and I have been
rich. Of the two I would prefer to be rich. I walk my Cheshire acres
now and feel a supreme satisfaction that this isolation and beauty are
mine to enjoy. I love every inch of them. I love the tennis court, the

swimming pool, the cricket field. I feel like an old colonel in the inner reaches of my house. I have space and time to do as I will.

And yet, deep down, I know, too, that there are people out there working with their hands, toiling for some pension, whom I love and revere and respect – because I have had the privilege of being one of them, working with them – and it would not hurt too much to give up what I have and return to this basic form of creation and satisfaction.

Did the Sixties generation betray itself? I think every generation betrays itself. The world of the Sixties, with all its revolutionary fervour, did not effectively change anything. It dissolved. We all moved on. We became different people. Some of us tried to retain the principles of the Sixties, however submerged they were in our psyches.

GAMES PEOPLE PLAY

—

One night I walked into The Daisy Club in Beverly Hills and George, the maître d', said: 'I have a lady for you.' If you were to paint a picture of a French beauty of 28 to 30 you would not create anyone more physically or erotically exciting than Danielle. Cascading black hair, heavy gold jewellery. She wore Chanel suits, high heels, black silk stockings, jewellery, everything perfect, whereas everyone else around her wore jeans. She was unnatural to the California environment. She drove men crazy. In particular, she drove me crazy.

She had a woman friend, Dany Saval, an actress, and I introduced her to my friend, Eddie, the one who saved me from a punch-up. We took them to the Trips Festival in San Francisco. This was three weeks before Monterey, the first acid pop concert ever. It involved Jefferson Airplane, The Seeds, Big Brother with Janis. There were colours and streamers and here were these girls walking around in mink coats, out of place.

Danielle made love like a mature French woman and she devastated me. I was suddenly made to feel young and inadequate. I got myself totally

1967

HAPPENINGS

The summer of love.
Monterey Pop Festival.
Trips Festival . . . San Francisco.
Draft resistance.
Washington March.
Draft card burning.
First heart transplant . . . Christian Barnard.

MUSIC

Pushing Too Hard . . . The Seeds.
L.A. Woman . . . The Doors.
Janis Joplin.
Incense and Peppermint . . . Strawberry Alarm Clock.
White Rabbit . . . Jefferson Airplane.

Flower in Your Hair.
Dock of the Bay . . . Otis Redding.

MOVIES

Rosemary's Baby . . . Mia Farrow.

TV

Laugh-In . . . Rowan and Martin . . . big show.

entangled and, in my madness, and on the rebound from Claudia Martin, I married her. We drove a million miles to Las Vegas for the ceremony and came back the same day. By the time I got back, I knew I had made a mistake.

Danielle had two children, twins aged three or four. She was part of the international jet set and lived in the fast lane of life. She knew everybody. She was very much at ease in the Beverly Hills Hotel, or the Polo Lounge. She introduced me to lesbianism and followed her inclinations before my eyes. She would have dinner parties and invite a woman friend. Not some little girl: a woman with maybe three kids. I saw her making love to these women, a mind-bending experience I shall never forget.

We got ourselves a big house with swimming pool and she became domesticated, taking over my life, my business, everything.

We had a group called The Lollipop Shoppe which we promoted through a tremendous advance from a recording company, but all the time I had trouble with Danielle.

I would not call a lady a liar, but she was something of a fibber and I never quite knew what to believe. She seemed to know some of the most famous men in the world. She told me she knew Sophia Loren, Brigitte Bardot. There was no reason to disbelieve that. In her world, I was a toy boy. She could get quite angry. She taught me a lot about life, but other parts I would prefer to forget. I never knew who she was sleeping with, man or woman. She acquired diamonds and someone other than her must have been paying for them. She treated money lightly. She would say she had borrowed $10,000 from someone or other. It took me a long time not to be gullible.

All this was around 1967. I started my own record company, but the odds were too great: she literally ran me into the ground. The sexual part was erotic and exciting, but there was nothing beyond it to compensate for the pain and frustration.

If a man were paying $1,000 a night for a call girl this is what he would expect. She was probably one of the worst events of my life and the experience lasted just over a year. In some ways she was magnificent. She wore black underwear as few women can wear it. She is best forgotten, but eminently unforgettable.

Once, after our divorce, she invited me to the Beverly Hills Hotel where she was staying, and had a massage from a Swedish woman in front of me. Ah! I thought. Up to your old tricks again! I had a joint, marijuana, in my pocket and for once she felt like a smoke. I forgot to tell her that when you live on the streets the cannabis is much stronger than the stuff you get in rich houses. She took a couple of gulps of the smoke and announced that she was dying, going under. We had ordered dinner, but I ran for the door. I have not seen her since. Last I heard, she was very wealthy and selling islands. It figures.

My E-type Jaguar was stolen one night. It was found wrecked. That did not improve my spirits. I ended with pretty much nothing. I got out and moved into a house further up the road, went out and bought furniture. It was wooden, and I painted it. I was happy to be rid of a problem, but I had many more on the horizon.

Then I moved out of my house and began to sleep on a friend's sofa. This was my low ebb in life: the grand dream diminished to minuscule proportions.

After Flower Power a man named Bob York, vice-president of Capitol Records in Hollywood, met me for drinks on Vine Street and basically he said:

If I become president I will assign you to Capitol and you will have five or six special projects every year for me. But in the meantime I want you to promote a singer.

The singer was Joe South, who had a record called *Games People Play*. Bob York gave me an open flight ticket to anywhere in the world and something like $1,000 dollars a week. He said: I want gold. The Grammy (the 'Oscar' of the music world). The record went to No. 2 in England and it was recorded by more than 50 different artistes and we won three Grammies.

For the promotion I flew to London and stayed at the Mayfair Hotel. I bought 2,000 copies of a book called *Games People Play* and had a folder made up. All the publicity went into that folder. I did an 18-page biography of Joe South and people said: 'Who is going to read all that on a new artiste?' But it worked wonders.

A producer named Wayne Schuler had been sent along with me as part of the team. So there we were, Wayne, Joe and myself pushing for the skies. Joe was not outgoing and kept to his room. He wrote beautiful songs: *Walk a Mile In My Shoes, Hush, I Didn't Promise You a Rose Garden*. Wayne and I went on the town.

I was in black velvet jacket, white ruffled shirt, with three or four chains around my neck at that time; suntanned, hair long, 28 years of age. And in a bar were two Brazilian ladies, one about 40, the other around 30, and within a short time a waiter came over and said these ladies would like us to have a drink.

We discovered that the younger of the two went on a 90-day trip every year with the elder, who was the chaperone. We went to Tramps, and I must have popped one of my little Purple Hearts because I was having a great time talking to Art Garfunkel, Lady Somebody or other and a third person who played rugby for England.

Back at the hotel with my bronzed Brazilian blonde I tried to get into the room I was sharing. The door was locked. She said, 'We can't go to our room. We have another friend with us.' I saw a door, opened it, and found it was a broom closet. I threw her mink coat to the floor and that is where we made love.

My friend came down the hall with the chaperone, heard noises from the closet, opened the door, and there I was in horizontal action surrounded by mink, the questing digit seeking its rewards.

Next day, my Brazilian lady came to my room and said, 'I'm off to St Moritz. Come with me.' It was a splendid offer. But hey! I had Hollywood to go to.

Joe and I had some good talks together. He said, 'You're a writer like me. You're a poet. Why are you doing this publicity stuff? Go in there and write your own songs.'

Back in Hollywood, I walked out of my office saying, 'I am going to the beach and I am going to play tennis for the rest of my life...'

I was a total product of the LSD generation. Capitalism and its old ethics were boring me. It was not what I wanted any more.

So I had lost my house. They repossessed the E-type. I bought a cycle (for two dollars) and painted it red, blue and white. I was exposed to a basic truth: that in Hollywood money runs out fast. I still had my Beverly Hills friends but did not feel at ease with them. I still did not

like their behaviour; the way they treated waiters and servants and girls.
I did not like some of their conniving ideas.

I had a photographer friend, Nik, who was married to a French
journalist, and I slept on his sofa. One night he said: 'It is no use being
sorry for yourself. You have got to get out there and meet people.'

So at 11 pm we went to Barney's Beanery, a famous eating place in
West Hollywood, and found a group of three girls speaking French. I
asked them whether they were French and they said no, they were
Swiss: two sisters with a friend. One sister was beautiful, like a Grace
Kelly, but a Grace Kelly who was
hippie. She had red corduroy
pants with paint stains and a
heavy sweater. We followed them
outside and she had the tiniest car
I had ever seen. She called it
Phoenix, an 850 cc Fiat.

I said, 'What a beautiful toy!'
It was painted purple, a present
from her grandmother. One sister
said goodbye and left. The friend
said, 'Bring him home for a
coffee.' I jumped in my friend's
car and we followed the Fiat.

Trees, steps, courtyard, and
then this incredible room where
every wall was painted a different
colour. Books, books all the way
round. Tiny hotplate in the

1968

MUSIC

Sunshine of Your
Love . . . Cream.
Born to be Wild
. . . Steppenwolf.
Hello I Love You
. . . The Doors.
Love Child . . .
The Supremes.
Jumpin' Jack
Flash . . . Stones.
Hurdy Gurdy Man
. . . Donovan.
Mighty Quinn . . .
Manfred Mann
. . . (a Dylan
song).
Macarthur Park
. . . Richard
Harris.

New York Mining
Disaster . . . Bee
Gees.

HAPPENINGS

My Lai Massacre
. . . March 16th.
Assassination of
Martin Luther
King . . . April 4th.
Assassination of
Robert Kennedy
in L.A. in the
Ambassador
Hotel . . . June
5th after he had
won the Primary
Election in
California . . .
changed the
course of history
in America.
Democratic
Convention in

Chicago . . . the
Chicago 7 . . .
Tom Hayden . . .
later to marry
Jane Fonda.
Nixon elected
President.
Drugs . . . Jesus
freaks . . . Hippies
. . . Flower
children.
10,000 young
Americans learn
how to avoid the
draft . . . Canada.

MOVIES

Easy Rider . . .
Jack Nicholson
. . . Dennis
Hopper . . . Peter
Fonda . . . what
happened to
Chris Jones?

corner. Tiny shower and bathroom. Tiny bedroom where there were
two doll-like beds. Giant cushion in the middle of the floor. We made
love on the cushion that night.

Kathy had short-cropped hair in the style of Jean Seberg. Her
father was the famous old travalogue movie director James A.
Fitzpatrick. She changed my whole attitude to life. I moved in around
three days later.

Here was a girl living a Bohemian life; aged about 27. She had been to finishing school in Switzerland after Beverly Hills High. Her grandfather owned a bank in Chicago and discovered oil in Oklahoma and gold in Alaska.

She was real, old, blue-blood American. Her mother's family were involved in an American soap company. For the first time in years I felt a warmth beyond superficiality. She was not interested in how many dresses she owned. One good dress was all she wanted.

She was not concerned with painting her nails, or with how much somebody paid her for doing a job. She was a Kelly girl. She might have a job for a week, then another the following week. She was a talented designer with a degree in theatre arts – set designing.

At Thanksgiving I met her whole family: two brothers, three sisters. For the first time I was walking into a world I had left long ago: of books, theatre, opera, business. The family had connections with flour, oil, newspapers. I basked in the warmth of this family. It was something I had missed. My parents' divorce had removed such intimacy from me.

Like all ladies of the blue-blooded kind, Kathy liked the rascal, the cavalier, the outlaw. I do not suppose I would have been her father's choice. After about a month the friend left and we took the place over for ourselves. She bought me a tennis racket and a can of balls and said: 'Go play tennis. Go do something. Don't sit there dreaming about the glory you've had.'

ASK FOR A PERCENTAGE

—

This was a tranquil and good period in my life. I never once saw Kathy lose her temper. She seemed incapable of raising her voice. She was kind beyond any call of kindness. She was never bored, and loved to create. She was always doing something: sanding a floor, putting up tiles. She taught me how to use my hands and thereby enriched my life. I do not think I had ever hammered a nail into a piece of wood before I met her.

She would know how to take a big sheet of fabric and cover a sofa, using a staple gun in a way that made the end product look as if it had just emerged from a store. She would work all week for 80 dollars, then spend 72 dollars on a brass chandelier: the perfect, tranquil, well-balanced American lady.

She always knew she had two or three thousand dollars in the bank and that was her security. She was always happy, never jealous of my promiscuous behaviour, and accepted the fact that I made love to other women. Sex was not something that overawed her. She accepted it as a part of life, not the beginning and

1969

HAPPENINGS

Visit England promoting the record Games People Play. Woodstock . . . 1.5 million people. Hudson dropout. Office on Sunset Blvd. First man on the Moon . . . July 20th . . . Neil Armstrong. Bombing ceases in North Vietnam. First 747 Jumbo Jet.

Jogging becomes a fad. Tennis becomes a fad. Vegetarianism begins in earnest in California. Altramont . . . The Stones . . . the end of the Sixties trip. Epstein dies. Brian Jones dies.

MUSIC

Games People Play . . . Joe South . . . my PR won a few Grammies for that one. Honky Tonk Woman . . . Stones.

Bad Moon Rising . . . Creedence Clearwater Revival. Sweet Caroline . . . Neil Diamond. Lay Lady Lay . . . Dylan. Everybody's Talking . . . Nilsson. Aquarius . . . Fifth Dimension.

THEATRE

Hair . . . Musical.

Doctors . . . Dentists become hip to Flower Power.

end of it. She was wholesome.

Her family were the first academics I met in America. Her father loved England and people remembered him there – still do. America forgets its heroes and is forever seeking new ones. To English cinemagoers, James A. Fitzpatrick will always be remembered in the phrase, 'As the sun sinks slowly in the West...' It was part of their youth when the cinema screen was paramount.

Kathy made me fill my space with things without worrying about what I had not done. She bought me a fur coat for Christmas – in California!

So there we were – happy, but not particularly affluent. When a man falls off his pedestal, as I had done at the radio station, the world seems an alien place and a phone call is a million miles away. If I had called someone I might have had offers. But I had said so many crazy things through newspapers that I doubted whether any radio station would touch me. They preferred to hire safe people – people with secure backgrounds, tied to kids and mortgages, the hostages of fortune. I had been very much anti-establishment. And radio, in any case, was becoming more and more automated so that it did not need personalities. Personalities demanded too much money. The Machine preferred money to personality.

There were compensations. Around that time boot sales were starting. It became very in to buy second-hand things and not have flashy cars. I had always been adventurous in style and found that a £3.50 pair of painter's overalls could overpower all the smart, expensive suits at a party. They were copied by people with far more money than I had. It was very out to look rich.

One day, my accountant said, 'I am a bit worried about you. You have no money. I hear you are living in some garret somewhere. Have you ever thought of being in the property business? I have friends who are the biggest property men in Beverly Hills. You could make a lot of money selling.'

I did not want to know about people like that any more. I had a fine girl friend, a place to live, a cycle, her car when she was not using it for work; I was playing tennis and going to the beach where I had a beautiful German girl friend with that Prussian look I love.

I had a phone call from an entrepreneur named Pierre, who invited me to dinner. I took the German girl along and that probably hurt Kathy, but I did not want her to be part of that business world. Pierre said: 'We are buying a night club in New York. It will be the biggest in town. We want you to manage it. You will go on the *Johnny Carson Show*, meet Jackie Onassis and others like her. We will pay you $500 a week plus [I seem to remember] 6 per cent of the gross.' And I said: 'I want $750.' The truth is that I did not want to go. In spite of my wanderings, I like my roots. A colleague of the entrepreneur came to see me. He said: 'Do it, Tim. It is the chance of a lifetime. New York City is yours. Night-club owners in New York are better known than rock stars.' I was unmoved.

My accountant then said, 'Look, I have some property in Hollywood: fourteen little rundown shacks. How would you like to be involved with me in this? I will pay you $75 a month.'

I drove to this dilapidated piece of property – destination zero, one step from the welfare office – and I fell in love with it, absolutely. Here were old, wooden slatboard houses. I had a vision of the way they could be, the gardens that could surround them. A friend said, 'Go in there and ask for 25 per cent of the business.' I said, 'You're crazy.' He said, 'Never ask a Jewish businessman for money. Ask for a percentage.' I was learning. So I went back to my accountant and said, 'I'll do the whole thing, 20 per cent,' and he said, 'You're on.'

I renovated that place with love. I painted those houses the colours of the rainbow. I did the windows, the roofs, the gardens. I sanded, I chiselled, I brought them back to glowing life. Monroe and Brando had lived here at one time as well as many celebrities, including painters and photographers of a Hollywood bygone era. And it had gone to seed. It was like renovating something in a British dockland. Here was an area of Hollywood deep-down depressed, although the property around was quite good.

I had Linda Ronstadt, Jackson Browne and members of other famous groups living there. The Eagles were formed there. I had the rich people, the fêted people, and I had call girls. Rents soared from $75 a month to $500 and I was doing fine.

This was the Highland Camrose Estate, built originally by one man. He had one major house, three-storey, wooden, and he built houses for his family at around the turn of the century. The intention of the authorities was to knock it down eventually and rebuild it on the other side of the road, where there was a car park. That never happened. Now this property is a State monument (Californian listed buildings).

It was here that I met my Howard Hughes.

He was known as the Highland Camrose Hermit. We were going to have bumper stickers made at one time which said: 'Howard Hughes is alive and well and living at the Highland Camrose'.

His name was Raymond Arbeley and he had lived on the estate for twenty-seven years: same little flat. The lady next door had not seen him in the fourteen years she had been there. Groceries were left at the back door and a cheque would be left in their place. He would wash empty cans of beans, remove the labels, and pile them up. He had uncashed cheques in a box two feet long and they filled it to capacity. These were dividends from oil companies and so on.

We were friends. I was his only friend. He wore the same clothes every day and had the same physical appearance as Howard Hughes. His 1930s shoes were expensive, but now his corns stuck out left and right where they had burst through the leather. His pants were worn rolled up and his legs looked rusty and mouldy. He had a Cashmere sweater, grey, with holes and a shirt with no collar. I do not think he changed a shirt more than once in four years and he never took a bath. He just smelled musty.

He was terrified of germs. Everything he had was covered in an inch of dust. Nothing had ever been cleaned. In all his drawers he had brand-new shirts, collars, shoes, a whole row of beautiful clothes he never wore. Oil magazines were piled up to the ceiling, plus all the magazines from the Los Angeles Country Club and various athletic clubs peopled by upper-class Christian people.

He had a 1938 Buick, rusty, parked at the rear of the property. I persuaded him sell it for $300 and the fellow who bought it pumped up the tyres, turned the key, and it worked. He went out only at night and listened to news all the time.

Always he thought people were coming to get him. He had grown

up in Washington, DC. His father, he said, was a surgeon and he had
done a world tour in 1907. I got the impression that he had knocked
someone down while driving and that he had killed him or her. After
that, he ran away to the West Coast and got involved in oil. He never
married. And in his paranoia he locked himself away.

He spoke only to me and gave me a little box from Constantinople.
He liked the fact that I was English and had time to talk. Everybody
else went to work or slept. He said he knew that one day I was going to
be a millionaire and gave me maps of oilfields in Colorado, Montana,
Wyoming. He predicted the oil embargo. I think he had been a
wildcatter.

He had crates of 1928 champagne, and 1940 wine. And one day
they took him away. He simply vanished. Who took him? I do not
know. They said they were the health people.

Here was a real American gentleman, mysterious to me now as he
then was. Here was my Howard Hughes. I believe Hughes was alive
and well and living at the Highland Camrose and that is my story, make
of it what you will.

PLAYING TENNIS

—

The finest billboard on Sunset Strip had four-foot diameter beams, and that is where Kathy and I went to live. Not precisely on the billboard, not precisely under it, but sufficiently close to have it dominate our environment.

Here was a piece of property owned by a man named Pinzner and it had two shops: one a tattoo parlour, the other a rent-a-car place. Beneath were two flats looking down to a courtyard. In the courtyard was a two-bedroomed bungalow once lived in by Errol Flynn. Next to that was a monstrosity of an old building that, in its time, had been a club, a restaurant, many things. At that period it was rented to a man who ran a church for wayward children: one Arthur Blessett, who pulled his Cross right across America. The Flynn cottage is where three or four of his ministers lived and it was in a depressing state.

You drove your car through the car park round these little buildings and there was this gorgeous little Flynn cottage and above that – us. Steps up to us on the right, and further up the steps, Sunset Strip.

The great thing was that you could not hear a sound. Nothing apart from an occasional rumble. Trees were all around. We watered plants all the time and everything started to grow. I think we were paying 75 dollars a month at a time when little flats in Hollywood rented for 150 to 200 dollars a month.

Kathy and I would play Monopoly out on a huge patio we had built. The flat next door was up for rent and I said I would take it. Kathy's look said: but how are we going to pay? I went in, painted it all up, put in this and that, took out bits of it, and re-rented it for double what I was paying. Suddenly we were living free.

Kathy thought this was fantastic. I had my other property where I was getting 75 dollars a month guaranteed (from the accountant) plus 20 per cent of the moneys coming in.

Suddenly, from losing the Jaguar to buying the cycle to Kathy's Fiat painted purple, we aspired to a 190 Mercedes SL. A fantastic car. It cost 175 dollars, and was born in the late Fifties. It had a superb, wooden dashboard, and a gear shift on the wheel; it was compact, strong, and we polished it up so that it glowed.

Nobody was driving old cars in Los Angeles at that time so we were part of a thing that became a vogue. We liked to think we had style. The admiring looks of passers-by confirmed that feeling. Our excitement was to go to a big DIY store and spend 30 or 40 dollars on paints, rulers, pads. We had no luxuries: no chocolates, no cookies. We were eating organic: egg plant, soya. Nuts were a luxury. Oatmeal, brown bread (no white), margarine not butter, nothing from a supermarket – this was our life. We made our own muesli – in 1969. Work boots were our badge of office. We both wore them. We both wore overalls. We had tartan shirts over T-shirts. I had a blue baseball cap, and embroidered on it were the words: Highland Camrose Estate, Hollywood.

So my cap reflected my property.

I would go to bed around 8.30 at night and be up at seven. Tennis court 7.30 to 11. Home, shower, lunch, then work on the property. I had become a gentleman of leisure.

The weather was perfect. It did not cost a penny to play tennis. There was a pro shop and an orange juice machine. I began one of the most enjoyable periods of my life, a good seven or eight years.

I became a good player with a big serve and I had a tendency to beat better players and lose to weaker players. I was a serve-and-volley man. I never got the temperament quite right, but I reached a situation where people would stop and watch.

There, I met the most beautiful, kind, most interesting people of

1970

MUSIC

Lola . . . The Kinks.
Instant Karma . . . Plastic Ono Band.
Bridge Over Troubled Water . . . Simon and Garfunkel.
Let It Be . . . end of The Beatles. Letter . . . Joe Cocker . . . produced by Denny Cordell . . . wasn't that a hit in '66 with The Box Tops?
War . . . Edwin Starr.
Woodstock . . . Crosby, Stills, Nash and Young . . . written by Joni Mitchell.

my whole stay in America, all from different walks of life.

Among them were Manny, an Israeli professor teaching economics at university – a little, rotund man, always with a glint in the eye (I think he was fascinated by my amorous pursuits and I never once remember him being rude or critical); and Rusty, an insurance broker's wife who lived in Hancock Park, the wealthiest Christian area of Los Angeles.

Los Angeles is divided. Hollywood and Beverly Hills are basically Jewish-orientated. Hancock Park is made up of beautiful houses built at the turn of the century by the great old families of industry. This was the original Los Angeles. Everything grew from there. Rusty would invite Kathy and myself once or twice a month to meet her friends. They had a lot and we had little, but they were kind. She taught me to play tennis. I thought I could play already, but I was wrong. She would bring iced tea and cigarettes. I had a big white Samoyan dog and he sat under a bench the whole time, never moving.

I met three groups together for the first time: Jews, Italians and blacks and was at ease with all three. I became very radical. I would not allow newspapers or magazines in the house. I never watched TV apart from football. I did not know anything of what was happening in the world and I did not want to know. I was on my Hulot's holiday in Hollywood: bearded, healthy, 29 years of age, and able to play five hours of tennis straight. I had my Mercedes, my white socks, my white pants, my wide-open shirt, my bronzed body and I must have met, and experienced, more beautiful women than most men have in three lifetimes.

One regular on the courts was a porno-movie star, big and blond and good-looking but no Romeo. Another was co-host in a TV show. A third was Paul Mazurski, the movie director (*I Love You, Alice B. Toklas*, the 1968 film about an asthmatic Los Angeles lawyer escaping from his bullying fiancée by joining the Flower people). He was rather rotund, older than me, a good player, and he came from New York. He had been a stand-up comic.

He knew I was Lord Tim, but never acknowledged knowing. He said one day, 'I'm making this movie and I want some guy to be a hippy. What do you think of James Taylor?'

'Ah, no,' I said.

'What about Kris Kristofferson?' I say, 'That's the guy.' The movie is called *Blume in Love* and I swear to this day he used to mould his characters on me.

He saw me coming in a Jaguar, then on a red, white and blue cycle, followed by a little Fiat and a 190 Mercedes and, later, a VW bus. Now are they not the trimmings of a hippie?

He brought an incredibly beautiful lady to the courts: around 37, blonde, Swedish, body like Marlene Dietrich, the shortest white shorts any woman can decently wear, and with the most natural Californian sun tan: about 5 ft 5 in of perfection. I heard she was the wife of Mazurski's best friend, a dentist.

1971

MUSIC

Maggie May . . .
Rod Stewart.
Brown Sugar . . .
Stones.
You've Got a
Friend . . . James
Taylor.
My Sweet Lord
. . . George
Harrison . . . the
great rip-off . . .

what was the
name of the
group???
Shaft . . . Isaac
Hayes . . . big
man.
Riders on the
Storm . . . The
Doors.
It Don't Come
Easy . . . Ringo
Starr.
She's a Lady . . .
Tom Jones.

HAPPENINGS

Manson.

Beautiful women bounce. They can feel the lusting energy of those who look at them. I personally lusted after this woman. Kathy was always just taking a little job. She was personal assistant to an art director at a cosmetics company. I was making money. She was making money. We were having a good time. What else does anyone want in a relationship?

Our Friday-night friends became Leonore and Willy Crystal, both rotund, both short. Willy had an Afro stand-up haircut. His wife was book-keeper to my accountant. They were into ballet and had a swimming pool and a Corvette – everything a Los Angeles couple would hope to have, but no kids yet.

Willy was an engineer. His wife had talked one day about Lord Tim, this English fellow who had become a hippy, and Willy decided he wanted to meet me. We all became constant companions. They would take us out on Friday nights to a pancake house for stuff that was bad for us. This was also a time of middle-class experimentation with drugs. We used to take LSD and we would spend until the early hours of Saturday getting high. We would listen to Moody Blues records. I was into Wagner and, by this time, reading all the underground papers.

One night, Willy, confused by LSD, wanted to call the police. He said we definitely needed help. I said, no, we did not need help. Kathy, meanwhile, put herself in the garbage can. We were hallucinating in our own little world below Sunset Strip.

The deal on the rental of the flat next door was that we would share the kitchen with the tenant, Little John, a gay from Ohio, who liked girls as well. We became a family. He made marvellous dinners. We all became very good friends. I was independent. Kathy was independent. Her father was always going on trips to Europe or Mexico and she would go too, so my promiscuous behaviour was not thrown in her face.

One night I went to a party at a big house in Beverly Hills and wore my white overalls and tennis shoes. There, I saw this beautiful lady. Prussian. Aristocratic. And I watched her all night; never danced with anybody; hardly spoke to anybody. And right at the end, we spoke. She said she was working as a translator-assistant. We parted.

Next day, Little John said: 'There's this beautiful lady in our office. You must meet her. I'm bringing her back for lunch.' He began to describe her. It was the girl at the party. By this time, on the patio, I had a round table with an umbrella over it. She lunched with me. John was not there. I served lettuce with strawberries and brown bread; fresh water. She had never seen a lunch quite like it.

Her father was something in the German government. She wore a Pucci dress. Her hair was beautifully blonde and combed. She had seamed stockings. And I did not so much make love to her as devour her. In the garage.

That night we drove up into Topanga canyon with a friend of mine driving and we made love on the back seat of the Mercedes as we drove to a restaurant. We went to the beach and she wore a white T-shirt with nothing underneath. Her hair was flowing in the wind. I wanted to love her again and again, and to marry her. I was full of passion. She wanted sex. She had a strong, healthy body. Kathy was away...

HORTICULTURAL HOLIDAY

—

Kathy and I started using the courtyard downstairs for table tennis parties. We strung up lights. Three hundred people would turn up, all bringing booze, and we would have enough to drink free for the next three weeks. One night we had Eric Clapton playing guitar. Manfred Mann came ... several members of a group called Bread. The people who were not coming were the ones in seersucker suits and crocodile shoes. I had started to write my memoirs and my friends were saying: 'How can you do that at the age of 29?' It seemed simple enough: in my experience twenty-nine years constituted a lifetime.

I had money enough for my needs but not enough to live the high-level Hollywood life. I created a persona: the Englishman, the poet. I was trying to write songs. In the tattoo parlour on Sunset Strip I met a fellow named Bobby Buck. He had a guitar. I said, 'Do you play that guitar, boy?'

'Sure do, sir.' Then – 'Aren't you Lord Tim? Didn't you manage The Seeds? I met you in Amarillo, Texas.'

Bobby Buck was carrying a pack and wearing big boots and hitch-hiking through America. We began to write songs and the very first was: 'I walked into America ... Here at last America, the land of my childhood dreams, where the past becomes a future and the snow becomes a stream.'

We sold that first song for $200 each and the idea was to record it with John Wayne; but the guy who was taking the song to Capitol

Records in Hollywood got carried away and recorded the song himself. He was a voice-over man.

We wrote a whole musical called *America*. 'I couldn't get it all on a postcard so I stayed ten years...'

We teamed up with a girl named Dee Dee whose biggest record was *Thou Shalt Not Steal*. By this time she was a housewife in the Valley.

Our concept was that Bobby and the girl would sing and I would talk. It would be the story of how an Englishman and a Texan swapped opinions of America. We got to a producer, an arranger, a publisher, a studio, and I thought (not for the first time): I'm going to be a star! But I blew it: I could not keep the three of us together.

A manager took the musical to New York and he said, 'It's a great first act. Where's the second act?'

During this time I got busted twice in three days for marijuana. Bobby Buck and I were driving along Santa Monica boulevard when a girl stuck out her thumb for a lift. We pulled up, she jumped in, and said, 'I live just up the road near Sunset.' We went to the house and were playing songs and singing. Bobby and her room-mate walked to the corner store to buy newspapers. While they were gone, there was a knock at the door: a postman delivering a parcel.

The girl was all smiles. 'I've been waiting for this – it came from Korea.' I did not think anything about it. Bobby returned with the other girl and we were sitting there rolling a joint. There was another knock. Bobby, who knew nothing of the parcel, opened the door and found himself looking down the barrel of a .38.

Behind it was a narcotics hippy cop, service badge in the other hand.

'Do you live here?' 'No, sir.' 'Why did you open the door?' 'Because I was closest.' Next, we are all sitting on the floor, hands behind our backs, handcuffs on. Bobby turned to me and said, slowly and deliberately, 'Just-tell-the-truth. This is no time for humour, Hudson.'

The place was being ripped apart in the search for the parcel. We were interrogated. They separated us. Then they were all smiles. They let us go.

'You'd better be more careful when you're looking for a piece of arse in future,' one cop said.

Two days later, I was having dinner with an old friend in her apartment and sitting in an easy chair opposite the front door. We were smoking an after-dinner joint. There were several people in the room. I was actually holding the joint. Again, a knock. In walked two sheriffs, one around 40 years of age, the other a young buck in his twenties.

'Hello, darling,' the girl who lived there said. 'Would you like a drink?' 'My usual.' 'And how about your friend?' 'Just a Coke,' says the young sheriff. He never took his eyes off my left hand, the one holding the joint.

He said, 'If I ever see you again, watch out.' The older sheriff finished his drink, and after ten minutes he said, 'Bye.' It seemed time to vanish for a while.

Bobby Buck said, 'I'll show you America.' He had a bread van painted white by this time and I can still hear the gear box grinding. He took me up to Big Sur, down to the Grand Canyon, to a beautiful part of California above San Francisco ... into the gold-mining towns, to the ski resorts, and he wrote a song called *Truckin'*.

1972

MUSIC

Without You ... Nilsson ... soppy music ... what happened to Rock and Roll? Nights in White Satin ... Moody Blues ... Beethoven's Symphony No 7 in A major Opus 92 (beginning part). Who ripped

who off? School's Out ... Alice Cooper ... he waited a long time for success. Family Affair ... Sly and the Family Stone. Rocketman ... Elton John. Morning Has Broken ... Cat Stevens. Your Song ... Elton John. Horse With No Name ... America.

HAPPENINGS

Started to experiment with the format of Hudson's Theater of the Mind ... no intros ... no extros ... no time ... no name ... radio musical theatre ... nobody wanted to know the Hollywood Picture Show ... thanks, Marty.

One night, back home by the billboard, my friends and I were playing Monopoly and this time we were all taking mescalin. It was the big drug, then. Pure stuff. And I looked down from the patio to where Errol Flynn's old cottage was and I had a vision: St Tropez in the heart of LA.

By this time, no one was living in that area down below. Arthur Blessett the righteous, the fella who pulled a cross across America, had left, the cottage had become a crash pad, and my friends in Beverly

Hills would never go down to that end of the Sunset Strip. It was too far into the wrong part of town.

But I could see beyond what existed: I could see laughter, good food, people, lights, umbrellas. A restaurant, no less.

There was no such thing as an organic health food place for the upwardly mobile. It was still a cult of the hippies. There was a further incentive: my girl friend could not cook. In the early hours of the morning, I phoned a friend. He said, 'How much do you want to build it?' 'Ten thousand dollars.' 'You got it.'

He was a property developer. I phoned a well-known lawyer, got him out of bed, told him the idea. 'How much?' 'Ten thousand dollars.' 'You got it.'

It cost $34,000 to open that restaurant and I owned 40 per cent. I said, 'I am recreating the dreams of when I was in England – afternoon teas under umbrellas in summer. Plus memories of the South of France.'

I built that restaurant bit by bit. Kathy put in eighteen stained-glass windows. We worked day and night. You start with $10,000 and quickly reach $34,000. That is when my stake dropped from 50 to 40 per cent. It was to prove a crucial factor.

Pinzner the landlord charged $450 a month rent because he could not believe that a man could operate a restaurant there. I got parking space. I drew my own plans. I did everything I wanted to do, although I did not know what a restaurant kitchen was supposed to look like.

I got a fireplace that was all old wood, burned off the surface, and carved it. I found three artists who painted a mural all the way around the main dining room. I would take different pieces of wood, cut them into varying shapes and nail them on a wall.

I got the big spools that carry cable and made them into tables. A fellow in a funky junk shop where I used to buy my stuff said, 'Just build the bugger. If it falls down you can always build it again, but don't sit around thinking about it.'

I got away with everything, including the name: Horticultural Holiday – environmental eating. Look up the words in Webster's, they do make sense.

Can any man imagine a Jewish partner allowing him to get away with a name like that? I got away with it because my associates could smell money. They knew there was substance in organic restaurants. The rich were ready to move on to hippie food. This was to be a prototype for restaurants all the way across America.

There was no hard liquor: just wine and food. It was 1972. The third day of opening the restaurant grossed $1,000. The *Los Angeles Times* called it 'The dream as it really should be'. At lunch we would have serving wenches: good bodies, healthy skins, low-down *décolleté*, peasant dresses. They served brown bread, soups, salads, everything healthy. At night: handsome men serving, no women. And I hand-picked the hostess, Sally. She was a Veronica Lake. She looked and breathed everything that was best about American sexuality – pure *Philadelphia Story*.

I had three patios ... the Newport Beach patio subdued behind the bamboo trees ... mistresses would meet their lovers, blue and white canvas director's chairs ...

The 'I-want-to-be-seen patio' ... with bright reds and yellows, etc ... and the organic patio ... the earth shades of greens and yellows ... 'I want to be alone'.

You name the stars, they came in droves ... 'Hello, Lord Tim' ... people came from all over LA to be seen at the HH on the Sunset Strip. My friends became my acquaintances and acquaintances became my friends ... that's the restaurant business.

And I married Kathy.

I married her on the 'I-want-to-be-seen' patio beside the Magic Fountain, and a lot of well-known people came. It was like a pop star's wedding: fancy dress, tails and hats: a superb day. The colours were radiant. So River, my daughter, was conceived at 8424 Sunset Boulevard under a giant billboard and that was my *Dynasty*.

She was conceived on the very first night we opened and Kathy never thought she could get pregnant. Never considered it. She was 32. We had never taken precautions.

I walked into the restaurant at night with my black velvet jacket, white ruffled shirt, moustache, hair cut shorter than it had been and I was playing the role of Errol Flynn. It was my fantasy. My fantasies

1973

All the women are getting broody.

MUSIC

Let's Get It On ... Marvin Gaye. Crocodile Rock ... Elton John. My Love ... Wings. Love Train ... O'Jays.

Bad Bad Leroy Brown ... Jim Croce.

HAPPENINGS

The River Hudson was born 13th January on the Sunset Strip in Hollywood ... the hottest January day ever in L.A. 96 degrees. Vietnam ... 12 years of war ends ... 27th January.

occasionally overcome my realities.

I have never quite understood what other people call reality: I have never worked nine to five in my life apart from the period when I was three steps behind father.

It was a great and good time. We entertained leading politicians, show-business personalities, and we had fun. A party of 40 was coming one night and I forgot to tell the chef. The chef walked out. I had 120 people outside who had booked dinner under the trees and 40 people inside. I made an announcement:

'Folks, I'm sorry. All I can give you are hamburgers.' And Willie Brown, the leading Californian black Democrat politician, stood up and said, 'You're on.'

We were making so much money and people were having such a good time that my partners decided we had to bring in a general manager. They took away my power and made me a figurehead. Reducing my holding to 40 per cent had proved a mistake. Then pilfering began. Nobody could understand how lots of money passed throught the tills with no profit coming out. After around a year, a buyer came in offering an amazing sum. Horticultural Holiday became Butterfield's. It is still there.

I went off to live in a gorgeous old three-storey house on top of the hill overlooking Highland Camrose which people were calling Timmytown. Bela Lugosi had lived there. It was a period from 1971 to 1975 when I lived the most glorious, tranquil, happy life. I gardened. I collected my rents. I played tennis. I saw my daughter grow. My wife would go off for trips with her father. We decorated the house in a sophisticated-poverty way: different coloured walls. We were always collecting junk. Between the junk, we would have something expensive. I had a workshop.

I was going to bed at 8.30 am and getting up at 6.30 pm. During the day, everyone else in Timmytown slept. I never saw anything move apart from the odd curtain. I would be out there gardening, my daughter toddling, and I was organic.

They used to say that after 8.30 pm, suddenly, long black limousines would begin to arrive and rock and roll stars would jump out and everybody was dealing drugs. I never saw any of it.

With my wife away, I would go wild and for days at a time I would be missing.

My friend Willy Crystal was always talking about T-shirts. T-shirts and their potential intrigued us both. I saw them as the cheapest form of advertising. They were an integral part of Californian life. People would have a T-shirt, a sweater, a pair of jeans, and tennis shoes, and they did not need much more.

Willy said, 'Let's open a T-shirt shop at Laguna' (a Californian seaside resort). The idea did not work out but it led to other things.

One of the people renting a piece of property from me was named Marty Schwartz, from New York. He, too, had been intrigued by the T-shirt possibilities. We decided to sell in England. We called a major company manufacturing transfer machines and talked to its head, Bob Cohen.

He said he had just sold the rights in England but thought it might be an idea for us to liaise with the English businessman concerned. This businessman visited my house in the hills and said, 'You come to London and you can do the advertising, the concept.'

So, suddenly, it is 'Going to England, darling. Off for the summer.' Marty was a location scout for a film company and could get the time off.

So off we went to London. They offered us, I think, $600 a week each, plus a Daimler or Jaguar. We booked into a Holiday Inn and no one called us. We arrived at the office in Mayfair on a Monday morning and it turned out to be a Bank Holiday week-end. The office location was great – a fine building on Brook Street, opposite Claridges. The two businessmen concerned always seemed to be involved in meetings behind closed doors.

I got the impression that the American company had provided $100,000-worth of machinery and a similar value in transfers.

We next rented a flat, and the very first day on the tube, I said, 'I am going to have a magnificent love affair in London.' And I did. Coming up the elevator at Baker Street was a glorious apparition of a girl: blonde, Swedish. And I said, 'Hello, how are you? I'm from America.' She said, 'You are not from America,' which was partly right

1974

HAPPENINGS IN MUSIC

Virgin Records begins with Mike Oldfield and Tubular Bells. Steely Dan.

and partly wrong, but at any rate, the ice was broken.

I took her to lunch at a health food restaurant, the only one in the West End, and began a great love affair.

At the business, I started to organise and advertise and say what T-shirt colours we needed. The shirts were all black and purple, and not the right sizes, and it became apparent that these London people were buying stuff they could not afford to pay for. Fifty per cent of the transfers were not suitable for the English market.

I said, 'Let's get some more from America.' I contacted Bob Cohen in America. He said, 'I am not sending any more because I have not had any money.'

The whole thing lasted maybe seven or eight weeks. We always got paid but were stuck with the rent for the car. I decided to return to America and explain to the boss what was going on.

Cohen made me a sort of personal assistant. He knew there was a market in England and I explained to him that the biggest market was in rock stars. I said that in England a photographer owned the copyright to his pictures and that I had met one who had portrayed all the rock stars.

I said, 'We can do a whole series in America.'

In the meantime, his family and associates were getting a little nervous at having me around. I had stepped into a family business. Marty, who went with me on the first trip, decided to go back into the movie business. I went back to England.

I got the pictures I needed and returned to America where we had samples made. But I made the mistake of letting the manager of a group see them. He threatened that if we printed the designs they would sue. Cohen said, 'You take the lawsuits and I will print them.' No deal. I was despondent. I was confused by this time about the business; confused about love and life and everything else. London was cold. It was no longer my world. I went back home, and my wife had left me. I had to start again.

WHERE WERE YOU IN '65?

—

I had lost my wife, my child, my direction, and it was my own fault
that Kathy's mother and father had taken her away. When you are
dealing with a strong family and your father-in-law decides to whisk his
daughter back, then I guess the relationship is very much over. I don't
disagree with that action, if it happened to my daughter, I'd steam in
and tell the guy to piss off, or whatever. That is what basically
happened. Kathy's father decided that our relationship was going no
further. I still think he was wrong though. We were a very good couple,
we had a wonderful time together and, to this day, we are still the best
of friends.

My only redemption was to work hard, and with my hands. The
Highland Camrose estate had been sold to an Oriental businessman and
I offered to work for him. He agreed. I was roofing, concreting, making
patios, and living in a rough sort of way. A bottle of wine, a lot of
women: that was the pattern.

One day, an English friend came from New York and he was
reading one of my poems. I was going to write The Great Novel. He
said, 'Are you writing the story of your life in America? I will write it
for you.' Then – 'Have you any dollars in your pocket? Let's get the hell
out of here.'

There was a Renaissance fair in Los Angeles – a sort of medieval
thing. We went to this and I took my dog, a little Jack Russell, a nut of
a pooch with a bandana around his neck, and string for a lead.

I was wearing my work boots and cowboy hat and the most

beautiful girl in the whole wide world came towards me.

This was the countess.

We talked in French. She said she worked with stained glass – a curious coincidence in that Kathy was practised in the same sort of business. We exchanged a few words and then she was gone, lost in a maze of people. It was like a dream.

Next day, I was talking to Nik, my Yugoslavian painter friend, on the phone and I said, 'I met this gorgeous lady.' I described the circumstances, and he said, 'Is she tall, blonde, Prussian-looking?' That was the one. 'That's the lady I know. I told her about you. You wanted stained-glass windows for some house you were doing and I told her to see you. In fact, she is looking for a house to live in right now.'

I said, 'I just happen to have a house vacant.' She came over. I told her, 'You can't live here. It's tough. Not the part of town you would wish to be in.' She said, 'I want it. I have the money.' I made some excuse. I said, 'You don't have a green [work] card. If you get deported I am going to be stuck with the house. But why don't I take you out to lunch?'

We had a marvellous time. We went to the restaurant I had built. (I took my daughter, River, with me.) She took me to the studio where she worked. And I felt a growing excitement. She had innocence and elegance. Her father was German, her mother Swiss. Her name: Béatrice de Ballincourt. She really was a countess. The family were incredibly rich.

A few days later, I was standing outside my house in work boots, big rip across the front of my jeans, red bandana around my head, and she arrived with a silver bag. I thought: how inappropriate for this part of the world. I poured a bottle of wine. She said, 'I'll give you a call after dinner.' I had heard that a thousand times. The people who said it never ever called. I went to bed and the phone rang about midnight.

'Hello, this is Béa. How would you like to come down and see me?' I said, 'Where are you?' 'At my house on the beach.' It was fifteen miles or more away. But I went. And I do not think we left that house for three or four days.

It was one of the most erotic, enjoyable, stimulating three or four days of my life. This was my queen of the world. Lady Béa. I gave up

1975

everything. We moved to the mountains and bought Clark Gable's old hunting lodge and began converting it, stripping the walls. It was a large property overlooking beautiful terrain and ravines, thirty miles outside Los Angeles at Malibu Lake. We had movie neighbours, not beach people, and it was incredible. We married. We lived with her two children. River would come by, so I was living with three beautiful children all the same age. We were, to all appearances, the perfect couple and the relationship lasted two and a half years before it burned itself out.

I do not think we burned ourselves out. Other people did it for us. Béa always listened too much to what other people would say. She would believe them and tend to question me all the time. It wasn't really her fault, she was very beautiful, very sophisticated and she attracted people like flies, they were very subservient to her. But they were very critical of us, as a couple, of the way we lived. Also, at that time, I really wanted to do my music. I was writing a musical and perhaps I concentrated too much on that. However, although we had everything we wanted as a couple, piece by piece others were nibbling away at us, bitching away at the corners.

We just went to a lawyer and that was it.

Around 1977 The Sex Pistols were happening. There was a resurgence of music from the 1960s: the underground music, the garage bands.

My old friend, Bobby Buck was around again, singing his way through California, and he bumped into an old Hell's Angel called Big Al. Al had worked in

1976

1977

1978

the mailroom at KFWB Hollywood in the late Sixties and Bobby was
talking about his mate, Lord Tim, who lived in the mountains with the
countess. Big Al said, 'Is that the same Lord Tim I remember? I've got
to meet him.'

He owned a club in the San Fernando valley and next thing I knew
I was putting a show together on stage there. It was called *Where Were
You in '65?* So twelve years after I had hit Hollywood, I was coming
back. The show was multi-media: slides and music backdrops with
myself on stage. It sold out nearly every night. I was in magazines,
newspapers. I had money, but I had turned drifter, sleeping in my car
or the house of any girl I picked up.

I had wanderlust. Eventually I moved into a house on the beach in
Malibu with a girl named Tabatha. She was a fun-loving basketball
sports-mad Californian, more like a 'mate' than a girl, and it turned out
she knew me from the Sixties.

One day I was listening to a college radio station – KXLU on the
campus of Loyola Marymount – and it was like listening to the BBC: no
commercials, a combination of Radios 1, 2, 3, and 4, heard both off and
on campus. It had everything; a mélange.

I called the programme director and said, 'I was known fifteen
years ago as Lord Tim in Hollywood. Everybody is talking about the
Sixties. I would like to do a show.' He said, 'Well, you know, great
idea, but–' That intrusive But. However, there was some interplay of
talk between Tabatha and Stella, a DJ at the station, who said she knew
me. This director, who was in his early twenties, showed interest and
said he would love to meet me. Thank you, Stella.

We talked, I at my usual breakneck pace, and we came up with an
idea: 'Hudson's Theater of the Mind'.

The condition was that I could do anything I wanted. I would not
be told what to play or say. And I would get three hours on air each
week. That relationship lasted four years. And Tabatha was my very
first producer.

Tabatha was a great girl and I lived an idealistic life with her. I
started another show, *Juke Box Saturday Night* – three hours where I
played daddy and some nineteen-year-old played daughter. I played
music of the Sixties and she played music of the Eighties. I took this

1979

HAPPENINGS IN MUSIC

Ian Dury . . . Sex
'n Drugs 'n Rock
'n Roll.
Joy Division.
Gang of Four.
Teardrop
Explodes.
Echo and the
Bunnymen.
Police just
breaking.

MOVIE

The Wall . . . Pink
Floyd.

95

1980

MUSIC

Ska ... Black and
White ... Selector
... Specials.
Pretenders ...
Brass in Pocket.
Jam ... Paul
Weller.
John Lennon ...
Starting Over ...
blown away on a
cold winter's day.
Dexy's Midnight
Runners.

1981

MUSIC

Adam and The
Ants.
Tainted Love ...
Soft Cell.
Police.
Simple Minds.

1982

MUSIC

ABC.
Human League.
Haircut 100.
Madness.
Culture Club ...
Boy George.
UB 40.
Thompson Twins.
Blancmange.
Spandau Ballet.

show to the bars and clubs and pubs, live. I got very confident. There
was no shortage of anything, be it love, drugs or money.

I liked the college atmosphere and the close proximity of the
students. I was flattered to be talking to professors and teachers. I felt I
was getting a sort of honours degree. I was getting press coverage. I was
buying sweat-shirts for the kids with the station call letters printed on
them. I issued buttons with the words: 'University of Loyola Smarties'.
I would pay the kids to work with me. And in the end I received one of
those nasty letters from a student who said I had taken advertising in a
newspaper to promote the station without authority.

It was my stab in the back and it hurt. The students misconstrued
what I was trying to do.

I left.

A few weeks before, with the Saturday night show on the road, I
went to the King's Head, the English pub, leaving my little dog in my
VW bus. When I came out my dog had gone.

Next morning, a phone call. A man's voice, 'Would you own a dog
named Ego?' He had it. I went to his house and he said, 'Aren't you
Lord Tim? I've been a fan of yours for a long time. What are you
doing?'

The *Los Angeles Times* was doing a feature story on me the following
week – 'Lord Tim Reigns Again'.

> Every Wednesday night at 11, Hudson's Theater of the Mind
> unfolds – a unique program that incorporates a multitude of
> musical expressions within a basic rock framework...

He said, 'My best friend's wife wants to get into this entertainment
business and she is very good. I will get her to call you.' Time went by
and then the phone rang, 'I'm so and so. I'd like to meet you at Alice's
Restaurant on the beach in Malibu.' 'No,' I said, 'come over to my
house.' She walked in through the door.

This was Maxi, my present wife, all ribbons and bows, high heels,
painted nails, the whole thing, and I said, 'I'll show you paradise if you
really want to see it. Really!', I went on, 'I know where Paradise is.'

'Well, show me.'

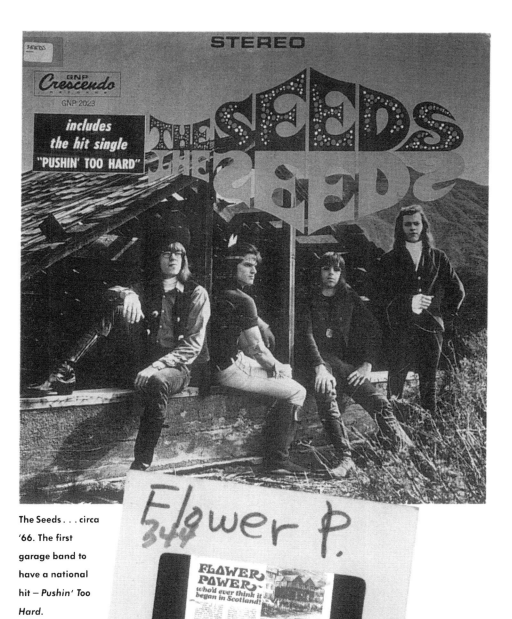

STEREO

GNP
Crescendo

GNP 2023

includes
the hit single
"PUSHIN' TOO HARD"

THE SEEDS

The Seeds . . . circa '66. The first garage band to have a national hit — *Pushin' Too Hard.*

Flower P.

FLOWER POWER — who'd ever think it began in Scotland!

#3

Flower Power.

Seeds promo . . . a concept later ripped off by The Stones. The flower girl in the photo, none other than Toni Basil, later to be seen in *Easy Rider* and, much later, had a huge hit with *Mickey*.

Sky Saxon.
Hollywood Bowl.

Getting married
on the Livers,
Lovers, Sinners
and Saints Patio of
Horticultural
Holiday on the
Sunset Strip.

Kathy Hudson
with Little John at
Horticultural
Holiday, 1970.

The Statue of Liberty, the gateway to America. River Hudson.

River Hudson playing cards.

Hudson with
Ozzie, gardening
at Timmytown,
Hollywood, early
'70s.

High times in
Malibu with
Lady B and Bobby
Buck.

The countess . . .
Lady B, The Queen
of the World.

Digging ditches,
circa 1975.

Freedom in
California, 1976.

Danielle, my
Parisian amour.

The old
headmaster —
W.N.S. Hoare,
Strathallan
School.

Back home in
England, '74.

I got behind the wheel of her brand-new Corvette. (The Corvette was the car of the era together with the Ford Mustang, Corvair, Dodge Charger and Barracuda.) She threw me the keys. It was a beautiful day. And I took her up into the mountains, past Gable's lodge, where I had lived, up, up to the top so that we looked down on the lodge and the whole 360 degrees of Los Angeles: ocean, mountains, valley. She had never seen it in her life.

She said she wanted to manage my career, and the sequence of events was amazing. We went off to San Francisco together and bought a house on the beach and she left her husband. Just walked out. Finished. Had enough. It was not love at first sight, purely a business relationship. Our love affair was something that grew and grew. I was still shattered by what I had been through with the countess: an erotic, physical affair.

We talked about England and my roots, the whole thing. She said, 'Let's go!'

TAKING STOCK (THE LAST OF THE ENGLISH ECCENTRICS)

—

In the 1970s, when commercial radio was stirring into life in Britain, an American friend named Larry Shane, a leading music publisher, used to say, 'It's time you went home, Hudson. You'll do very well there.' He was a fatherly man who, at one time, felt I might be a successful lyricist. I did not take his advice. The pull of California was too strong at the time; and in any case, there was no catalyst to make commercial radio in Britain the big thing. You do not miss what you have not had.

But around 1980 the *Los Angeles Times* printed a full-page feature about me based on my 'Theater of the Mind' show on a university radio station (no commercials; I did not like those), and the headline was on the lines: 'Lord Tim Rules Again'. I remembered Larry's advice: 'Hudson, you're the genius – go out and prove it.'

There is a theory that if that particular newspaper prints a full-page about you on a Sunday, you should, on the law of averages, be able to turn it into a million dollars within the year. Which is fine as theory. How to actually do it – that was the question. My peak time had come and gone with the Beatles/Stones era, the Sixties; and here we were turning into the Eighties where the young did not remember Lord Tim and

1983

MUSIC

Blue Monday . . .
New Order (Joy
Division).
Girls on Film . . .
Duran Duran.
Let's Dance . . .
Bowie.
Men at Work.
Michael Jackson
. . . Billie Jean.
Wham.

Eurythmics.
Heaven 17.
Hip Hop from the
Bronx . . . Grand
Master Flash.
Haysi Fantasi . . .
Hello John
Wayne.
1999 . . . Prince.
Aztec Camera.

MOVIE

Raiders of the
Lost Ark.

where I might be looked upon as a piece of memorabilia.

Why try to crack Los Angeles all over again? Maxi thought it would be a good time to go to England, play a little cricket, and do a little business. 'Why not', she asked, 'try to fulfil your ambition to be the next Alastair Cooke?'

So we got ourselves a London flat in the King's Road, and made our approaches to the BBC. We pursued the BBC for an entire summer and ended with an appearance in one show, *Round Table* on a Friday night, and that is as far as I got. Radio 1 implied that it was looking for 26-year-old blue-eyed DJs, not 45-year-old nostalgia freaks, and recommended Radio 2. I did not fancy six further rounds with new antagonists.

I did, however, take the opportunity to talk to various music groups of that era and sent the material back to Los Angeles. Much of the commentary went over people's heads: there was to be a delay of six months or more before the groups became better known Over There. I was seeking out the flower of the second British invasion.

It was a frustrating time. I was storming the barricades and they were high and showed no signs of yielding. We went back to America unsure of what to do next.

The pull of Britain was becoming stronger, partly by chance, partly by design. It was chance that made me buy our old gardener's cottage in Prestbury as a £37,000 part-time hideaway that seemed right for the time; chance that produced Fanshawe Hall (friends told us about both), the substantial Cheshire home in four and a half acres which we occupied before Birtles Old Hall.

Vicars always have wonderful houses in the country. Fanshawe is a splendid Cheshire Victorian vicarage with six or seven bedrooms and a big, winding circular staircase. Very romantic. When I was at prep school, I had a friend whose father was a vicar and we used to go to his home for Sunday lunches. There were big old pots suspended from the ceiling, overgrown gardens, tennis court. Vivid memories for a romantic. I am in love with overgrown gardens. Fanshawe was big, big, big, with a brook, not a stream, running through the garden. Maxi always loved it much more than she did the Old Hall.

Birthright.

That is really what it was all about.

It was time to reclaim my birthright.

When I left England in 1964, I was virtually no different from somebody being shipped out to Australia 100 years earlier. I had to leave. I did not need a magistrate to sentence me. Circumstances had done it for me. I was guilty of no crime but that of urgent need. I virtually had no scope in England: two O-levels, a degree of desperation, no job, my parents divorced, my cricket in tatters. I was not qualified for anything and the message was clear: Go West. As I headed West on that Air Canada plane I exorcised England from my mind. There could be no lingering regrets. The break had to be decisive and absolute. So England ceased to exist for me and I became, I think, the most Californianised Englishman it is possible to meet.

It was LA Raiders on Sunday afternoons and Monday night, sun, sea and an uninhibited lifestyle; a floating of the ego on the high seas of opportunity in the least-inhibited society on earth: and who could deny the charm of it, the lure of it? But it was not choice. That is the crucial point. I do not think anybody emigrates unless they have to. They do not say, 'Hey, I'm going to California because it is the best place in the world to live.'

I wanted the birthright.

I had begun as a cricketer with Lancashire County Second Eleven and I felt that, in the course of half a lifetime, I had acquired sufficient experience and skill to be of service to that same club as a committee man or – and why not? – its chairman.

The upshot of all that is that I have fought with the then chairman, Cedric Rhoades, and have seen him replaced. I have not been elected to the committee in spite of repeated attempts, but in a curious way I have achieved all I set out to achieve: an influence on the sidelines, through friends, which shows itself in the club and which has brought it nearer to my appreciation of what it should be: this past season has been much happier for it and for me.

If my parents had not divorced, I think I would have captained Lancashire and toured with England as a batsman/wicket-keeper; A. C. Smith did, why not Hudson? When you spend more than a decade of your teenage years dedicated to cricket – sacrificing your academic work just to become a cricket player, which I did – you have to feel the pain when the effort does not produce the proper reward.

The divorce destabilised many things and affected my anchorage point in Prestbury. It was a different village then: more predictable in its moods and habits than it now is, and more aware of its past; very much a small and intimate community.

It was good to re-establish roots in this area, whatever the means: homes, cricket, radio stations, come what may. Every man has to 'belong' because, by nature, he is tribal. I now want to turn my coach-house into part-home/part-museum with an art gallery upstairs where I can exhibit all my paintings: my Bellanys, my memorabilia of rock and roll. That, too, is part of 'belonging'.

And I have just become Lord of the Royal Manor of Birtles, which seems fair justice for a man who was known to Southern California as Lord Tim. I had to buy it, of course: for just short of £70,000. I might have got it for less, but there was a lady of the Cartier family competing and gallantry in these matters must have its limits. She lost.

This is a Crown title, which is unusual – the first to be auctioned by the Crown in living memory – and I have the family tree showing its origins. Supposedly, the first Lord of Birtles existed in 1250 and that is the date I am going to put on the front of the reconstituted coach-house: *Birtles Manor, 1250 AD*.

I am a toytown builder at heart, you see – I build images and illusions through my imagination. In Cheshire, I am continuing a trend I began in America. I took fourteen dirty, old, ugly, worn-down, forgotten welfare-assisted wooden houses in California and today it is a State monument to old Hollywood, incidentally next door to the Hollywood Bowl.

If I had not gone in there and dug the ditches and painted the houses and spruced up the place, no one else would have done it and the vision would have been lost.

So here I am, Lord of the Manor of Birtles, building my walls, and landscaping on a large scale, and it is nothing whatsoever to do with lording it over anybody. Thank heaven the money did not come from forbears who sent twelve-year-old kids to work eighteen hours a day in factories in the 1800s ... That is not part of the heritage I wish to claim.

I have transformed this Cheshire mansion so that it sports my four colours in every conceivable nook and cranny – this to the consternation of some of my very worthy and respectable neighbours, one or two of whom would rather die than draw attention to themselves (although they frequently draw attention to me).

Since the Englishman's home is his castle, I fly the rebel Californian flag at mine, together with skull and crossbones. My dogs come and go and they tend to wear men's neckties bearing my colours.

I have been vegetarian for over twenty years, and do my share towards keeping Aqua Libra water from going into disuse. I am a veteran of the Sixties drug scene and in my middle years have put it far behind me in the cause of healthy living.

I am the black sheep returned to the Cheshire fold and people I knew in my formative years stop at the gate in their cars and say, 'Yes, that's where he lives – you wouldn't have thought it, would you?'

My stepfather is dead, and my mother has lived to see it all...

Whereas I used to look out of Dean Martin's window at *his* tennis court, I can now look out of my own window at *my* tennis court (though I concede that Jimmy Connors has not, so far, appeared to play upon it, though Vivian Richards has).

Many of those who come to my door are clear-headed on arrival, but confused upon exit – particularly those who have to write about it:

'The pony-tailed eccentric property developer, ex-DJ and restaurant entrepreneur today described his plan for transforming county cricket...'

Nothing connects, you see. My life seems logical enough to me in its progression from Lancashire textiles to cricket, to rock and roll, to DJ, to property, back to DJ, to real estate, back to cricket, back to textiles, back to Lancashire (the club) and Cheshire (the county), taking in along the way four wives, cannabis, LSD, mescaline, a couple of homes in California and a couple of homes here in Cheshire and a penthouse in trendy 'South Chelsea' (Battersea), overlooking the park. It is totally baffling to everyone else.

To compound the confusion, I have been young tycoon, sartorial Beatle, Errol Flynn, honest craftsman, squire, poet, hippie, lover and guru. Compressed in the fashion of newspapers this makes little sense: it is as if they write about a dozen different people. And since writers are confused, viewers and readers are confused. There is too much detail to be absorbed in a couple of thousand words. And as that appears to be the optimum number in newspaper or magazine articles, the mystery of who and what I am (so far) remains; though I hope I am now dispelling it with some success.

'Hudson', says one English writer, 'is the last of the English eccentrics'. I hope not. I trust not. Eccentricity must live! It is the only thing that gives normality a yardstick by which to measure itself.

In my own mind, the aim is clear enough:

To get the best out of a situation at any one time for the good of the majority.

Now what's wrong with such an objective? That was my commitment to, and on behalf of, Botham; my commitment to cricket (*whose administrators are invariably dull, rigid, uncompromising, unimaginative, and frequently inept*); my commitment to radio (*why are the DJs all alike, speaking not an ounce of sense between them, and where are the stations ready to employ people in their place who not only have intelligence but who are allowed to use it?*); my commitment to textiles (*people's lives should be more colourful, more varied, more adventurous*); my commitment to life (*where all things are possible in the light of a new day*).

I am eclectic in the people I admire.

I admire the man who uses his hands, Uncle Charlie, Brother John, the anonymous man, the working man, the man with skills, honest intentions. I admire him from experience because I have done what he does and been proud of what I have shaped and created, like him. There are times in life when there is no choice: circumstances put you down. The only way forward is a hard way. When those times come you dig and you toil and you work your way through to something better.

I have relatives and friends like that, and I will forever regard them fondly.

I admire the rich who have the foresight and skill to acquire their riches against all the odds, for they are like great cricketers or great gladiators in the arena of competitive life. But if their riches bring pettiness, if they live meanly and falsely, and if they use their powers to humiliate or degrade others, then I will put them down if I can and

103

humiliate them in their turn.

I do not admire the in-betweens: the aspiring people of doubtful worth now known as Yuppies. A curious breed, I feel, of no real account except to themselves.

Here, then, are the values I hope I represent in this middle period of my life, where my roots are established on both sides of the Atlantic, where my wife and partner, Maxi, increasingly likes, admires, and feels comfortable in the English ways; and where, gathering mushrooms on my cricket field, I can leap over the fence to say hello to someone passing by from the long-gone days of my youth.

Tranquillity is here, but conflict is never far away. There is much to be done. I would not like to think that the administrators of cricket, or radio, or TV, or any other area where I have a restless interest, will forever sleep easily.

Meanwhile – on to cricket, and Botham, and 1985.

BY CHOICE, BOTHAM

—

I would love to see cricket totally orchestrated: Pink Floyd playing
and the game going on. Here (at my Cheshire home) we hope that
when people come to watch cricket, grandfather will fish in the
lake, a wife will play tennis, kids will have swings and paddling
pool, a brass band will play for grandmother and at night the
young daughter-in-law will come in because the calypso band is
playing.
Tim Hudson, *Daily Express*, May 1984.

Becoming the friend and adviser of Ian Botham was a supremely
satisfying achievement. I felt I understood him. I lived my cricketing
fantasies through him. I did not get to play for England, but my man
was the star.

For love of cricket I had acquired, first, my own cricket field in
Cheshire, and then the old hall and grounds of which the pitch is a part.
For love of cricket I organised there a Boycott v. Botham game which I
billed as the Heavyweight Championship of Cricket – £10,000, winner
take all. Jack Ikin had been my childhood hero. Ian Botham was my
adult inspiration because he towered over everyone: strong, masculine,
dominating, flamboyant. He is the man who, says Maxi, epitomises in
one frame every woman's son, every woman's lover, every woman's
bastard. To me, he is magnificent, unrepeatable, and greater than Dr
Grace – fallible, volatile, a precious commodity, and, in the manner of

larger-than-life people, not infrequently a boor, a bore and a gross irritant.

I acquired my cricket ground almost by accident. I returned from America with the intention of playing cricket and buying an interest in a commercial radio station. Ian Botham was far from my mind.

My initial return was instigated when an old schoolfriend called me when I was in LA and told me that the old gardener's cottage in Prestbury was for sale. Bascially I bought it as a family memento; what could have been more romantic than that? I just thought it would be good to use during the summer, and rent out in the winter.

We came over in 1982 to send back a rock show once a week to KXLU in Los Angeles, reporting from England just after the Falklands war. A good year for music. I interviewed all the bands. We had a flat in Chelsea, on the King's Road. We spoke to everyone, Mari Wilson, Simple Minds, Viv Westwood, Richard Thompson ... we went to one of the huge Futurama concerts ... we recorded shows, walked down the King's Road, and had a great time. I was last in England in 1977, so I saw the beginning and the end of punk.

I was also playing a lot of cricket. I was playing for Prestbury on Sundays and driving straight back to London at night. A guy at the IBA in London told me about Signal Radio in Stoke-on-Trent. The station was just starting. I thought it would be good for the Midlands ... and for Macclesfield, which was near by.

One morning I drove out to look at Signal Radio station. I was looking for financial involvement. I was staying at the gardener's cottage in Prestbury and we were driving along a country lane when Maxi spotted a For Sale sign. Here was the cricket ground where I had once played in an under-13s game, and I told her so.

She said, 'That's nice – let's buy it.' At the first available phone box, I called an estate agent and childhood friend, Mike Higson, and told him of my intention. His immediate response was, 'What the hell do you want to buy a cricket ground for?' 'Will you', I said, 'get Tony Neary (a solicitor and former England rugby international) to go along to

1984

Isn't this the year of Big Brother and the end of the world? Marvin Gaye dies.

Frankie Goes to Hollywood. Wham ... Splitsville. Band Aid ... Do They Know It's Christmas.

Madonna ... Like a Virgin. Prince ... Purple Rain film. Billy Idol. Pet Shop Boys. Tina Turner and Eric Clapton come back.

TV

The Tube.

MOVIE

Ghostbuster.

the auction to represent me and buy the ground for me?' He said he would call back, so I stood in the box and the return call said Tony was not available but that I would be represented by another solicitor named Tim Lomas.

I went to the radio station. That night, at the auction, Maxi leaned across to the solicitor and said, 'Buy the cricket pitch at any cost.' I had not even seen the ground. We had not had the time. All we had seen was the sign. At any rate, we bought it for £18,000 and I remember feeling very hot and sticky and people were saying 'Congratulations' and I thought, Wow! I have my own pitch. Or rather more, as it happens, in fact ten acres.

Next day I went to this ground and found it to be a cow pasture where they brought the mower out on Saturday or Sunday mornings to cut the wicket. There was a little ramshackle shed. You could not hit a cover drive for four. You could wham the ball as hard as you liked and it would only go to short extra-cover. I played a game with the village side and I think we had only eight people in our team. But something far grander existed in my imagination. I could see my cricketing Hollywood Bowl, the Birtles Bowl. Everything had to go, the village side included. I could not paint my grand picture with everybody playing on the green. The inaugural game of 4 July – my grand Independence Day – had Farouk Engineer and Roy Collins. We had a big tent in the middle of the field and we hung out our flag to proclaim our presence.

I cannot say, in truth, that some of my Cheshire neighbours were happy with what was to come … either the brass bands or the prospect of promixity to the greatest cricketers of the day. One neighbour was quoted as saying: 'You can't send Mr Hudson back to California, can you? I thought Flower Power died back in the Sixties.'

Boycott v. Botham … The Heavyweight Championship of Cricket … £10,000, winner take all … at the Birtles Bowl, the Superbowl of cricket … Tuesday, 8 May 1984. I think people are aware that what I am doing is not just getting money: it is a new direction. People say: How can you paint the pavilion green, with touches of black, yellow and red? Why isn't it green and white? They say that is disgusting. Others say: How delightful! It is very hard to please everybody. How much did I lose (as a result of the day's game)? It could be £25,000 or £30,000. I do not know until my accountant tells me. But the day was beautiful, the game was completed, and I was happy, totally content.

Tim Hudson to the Press.

A year later, after that game at Birtles, on a day in January 1985, I was out by the pool in Palm Springs reading my *Wall Street Journal*. The temperature was 80 degress, quite mild for that part of the country. It was a good winter's day and I was at peace. Maxi came screaming from the condominium – 'the condo' of one-level apartments around the pool and tennis court where we have one of our Californian homes – and what she had to convey was shattering: 'Botham got busted.'

That term can mean only one thing in California. Drugs. She showed me an English newspaper and there was a picture of Botham wearing suit and tie walking into court with his solicitor. This, it became obvious, was something to do with roach or seed. Cannabis.

My immediate thought was for the man. The attitude of California towards marijuana is in no way similar to that of England. In something like twenty-three states of America possession of less than an ounce of cannabis is a misdemeanour akin to getting a parking ticket. The vast majority of people in California, of whatever social or financial level, have taken drugs at one stage of their lives. Marijuana is taken for granted. Cocaine is often openly available at parties, like nuts or crisps. Make whatever moral judgment you will: this is a fact of Los Angeles life.

From what I had read, Ian Botham had not molested any little girls. He had not corrupted anybody. He had not raped anybody. Yet here he was, pilloried, guilty or not I knew not. I recalled my years growing up in the English countryside: people boozing, driving their cars in narrow-lane pile-ups. And the inconsistency of attitude between marijuana and drink was something I found totally illogical.

I phoned Botham. I was not managing him at the time and had to get the number from Brian Close. I was just a guy on my usual winter visit to California, staying at my weekend home. I felt I had to help him. I had happy memories of his appearance at the cricket match he played for me, and felt the £10,000 I handed to him then had been money well spent.

I had spent around £50,000 doing up my pavilion and maybe another £20,000 on machinery and I did things that the normal Englishman would not be able to afford to do and things the wealthy Englishman would never dream of doing. Love of the game was at the heart of it. Respect and admiration for Ian Botham was a key part of that love.

After speaking with Botham on the phone, Maxi and I told him we would be returning to England in March and it was agreed we would get together with him and his wife, Cathy, to talk. He was unhappy with the people surrounding him. We met him on our return and I guaranteed him £20,000 more a year than he was currently getting, telling him I did not want to manage him in the conventional sense.

I had a concept for the game and I had a concept for Botham. The game had to change radically. Botham had to be given the true rewards of his talent. There is a feeling in England that the heart of cricket is the three-day game, and what surrounds it is sacrosanct. It is a man with sandwiches in a plastic bag alone on an otherwise empty seat contemplating, from beneath a straw hat, the inner mysteries of motion. It was not my concept.

I felt cricket had become more and more watered down. It began with big wagers and should go back to them.

Cricket should be the Coliseum with gladiators, thumbs up or down, with room only for winners in the arena. It is not the sound of ball on willow. You cannot support cricket by old school ties. The whole idea is catering for the family: food, drink, merriment, rock and roll charisma, promotion, whatever you care to call it. I was trying to take that rock and roll audience that grew up with me in the Sixties, now with kids in the Eighties, to a new dimension, so that they would say:

'Hey, I'm going to this cricket match because they have a brass band playing during the game, and after the game they have a calypso band, or a reggae band.' The whole thing encompassed in a day.

Americans go to an event of some kind at week-ends. The English see week-ends as an uneventful sandwich for the dark, toiling week.

Excitement is needed, and Ian Botham is excitement. I saw him as my rock and roll Superstar.

> Cricket changes with its social background. The quality of it, the tempo of it, the aim and character of it changes in any period. It was a gambling vehicle in the days of Regency bucks, a game of muscular Christianity and eminent respectability in the Edwardian age, alternately promising and threatening between the two wars, increasingly technical subsequently, and nowadays it is promotions, sponsorships, entertainment through television. It reflects its society.
> John Arlott, April 1980.

Stars, names: these are the things that matter. Botham and Richards turn the turnstiles because they are great cricketers and larger than life. And why not Gooch v. Boycott? The more you see rock, the more you realise it is Mick Jagger *and* the Rolling Stones, Bruce Springsteen *and* the East Street Band.

You need the team; you need the back-up, but above all the leader must be inspired. You do not talk about the British Army but rather of Wellington, or Montgomery.

You do not think of the wartime Cabinet; you think of Churchill. The inspired leader is what makes the boys join up. Observe the cricket posters: 'Lancashire v. Somerset'. Is that the way to sell? Where is the inspiration? Where is the big picture of Botham in action labelled: 'Here today – THE GREATEST!'

In Hollywood I had become accustomed to star status. I am probably one of the most knowledgeable Englishmen in the arena of American football because I follow it, and watch it, compulsively. Great stars earn vast amounts of money at an early age and I see nothing wrong with that. If money is indecent why do some people around the periphery of cricket have so much while many of the players have so little? If footballers can earn £2,000 a week for kicking a ball into a net, why should a batsman not earn that much for hitting a ball to the boundary?

I remember reading how Botham had said Mick Jagger went round to congratulate him after he had a big knock and he was overwhelmed by that event: flattered beyond measure that Mick Jagger (who, in any case, gives the impression of being unsure of himself beyond his stage presence) had made the effort. I said to Ian: 'He would love to be *you*. You are the biggest hero in his life. He would have given all his money, all his achievement, just to have had your name, your success. You are the greatest hero in the country. In America, sports heroes are royalty.'

My concept for my ground at Birtles, then, was to have two forms of cricket: world heavyweight championship cricket and a Hudson's Hollywood Eleven playing anybody for money. We put out a challenge to Mick Jagger for £20,000 and heard nothing back. I had a vision of playing Tim Rice's eleven for money. Elton John's eleven. And I could *see* it on television: £25,000 on the game. They do it for racehorses, why not for cricket players?

I think I was the first person Ian allowed to get on stage with him. I had the idea of him branching out in all directions.

Super sportsman Ian Botham is planning to hit the fashion industry for six. He is teaming up with millionaire businessman Timothy Hudson to become the image behind a new concept of unique and classic clothing. Fans will be bowled over by the English public schoolboy look that will carry the label 'By Choice Botham'. Ian Botham is joining the company of Hudson's Hardware as a director. It is to invest £1m to promote a new line of fashion wear that will range from brothel creepers to bowlers.
Press release, 7 May 1985.

Early in 1984, Maxi and I had started to develop a concept known as Hudson's Hardware, which involved the manufacture and sale of traditional-style cricket clothes – the old-school-tie collection: rugby shirts, cricket sweaters, striped blazers, white flannel trousers with turn-ups and buttons, and we adopted our flower motif of black, yellow, red and green in the styling.

Hudson's Hardware was to exploit the clothing range sold from a shop we owned in Prestbury.

Ian Botham agreed to promote the clothing range and, in return, was to receive a 20 per cent stake in the company.

In May of that year, it was agreed that Maxi and I would act as business managers to Ian in place of his then manager, Reg Hayter. We felt that Ian's commercial potential was not being properly exploited and planned to promote him as an international sports star, broadening his potential to a degree that no previous cricket player had achieved.

From around May 1985 onwards, we set about renegotiating contracts Reg Hayter had negotiated on Ian's behalf and sought new contracts to promote and exploit our player's reputation. As part of the renegotiation we approached Nike in the UK. Botham already had an agreement with them to wear Nike shoes exclusively. This agreement was limited to shoes.

On 20 August 1985, Maxi and I met John Caine, promotions manager to Nike International, with two ideas:

To interest Nike in our Hudson's Hardware concept – the English public schoolboy look with traditional British clothing such as the cricket flannels, blazers, sweaters and tracksuits.

And, separately, we discussed the idea of using Botham to promote the concept, particularly in America.

Mr Caine was not enthusiastic.

As a result, we contacted Rob Strasser, No. 2 in Nike Inc. of Portland, Oregon, and on 9 January 1986 we flew to Oregon at Nike's expense and attended a long meeting discussing both the Hudson's Hardware concept and the idea of using Ian to promote it.

Rob Strasser was enthusiastic about both ideas and figures were discussed. Items of Hudson's Hardware clothing and logos were left with Nike. It was agreed that a further meeting would take place in the UK to finalise the deal, and this took place on 22 January 1986, at Blake's Hotel in London where both Maxi and myself were staying.

1985

MUSIC AND HAPPENINGS

Live Aid . . . Wembley . . . US/UK tie-up. Simply Red . . . Manchester starts moving musically for the first time since Punk in 1976. International Club . . . brings in medium-size tours to the city. IYY Festival at Platt Fields. U2 . . . Unforgettable Fire . . . Bangles. Robert Palmer. Sade. Jesus and the Mary Chain. USA for Africa . . . (We Are the World). Springstein's big year in England . . . Born in the USA. Greenpeace.

MOVIES

Beverly Hills Cop. Brazil. Give My Regards to Broad Street . . . Sorry, Paul . . . You gave birth to a turkey . . . we've all been through it. Great idea, though. Cotton Club . . .

Agreement on management terms had still not been reached.

But considerable progress was being made with Nike. Botham's name was to be used to launch a new Nike tennis shoe, which could also be worn for cricket, and a range of clothing, the blazers, the white flannels, the sweaters, rugby shirts, etcetera, and Nike would spend between $300,000 and $500,000 in publicity on the range of goods.

In my view, the deal would give Botham recognition as a public personality in America which he would never get merely as a cricketer, and which could lead to films and other things.

As a goodwill gesture – since I had promised Botham would earn £20,000 more in his first year over his current earnings – I provided a car, and there is some considerable history to this, as we shall see.

We decided that the Guy the Gorilla image was over. My original idea was to get him a Rolls or Bentley with a chauffeur and I thought he and Viv Richards, whom I also had ideas of managing, would have a marvellous time riding around in this way.

That idea fell apart and I contacted Jaguar. I saw Ian as their image. The Jaguar point of view seemed to be that it was its own best image: the car not the star.

I wrote to chairman John Egan: 'I have the idea of taking Mr Botham to California just prior to the tour of the West Indies. I would very much like to see Ian Botham presented as a C. Aubrey Smith–Errol Flynn British-man's image to go with the Jaguar motor car ... I understand you are bringing out a new model later this year and do feel that an entire package involving Mr Botham could be of great interest to you and myself.'

The reply indicated that 'in principle we would not be interested in your promotion, but Graham Whitehead, president of our company in the USA, might be...' If he were, 'he would make contact with you direct'.

So a car for Botham did not materialise. I found that disgusting, particularly when I discovered that Bernhard Langer, the golfer, was given a Jaguar. I was told it came from Deutsche Jaguar, the German agents. I gave that story to the papers and they loved it. My line was that they could provide a car for a German but not for their home-grown hero. I signed the cheque for a £22,000 Jaguar for Ian in anger. I suspect it embarrassed the company because they gave me a 17 per cent discount.

The cost, so far as I was concerned, was to be reimbursed out of the first £20,000 earned during that current year in excess of Botham's earnings in the previous year.

Botham was later to claim that the car was a gift.

Nike (and this becomes important later) was always treated separately from the management arrangements. It was proposed that Nike royalties should be split 60–40 in favour of Botham. It was, in other words, being dealt with outside any arrangement agreement.

At the Blake's Hotel meeting, Nike produced a letter of intent confirming that Nike and Botham would enter into a new agreement to supersede the existing 1981 agreement.

Botham, meanwhile, had a contract with the Duncan Fearnley company to promote its cricket equipment and other goods which extended to leisurewear, although no leisurewear had actually been made.

After the Nike meeting, Maxi and I agreed a £6,000 reduction in fees to Botham from Duncan Fearnley in return for a release of Botham from the clothing obligations which might otherwise have jeopardised the Nike arrangements. It was agreed that he should keep the Jaguar. The management agreement was signed at that meeting, effective from 1 August 1985.

At this time there was a funny piece of gossip that ran from the Tytherington 'yuppie club' up the hill to the Prestbury Golf Club. It seems there was this very well-known young lady who frantically called the wrong T. Hudson in the Cheshire phone book in her search for the Botham. The crowd on the seven-past-eight train out of Prestbury to Manchester the next morning knew a lot more about Botham than I did. Courtesy of some fancy dancer ... I see them knocking on your stained-glass door ... with their words of this and that ... they glide across your floor.

On 13 March 1986, Maxi and I again flew to Oregon at the expense of Nike. The promotion of the Hudson's Hardware concept using Botham was discussed at length and Nike agreed to be a major sponsor of a cricket match to take place in September at Birtles Bowl launching Nike's new line. Nike had produced running kits for the April London Marathon using the Hudson Hardware colours. A draft agreement was prepared.

On 2 April 1986, *The Star* published its front-page story in which I was quoted as saying 'Doesn't everybody?' when questioned about Botham's alleged use of marijuana. So much for the bare outline of events. Now, to fill in the gaps.

Before Nike, I tried Tootals and Vantona. I needed a major company. The original idea, before Botham came along, was to sell by mail order.

I went to a cricket game one afternoon when Jaguar were playing Warwickshire. All the workers were there, maybe 1,000 or so. There were tents, food, laughter. Ian hit 80-odd. He was cracking sixes everywhere and I said, 'Look, you are being used. Are you being paid any money for this?' He said it was free because it was for a friend, Dennis Amiss; part of the cricketing code. I said: 'You are the one drawing the crowd. You only have so long at the top.'

I told him I did not want to hear the name Ian. 'You are Mr Botham. You are not I. T. Botham or Ian Botham. You should never be called Ian by youngsters. They should call you Mr Botham.' I was trying to create somebody bigger than life, somebody bigger than a billboard.

I walked into the office of Kelvin MacKenzie, editor of *The Sun*, and renegotiated a great deal for the column by my player. They upped the contract by a considerable amount and even offered me £10,000 a year separately. I refused because I wanted my lines of communication to the rest of the press left open.

I arranged a book with Collins – *High, Wide and Handsome*, written by Botham in collaboration with the journalist Frank Keating – for which a large advance was agreed.

I became obsessed by what I was doing with and for Ian Botham. I had a great summer as his friend and shadow.

Castle Hotel, Taunton … a vintage Jensen outside the door … my groundsman-cum-chauffeur to carry my bags upstairs. Ian was happy. Ian was making runs. Ian was getting lots of presents. I got to Arundel and along comes Colin Cowdrey. He drops Maxi and me off at our hotel. Fifteen minutes later, the phone rings. 'My wife and I would like to invite you up to our home. You shouldn't have to stay at an hotel.' We stayed two nights with Colin Cowdrey and Lady Anne. He even helped carry our bags to the car.

The next morning we were sitting in M.C.C.'s library and he blurted out, 'Yes, Hudson, you did play for Surrey Second XI v. Kent Second XI at Canterbury, 1962. You scored 1 in the first innings and 0 in the second innings – the same as Mike Denness who was making his début for Kent that day.'

July 1985, Lord's. Ian Botham bet me £5,000 that he would bag five Australian wickets and so become the first man in the history of Test cricket to capture a nap hand of wickets in an innings 25 times. Of course he did it. And with such style! He asked Mike Gatting, his fellow Test cricketer, to go around to the stand and give the ball to Maxi in front of the MCC bigwigs, England selectors and all.

I duly wrote out the cheque and sent it back. The look he cast in my direction when he took that fifth wicket was as memorable as anything in my recollection. He was the bullfighter presenting the ear of the bull.

In October 1985, I negotiated for him a new contract with Somerset to make him county cricket's leading money-earner by a wide margin. The committee members travelled to my house in Cheshire for the talks. I said: 'Only a one-year contract and we want a guaranteed salary plus bonuses, which will bring it up to £30,000 a year.'

I could see him and Viv Richards promoting Black and White whisky to perfection.

Ian spent a great deal of time at my house. He made it his own. The acres around it gave him the seclusion he could not achieve in his own home where there were neighbours to see every time he went out, every time he returned. He felt at ease, and would walk downstairs, just a towel around his waist, to find something in the kitchen.

The involvement I had with his affairs was such that it led to my wife giving me a choice: 'Him or me.' She was willing to stay with the business but not to have a matrimonial relationship, such was my obsession. Ian's wife may well have been uneasy, too. That crisis passed, but he was always a full-time occupation. He consumes people.

He takes over a room and the atmosphere in it with this huge, all-encompassing, powerful aura. He does not relax; not the sort of man who would sit with a book. He is action man.

I am fifteen years older than him and fifteen years slower. I find it difficult to watch three videos in a row. I am a man of regular habits. I do not mind going to bed at 9 pm and getting up at 7 am. Ian never appears to go to bed, and since he does not like to be alone his companions suffer the consequences of lost sleep and neglected matrimony.

He challenges everybody: the women in the room, the men in the room. A lot of athletes or rock people are very much used to the scrubbers and groupies and hangers-on of the circus. I was trying to take Ian away from such dangers.

I became the voyeur during The Both's Hollywood holiday … sitting and observing his actions. Being a lover of ladies I have been accustomed to feeling the sexuality in the air most of my life, but with 'Both' it's all so different from rock and roll. It's real heavy macho man … watching the ladies squirm in his presence … particularly in a night-club atmosphere … subdued lighting … hot music, etc.

Women certainly become uncomfortable … he becomes like a Roman gladiator at the feast of something or another. Women find it more than difficult not to cross and uncross their legs under his gaze. They seem to breathe much quicker and their chests begin to heave as the nipples push against the soft T-shirt fabric or the silk blouses. He's definitely every woman's piece of rough … in the long, long grass … by the lake … under a full moon.

I am saying all this from a writer's point of view … poetic licence. But I'm sure that the pretty blonde writer from *Penthouse* magazine at Tramps that Friday night would have to agree with me…

Maybe I was wrong. Scrubbers who hang around the periphery of stardom are never a threat to marriage. I was trying to take my man up-market. He looked good. He could have sold anything British. He was the bulldog. We started this I Am Bigger than Life attitude. I think now that he believes it. We created a Frankenstein. Upon our horizons the clouds were gathering and we did not perceive them.

DOESN'T EVERYBODY?

—

In December 1985 I took Ian Botham to Hollywood with the idea of broadening his horizons and furthering his career. It was part of a long-term plan. It was also, for him, a busman's holiday. It was not – as legend of the time would have us believe – the intention that he should be signed there and then for a movie. Fantasy would suggest that could happen. But who ever walks in and gets signed?

'Cricket superstar Ian Botham', wrote Frank Curran in *The Star*, 'is being tipped as the new James Bond. The man who reckons he is ready for the job is Hollywood starmaker Menachem Golan. The millionaire producer is ready to give Botham a plum role in one of his blockbusters. But he reckons his really big chance will come as the successor to Sean Connery and Roger Moore as 007. Golan, whose remake of *King Solomon's Mines* is America's latest box-office smash, said:

'He's got the looks, the build and the accent to be the next James Bond. I know they are looking around because Roger has hinted that he won't be in the next one. And Ian would be a live candidate if he takes my advice and puts his name forward.'

The *Daily Mirror* was quoting Ian at Heathrow Airport as saying: 'I am not going out there for a screen test or anything like that. I am just going to go over, take it from there, and see what happens.'

The *Daily Mail* was declaring: 'The opening innings of Ian Botham's Hollywood career is proving a spectacular flop. Rather than taking Tinseltown by storm, the would-be screen superstar has scored a duck. There are no movie directors summoning him for screen tests and

not one invitation to appear on a television chat show. Instead of living
it up in five-star luxury, he is dossing down in the garden shed of his
manager's brightly painted beach shack. And guests at a party thrown
for him were asking: "Ian who?"'

You pay a lot of money if you want to live on a beach in
California. That beach house is worth a million dollars. I spent $30,000
just converting my garage into a place I now think of as the Botham
Suite and it was finished – with fitted carpets and 50-channel TV – two
hours before he got off the plane.

He spent two and half weeks there and had a superb time. He
spent an afternoon on the beach with John McEnroe, Tatum O'Neal and
Ryan O'Neal. We went for dinner at Spago on the Sunset-Strip with
Bernie Taupin, Elton John's lyrics writer, and Bernie paid the bill which
must have been around $1,000. Thank you, Bernie. We threw a party at
the King's Head, the famous British pub in Santa Monica, for around
300 people and the British consul came.

I organised a feature cover story with *Sports Illustrated* that was
going to be done in the spring. I arranged for *Esquire* magazine to do a
feature on Ian's cricketing trip to the West Indies on the lines: The
biggest baseball player in the world does not play baseball.

Elle magazine agreed to go to the West Indies to do several pages
on Ian wearing our clothes.

He did, indeed, meet Menachem Golan, who said: 'All I want you
to do is put me ten cents on every seat.' I said, 'Botham will give you
ten cents; he'll give you a million kids in Britain, a million in Australia,
a whole lot more in India and Pakistan – wherever cricket is played.
That is what a movie star is all about.'

He said, 'Well, I've got to tell you he is better-looking than Tom
Selleck.' Botham struck out his chest then and got a little cocky. Golan
said if he was prepared to go to Hollywood to take acting lessons for six
months he felt sure he would be in demand.

I felt I had done a superb job for him in Hollywood. What stuck in
the craw was the *Daily Mail* reference to a shack. If all the world had
shacks like that it would be a better place. 'I thought everybody in
Hollywood lived in a shack on the beach,' wrote Frank Keating in *The
Guardian.*

It was fun time. Ian turned out for England against Australia in a pub match and was caught for a duck off the third ball. He drank Budweiser. He tuned in to a new kind of society and enjoyed what he saw. He was wined and dined from Malibu to Beverly Hills and, without doubt, was given 'the look' by the best beauties of Hollywood. He was a star on a first-class holiday.

After it all, he was quoted in the press as saying: 'I just wanted to unwind after the slog of my [charity] walk from John o' Groats to Land's End. I know Tim has got a few things planned from now on and I am looking forward to getting out to meet all the people he has been telling me about for so long.'

So nothing about his words suggested that he had been let down, or diminished, by his experience. Off he went to the West Indies and a series of misfortunes and protestations that were to lead to the souring of our relationship.

1986

New Order.
The Smiths.
Julian Cope.
Paul Simon . . .
Gracelands
Album.

MOVIES

Betty Blue . . .
sexy.
Mona Lisa.
Room with a
View.
Down and Out in
Beverly Hills.
Hannah and Her
Sisters.

'Guy the Gorilla's fury at tour umpire'. 'Botham fury as Gower makes Gooch deputy'. 'England tumble to 10-wicket defeat'.

'Botham has become a lone, reclusive figure who confines himself to his hotel room. He complains, with justification, that any move he makes in public will be distorted. He calls his room the bat-cage and broods there on the price of stardom.' Thus Ian Wooldridge, from Trinidad, in March 1986.

In five matches, 168 runs, eight wickets. 'Bye, Bye Both – It's time to pull your finger out or get out.'

March 1986: 'As England headed towards another humiliating defeat the question on everyone's lips was: Will England sack Botham?'

In that same month: 'Police are probing alleged misuse of drugs during Ian Botham's charity walk from John o' Groats to Land's End.' He refuses to comment. A fellow-walker describes the allegations as 'ridiculous'.

April 1986, and the *News of the World*, which has more lids to lift than a five-star chef, lifts the lid on 'the real story of Botham and drugs'.

'Blonde beauty Lindy Field has told how cricket ace Ian Botham snorted cocaine and made torrid love to her hours before he played for England in the West Indies.'

Accusations, denials, innuendo, trouble. The banana did not invent the banana skin. I suspect I know who did. Ian Botham was quoted by the *Daily Express* in these terms: 'If only a quarter of the things that have ever been said and written about me were true, I would be completely pickled by now and would have sired half the children in the world. I treat all these stories with the contempt they deserve.'

I was not involved in all this. I was in California intending to fly out to the West Indies.

Phil Elwell, who runs the King's Head in Santa Monica, is probably my best friend in California. He is from Birmingham, a 6 ft 2 in ex-military policeman who looks like Falstaff. He has a $3m Malibu home on a hill overlooking the ocean, with garden flowing down to the beach. A *Dallas–Dynasty* kind of house. Not bad for a fella who started off with a hot-dog stand less than fifteen years ago.

He held a party for maybe 200 guests. It was no rock and roll affair. The people there were largely English businessmen – suits, ties. The party began around 8.30. There was some conversation about police investigating cannabis following Ian's charity walk and Maxi and I were standing with three journalists: John Hiscock (then) of *The Sun*, Ian Brodie of the *Daily Telegraph* and Terry Willows of *The Star*. A cricketing group. We had all played for the English team with Mr Botham. In fact Willows had stood and talked with 'Mr Both' in the slips – a Judas Iscariot if ever there was one.

The question Terry Willows put about Botham's real or imagined use of cannabis was directed more at my wife than myself. As I recall it, he said: 'Look, we can believe maybe New Zealand. We can believe maybe Pakistan [these being references to various stories involving Botham]. But come on; we're not stupid. Off the record...'

The question has to be seen in the context of the time: a relaxed gathering after a few drinks, an enjoyable communion of friends, in a part of the world where cannabis has as much relevance to sin as virginity has to a hooker. It was not the sort of place where I felt threatened or on my guard. I recall using a soliloquy I have used many times:

'Ian Botham is a product of a generation that grew up on The
Beatles. To that generation, smoking marijuana was like our parents and
grandparents drinking a bottle of Scotch.' It was a reflex action: like a
boxer putting up a forearm to ward off a routine blow.

Terry Willows mentioned something else; I do not recall what it
was. And I said, off the cuff, 'Doesn't everyone?' Such was the
conversation.

John Hiscock never wrote anything, so far as I know. I believe
Kelvin MacKenzie, his editor [on *The Sun*], was not too pleased. *The Star*
used headlines of a size normally reserved for the deaths of Presidents,
the beginning of world wars or a falling government:

> BOTHAM DRUGS SHOCK – 'I know he smokes dope but
> doesn't everybody?' says his manager.
> Cricket star Ian Botham uses drugs, his manager said
> yesterday. 'I'm aware that he smokes dope, but doesn't everybody?'
> said flamboyant Tim Hudson. 'Ian does not have a serious drugs
> problem. Yes, he has taken pot, but that is not a drugs problem.
> He does not take cocaine to the best of my knowledge.'

Before publication, I had a phone call from John Hiscock: 'Listen, I
think something is about to explode in *The Star* from Terry Willows.'

Maxi and I looked at each other and said, 'My God!' The next
phone call was from another newsman – I cannot remember who – and
he said: 'Have you seen what is in *The Star*?' We had not. We were in
Miami, ostensibly on our way to the West Indies. We did not get to the
West Indies that night because the plane was cancelled. Then came a
phone call from Ian Botham. He had been in the coffee shop of the hotel
in the West Indies when he heard what was in *The Star* and Ian said to
me: 'Hudson, what the **** did you say? If you do not issue a story
through your lawyer threatening to sue *The Star* I will have no
alternative. I will either have to sue you or dismiss you.' And he added,
'Maybe both.' By this time John Hiscock was also getting worried
because *The Sun* and *News of the World* people were saying, 'Why didn't
we get this story?' So then he had to say he was a witness and Ian
Brodie said to me that John had admitted that he was a witness. 'And

with a witness and a tape recorder you can't deny you said it.'

I suppose I panicked. I thought, well, perhaps I did say it. Could anyone, involved in a convivial evening with friends, after a few drinks, remember, hand on heart, all that he had said? Would anyone, in social surroundings, expect a companion to be carrying a tape recorder? Would anyone, in a free and easy Californian society, seriously consider cannabis to be of any greater consequence than the state of the weather? The Puritans among us had extracted their blood.

I had not been criticising Ian Botham. I had been defending him. I contacted my own lawyer. He spoke to Terry Willows. Willows wrote the following letter:

> Dear Tim and Maxi: I am appalled at what happened with *The Star* and the gross error that was made in using my personal memo as copy. I know John [Hiscock] understands the error since it obviously affected him. I have not written a single word about yourselves or Ian since *The Star* story appeared and do not propose to do so in the future.
>
> I can only offer my apologies at *The Star*'s comedy of errors. I do know that steps have been taken by the editor to ensure it can't happen again. Once again, my apologies. I did not break my word as given to you on the night.
>
> Best wishes, Terry.

No comment! Meanwhile, Ian was obviously in trouble I did not know about and was worrying.

Ian said on the phone to me: 'Do you know about some woman who has given a story to the *News of the World?*' and I said, 'No.' I phoned John Hiscock and he knew nothing.

My alleged remarks were the final blow for Ian in his splintering world. It was almost like *Dynasty*. Pure theatre. And that was the last time I spoke to him. Ever. I returned to England and refused to make further comment.

Ian Botham will go down in history as a Robin Hood. He wore my colours for a painting by the highly-acclaimed painter, John Bellany, ARA. It hangs in the National Portrait Gallery and my grandchildren

123

will say, 'Those are my grandfather's colours.'

It will be long forgotten by then that I managed him for only a year. That is my Walter Mitty experience. He had said to me: 'There are only two people in this world who can tell you what to do – your daughter [River] and me.' I understood him. Botham was the most exciting thing in my creative life. By choice, Botham. By choice, good-bye.

My plans were left drifting with the tides of chance. As Botham dispensed with my services the contract with Nike was left unsigned. So far as I know the case is still in the hands of lawyers. We had gone as far as nominating the salesmen and one of them, Steve Smith, the England rugby scrum-half, ran with the ball and started his own company.

I felt, and still feel, betrayed. But I did not retaliate. On the contrary, when Botham was under fire over his 'gin-slinging' Test selectors speech ('Everything I said was in jest and I hope the selectors will accept it in that context') and already suspended from Test cricket over use of drugs, I offered him a two-month exclusive contract to play a series of eight games at my cricket ground, guaranteeing him a substantial fee, double what he was losing by not playing county and Test cricket. There was no question of managing him: it was a matter, merely, of acquiring his services.

I stated publicly at that time: 'If Mr Botham accepts this offer it will be the birth of The Outlaws and Carnival Cricket. We offer our hospitality to his family for this two-month period.

'We offer rest, relaxation, fishing, tennis and even cutting the outfield. Mr Botham needs rest and relaxation and his friends at my home will assure his privacy and security.'

It came to nothing.

The débris from all this, and a reassessment of my opinion of Botham, is perhaps relevant at this time.

CALLING CARD

—

The traumas of the Botham saga were many: the man is a bully. You have to be his servant to get on with him. Whatever he says, you do. He is volatile. He talks all the time. He is no academic, but after a few drinks he tends to pontificate on subjects of which he knows little or nothing to the embarrassment of his friends and the consternation of acquaintances.

He is a man of excess in most things, often unthinking, often unfeeling. His favourite subject is himself. He has a juvenile appreciation of money.

When we went to Bernie Taupin's house in California, Botham was very impressed by the pool, the black Rolls, the obvious opulence. 'I mean, this is money, Hudson.' That is typical of his way of needling people. The story also illustrates this childlike quality in him where he does not seem to comprehend that there is a level of wealth beyond which more wealth becomes obsessive. I have always been in the fast lane of life openly. He has been in the fast lane secretly.

Once, we were coming back from Old Trafford to Birtles in my Bentley and I made the mistake of letting him drive. I sat in the back with my friend, Peter Ross, and Maxi. My daughter, River, was in front. That ride was a nightmare I will never forget. He must have been travelling at ninety in a built-up area and Peter Ross's face was a picture. We had booze in the car. I became hysterical. 'For God's sake slow down,' I was shouting. 'We'll all end up in jail.' It was kamikaze stuff. He had disrespect for his own life as well as ours.

He is a lout's hero, and a nasty piece of work when the mood takes him. I do not think he is really into anything. But if someone were having a six-month trip down the Amazon, he would be the one riding the rapids. He could star (naturally) in a great series of TV shows where he would do Captain Marvel – frontiersmanship; Action Man; the greatest cricket player the world has seen, and fifty other unfortunate things as well.

I took him to the finest shop of its type in Los Angeles, The Banana Republic. An in-place making well-made, expensive clothing, hand-made flying jackets, marvellous dresses, and I said, 'How about something for Cathy [his wife]?' He said, 'My wife wouldn't wear that stuff. She's into Gucci and Dior.' I said, 'This is a different *style*. Everybody's got Gucci.'

1987

Michael Jackson
. . . Bad tour . . .
Terence Trent
d'Arby . . .
Beastie Boys.
Grateful Dead
comeback.

Stock Aitken and
Waterman . . .
Rick Astley.

MOVIES

La Bamba.
Radio Days . . .
Woody Allen.

The Sun contributed *mucho dinero* for Botham's trip to California. There were difficulties about his entry permit because he had a drug conviction. So we hired the No. 1 drug attorney in Los Angeles to get a visa.

He brought his minder, Andy, and John Border (brother of Allan Border, the Australian cricketer). He did not bother to tell us that there were three of them. He just brought them. Thank God I never gave him the *Sun* money.

I doled it out and made a list of how it was spent for Botham's accountant and mine. We were well out of pocket plus the cost of renovating our garage and turning it into living accommodation.

Maxi gave him a diamond earring on condition that he wore it. Maybe it was a crazy, silly idea. But I think he should have returned it. If he had any style, he would have done.

I gave him a beautiful watch Maxi bought me: a Boer War military watch. That watch has, so far as I know, been discarded for some gold timepiece.

He was the first cricketer to be painted for the National Portrait Gallery since W. G. Grace. But he was missing from the opening ceremony.

Probably his wife did not like me. My presentation of Botham was as a sex symbol, the greatest rock and roll cricket player in the world. I imagine no wife would be happy to see a man, particularly the father of her three children, presented in that image.

When we finished with him he was hanging out with movie stars and actresses. He went from looking sloppy to a very handsome man, beautifully dressed.

And, as we have seen, he almost cost me my wife.

I was managing him, and yet he did not sign a management contract until the day he left for the West Indies tour. So I was perpetually in limbo with his affairs.

A letter Maxi wrote before that signing sums up her feelings:

> Dear Ian: From the horse's mouth. Exactly one year ago today, your world and life went crashing around your feet. Now, one year later, you are a national hero. Magic? No. Witchcraft? No. Blood, sweat and tears? Yes. During this past year, without so much as a signature on a piece of paper, we, Tim and Maxi, have put our ideas, money, home, life, energy, talent and creative abilities at your disposal. Tim has given up his own writing and radio interests to pick you up off the ground and elevate you to the stature which he truly thought you deserved. He has hawked your talents to whoever would listen because he believed in you as a cricket super hero and a super person.
>
> He and I have argued a number of times about the invasion of Ian Botham into our private lives, as well as completely redirecting our business energies in your direction. Our office deals with your mail, phone calls, contracts, public image, etc., etc. We have scrapped all other business interests in the UK to concentrate on I. T. Botham. We have turned our creative energy into designing a line of clothes, 'The public schoolboy look', into a company which existed before you were on the scene and welcomed you and your image into it, also making you a 20 per cent partner and director. We have shared our Flower Power colours and logo with your image. Tim has turned the media completely around and today there is hardly a bad word written about you.
>
> Maxi/Hudson have withstood the hounding of the press at

Birtles and tried with all our power to keep them off your back. We organised to have your favourite sports writer [Frank Keating, of *The Guardian*] hired [to collaborate on the book] just for you. We have opened the doors of Birtles to you and your friends and family, and closed the gates behind so that you could have privacy.

Maxi/Hudson bought a car for your use when no other English company would do so. We constantly fought your adversaries with words and actions so that today you have become the super sports hero you deserve to be.

We have tried to look after your interests with kindness, consideration and love and still no signature on the dotted line. Maxi/Hudson purchased contracts [from the previous manager] and we have not even seen very much of their value because we have no I. T. Botham signature.

You, also, have worked hard for the company. You have been a superb model. You have exposed Hudson's Hardware at every opportunity. You have grown in self-confidence and become the Pied Piper of children. But you have forgotten that the road this year was travelled by us all. I think we have created a Frankenstein, bigger than life. We have disregarded those who said it would be so. We have disregarded the warnings of conceit, selfishness, rudeness and self-gratification. Yet today, one year after our association began, you don't want to share. You don't want to give us credit for our concepts, our ideas and advice. I heard you say more than once that you trusted us and our judgment, and yet you are questioning our ability today. We are a cohesive unit only if we respect our individual talents and creative abilities. You are a star cricket player. We are the creative and business mind. You play cricket. We make the deals. You are a star who is being managed by a star in his own right, who has shelved his personal creative talent to promote a man he believes in; so much so that he has convinced the whole country, and now America, that you are worth money.

If you want to play cricket, negotiate contracts, do your own PR, enter the entertainment world and continue to have a personal life, I wish you luck. Nike accepted the Hudson's Hardware concept, ideas, colours and Hudson's PR about your credibility. They

The greatest rock
'n roll cricketer in
the world.

The Adonis . . .
painted at Birtles
Old Hall, 1985,
now hanging
permanently in
National Portrait
Gallery, London.

Yours truly. I also
made it on to a
wall at the
National Portrait
Gallery, but only
for two months.

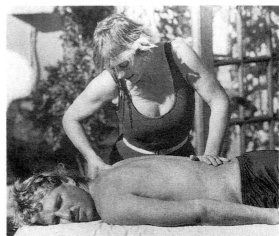

Mr Both. in
Hollywood.

An emperor, a lord, and a king. The best of the best.

The best team in the world.

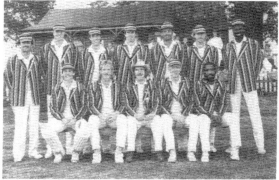

Press conference, Taunton '85.

The King's Head pub, Santa Monica, California.

Both. and Budweiser in Santa Monica with my good friends, the ever-beautiful Californian blonde, Mary Hughes, and musician Brian Auger's wife.

Both. in Hudson
colours.

A living legend.

accepted you as a super cricket hero to promote these concepts in
America. You could be on your way for the rest of your life or you
could screw up, as you have done in the past.

It is up to you. We love you, but cannot give our business
and talent free. We can pursue our other interests. You can pursue
cricket. Make your mind up. Whatever, Good Luck. Maxi.

We were once the best of friends. We liked each other. We began
to wear similar clothes and in a way, he became a clone of myself. But I
do not like his ethics. When he was banned from playing the game and I
offered him £16,000 for eight games at Birtles, he did not have the
decency to reply.

We gave so much away without a contract. I had made a dozen
pairs of cricket flannels for Botham with turn-ups and buttons and I paid
for those – at least £20 per pair. This kind of thing happened over and
over again. If I had half a dozen shirts made, I did not charge him. I
had shoes made for him.

Maxi is particularly irritated by the business of the car. We knew
he had sold it and it had not even been his. It was still in our company
name. Our car. And no contract signed. Maxi said, 'He's sold the Jaguar
and here I am driving around in a tiny car. There's something wrong
here.' By this time she was talking about 'my Jag'. I had to do a little
flannelling with her. That leads us to the day he left for the West Indies
tour, the day he signed the management contract.

Ian said, 'You gave me the car.' So it was a matter of meetings and
lawyers who expected a long bargaining session, and Botham said, 'I'll
give you 30 per cent but the car is mine.' And we agreed. The clothing
deal was separate.

We got into his new car, he had already got rid of the Jaguar, all
chummy-chummy, with his father-in-law in the back seat, and went to
Lord's for a goodbye reception before the team flew out. We spent that
night with Botham in his hotel room at the airport, and his father-in-law
was not there. That is all I am saying.

The next move was in America. We flew to Oregon and sat down
with Rob Strasser to finalise the Nike designs. They had scoured the
country for manufacturers using all our contacts as well. They put us in

a five-star hotel. They gave us gifts. In January, Ian started calling from the West Indies.

During February we must have had a phone call a week. The question was always the same: 'What is happening to the Nike deal?' We would say, 'The lawyers are talking. They take months to put these deals together.'

Nothing went wrong in February or March except England's cricket. Botham was taking few wickets, making few runs, and they were about to drop him. I called his wife and said, 'Look, Cathy, I intend to go down there next week and straighten him up. I am tired of all these rumours and nonsense.' She presumably took it the wrong way because he seemed to take the attitude: How dare I suggest I would straighten him up?

I said, 'Look, Ian, you have to get down to playing cricket. Cricket is what you are there to do.'

It was on then to the Californian party, *The Star*'s story, and the silence between Botham and myself which left the Nike deal in the great blue yonder – and with it my expectations for my own clothing business.

One day, on the back step of my house, after Botham had been playing Lancashire, I found two glasses and an empty champagne bottle: apparently left in the early morning. Was that the calling card of my diminished (ex-) hero?

BIRTLES BOTHAM BELLANY

BATTERSEA

—

It is mid-morning on an overcast day at the end of June 1989, with an occasional fine drizzle in the air. I walk the short distance from the old Cheshire hall that is my home to my cricket field nearby, and here is my monument, once founded on no more than hope, now shaping up nicely through hard work, hard battles and perseverance.

There is no Botham here, but the spirit of Botham is here. We parted but in some ways remained together, an invisible chord tying us, so that people still assume that a relationship exists. It does not. But here is my pavilion and my pavilion has a name and that name is Lord Botham.

I have been fighting the borough council, parish council, fighting all the way for three years to fill in the silted headlands of my lake and level out the cricket ground to the point where it matches leading county standards so that people from all walks of life can come here and help break down the barriers of the establishment and pursue my form of green revolution.

This bowl, the Birtles Bowl, this cricket ground, will be the Arundel of the North and probably is one of the most famous grounds in the world today. That is what I have been creating for so long now. My ground is more than Botham and more than me.

This piece of earth, once little more than a cow patch, for which Maxi and I paid £18,000, is a ten million-pound venture now. There have been enormous changes. Hundreds of thousands of tons of earth have been shifted to shape one end into an amphitheatre, a natural tier. In my mind I have been shaping it so that it reflects The Hollywood Bowl. I lived next door to that bowl on the so-called wrong side of town, with the hippies, the freaks, the weirdos, the transvestites, the prostitutes. I learned to be a carpenter. I learned to build. And this place is what I admired as I built.

Others build for me here in Cheshire, and the truckers are not just moving earth: they are part of the creation. It is their place too. And to prove it and to show my appreciation, I shall have their names chiselled out on a great stone at the entrance. There might be twenty names. The stone will record my respect for them and what they have contributed.

In the middle of the mound will be a real earth stage. All will be grassed. And eventually there will be a roof.

I fought in courts for what is happening here, for I have not been popular with neighbours whose ideas are often in direct contradiction to mine. When I first applied for permission to fill in the silted headlands of the lake my end vision was nothing like this. I had an idea but did not think it would come about. Either they would not let me, or I would not be able to afford it, or it would not work. But I got permission. Three years to do the job and it took eighteen months to find the right man to oversee the transformation. Roger Rathbone was that man. The man in charge. He is a good friend now. I call him the earth man. He is equally at home building a motorway.

The old hall was necessary to me when I bought the ground and now I have sold it. The cricket field is next to it and I needed the hall as a base for the transformation. I have retained the cricket ground and twenty-two acres and the Birtles lake and will build a new home, Hudson Hall, right here by the cricket field, on another grassy mound,

1988

Sergeant Pepper revival . . . Sixties comeback . . . Hello . . . Hello . . . I Think I Love You. Whitney Houston. Morrisey . . . Hello, Oscar Wilde and Cadogan Gardens . . . the Chelsea days are hereagain. Acid House . . . warehouse parties . . . The Smile T-shirt. Michelle shocked. Sinead O'Connor. Stone Roses. Happy Mondays. New Order at G Mex. Sonny Bono elected Mayor of Palm Springs . . . California. Michael Jackson Pepsi video. R.E.M. Bros. Waterboys.

MOVIES

Good Morning, Vietnam. Full Metal Jacket. Untouchables. Who Framed Roger Rabbit?

and to do that I will, no doubt, have to take on the establishment again.

But, meanwhile, I can have a house-boat on the lake or I can live in my coach-house which is now the Manor House, close by the main hall.

I walk alone in my pavilion on this June day. It reflects my style. Inside, it is deeply personal. A bar, sweaters and sweat-shirts lining the ceiling, lots of ties hung around – all used as ornamentation – and only members and their friends allowed inside (we had trouble with lager louts). No smoking here. No boots. No meat. People say I give them rabbit food for their £3 on match days. I have been vegetarian since 1968. Sure, I have strayed on occasion. We all do, but basically I have kept my beliefs.

I have a deep affinity with the Greens. I wrote about the Greens long ago in California, where there have always been lovers of nature ready to stand up for its preservation. So being Green for me is being healthy, being organic, starting with one's own body. It comes naturally – more naturally the better. I have an area of the estate devoted to organic food which will become Birtles Manor Farm.

I would like to make all this a Green headquarters. This should be its tabernacle, particularly for this area, though I would like it so for the whole of England. Why not?

Cricket has always been important in my life. It has remarkable facets. It can be philosophical, a battle, social, psychological. I would not be surprised if it were musical, since Sir Neville Cardus wrote music as if it were cricket and cricket as if it were music. For me it has had great pleasures but for the most part it has been battle. Battles with Botham. Battles on behalf of Botham. Battles with neighbours. Battles with administrators. And people have the cheek to call this just a game.

If life is seen as cricket is seen, here is a morning of some promise, the wicket firm and running true, the grass short, the sky not without hints of sunshine. The signs are good. I look back now on life's battles fought, won, lost, part won, and I can see where progress has been made, good progress.

At my Birtles ground I have Geoff Foley, Allan Border's protégé who has just scored 155 in his maiden game for Queensland, as resident professional and he has been bringing along a string of youngsters who, we feel, form the next generation of world Test players. We have become a haven, a home away from home, for overseas players from Australia, South Africa, West Indies, India, Pakistan ... the best of Birtles ... the heroes and the outlaws ... Hudson's Hollywood XI. And I have no doubts that Geoff Foley will play for Australia in the next two or three years, plus many of his friends he brought along during the summer.

I have reverence for cricket. When I look around my pavilion I see reflections from any kid's toy room. Maxi told me she had a toy room under the stairs as a child. Everybody has had a toy room. Even at university you had a room and it was yours. You stuck your posters on the wall. The pavilion is my tribute to my little toy room. I hope it never gets changed or moved and that people will always come to enjoy it. I am having a hard time because people are still coming to play cricket rather than to pay homage to something. I am trying to change people so that they make it an occasion, like going to Lord's. The ground will be truly born in 1990. I would like Prince Charles to re-open it. We have something in common. We both respect nature. We both want to preserve the best of our English heritage. We both went to Scottish schools. Why not have him open it? I think it would please him as it pleases me.

I wanted to be the Kerry Packer of English cricket and I believe that I am that. Many things happening in cricket now are what I talked about four or five years ago. Even the decline of the England team. Ted Dexter is not the man to be in charge. England needs an entrepreneur, possibly a man born to wealth who has increased it. A little of the Lord Hanson. It is a money game. Money on the table.

Nearby, at Lancashire County Cricket Club, Cedric Rhoades has departed and there is a new régime, for which I am grateful. I like to think I had a hand in his going but I never was elected to the committee. When I offered £100,000 to bring Botham and Viv Richards to Lancashire no-one took me on. King and Emperor these! Botham turned to Worcestershire, and sure enough it became No. 1, the San Francisco 49ers outfit of cricket. I like to think that the dash and style I fostered during my Botham years did not go to waste.

I feel at home at the Lancashire County ground now. I am out to pasture. I do not have a private box any more but I am a life member

and so is Maxi, the first-ever lady life member. I have good friends
there. Alan Ormerod, coach, David Hughes, captain and an old-timer
like myself, among them. They threw a few youngsters together and got
a good solid team. A battery of fast bowlers not being the least of their
assets. There is a new freedom in the dressing room which I find
welcome. People can say Castlemaine XXXX without getting worried
that some stuffed shirt will say, 'You can't do that here.' They're free.
Lancashire are two or three players short of a really first-class side, but
the signs are encouraging. I congratulate David Hughes and the county
organisation on a good job. I still think they need me in there with
floating executive status, because if I can do all this on my own ground
with my own resources, what can I do with theirs?

Maybe ... maybe some time ...

Meanwhile, I contemplate the age of 50. An Aquarian age of
Aquarius.

Cricket has a season, and cricketers have their seasons. The later
seasons just have to be taken a little slower. I have my seasons yet. And
there still are attitudes to the game to be discovered. Last winter, on
tour in Spain, a gentleman of the wicket-keeping fraternity, like myself,
said in an accent that reminded me of John Arlott that in every over of a
40-over game there had to be one bad ball and that if you hit that bad
one for four, the equation is 40 times 4 which is 160, quite a lot in an
afternoon.

I thought about that. Another friend, old 'Bloomers' from
Haileybury and ISC, a cricketer, same age, with a frightfully-frightfully
accent, all high chip and polished, spoke to me like a housemaster
would. 'Hudson,' he said, 'you were taught to play straight, yes? Bat
and pad. Play it bat and pad.' So I went out and hit 84 and he was quite
angry. 'Why the hell didn't you get 100?' he said. Next day I scored 126
not out, the first time in twenty years that I had scored 100. Never too
old, you see.

Never too old to find a new horizon, have a new vision, seek a
better way, fight a bigger battle and move on. I think we are winning,
Maxi and me. For this is very much teamwork too. I know she is aware
of my dreams and she is making and helping and pushing for them to
come about, always supportive. She has never once put me down,

walked away from me or been rude to me in public, and that is the height and strength of a woman. That is why marriage has worked for me this time. Of the women I have loved, Maxi is the one who made it work. Nothing to do with money. Money is great. Money is important. But to support, to push, to agree, to go for it, side by side – that is wealth, truly wealth. That is Ponderosa wealth, Barbara Stanwyck, big-country wealth that made the empire. It is through their special qualities and fortitude that women are stronger than men. I am a little boy who plays in a toy shop and I will probably never grow up. But I no longer have illusions of grandeur.

1989

The Malibu Sound.
Lou Reed.
Tom Waits.
Keith Richards.
Traveling Wilburys.
Cowboy Junkies.
Edie Bickell.

VIDEO AND MOVIES

Mark Almond & Gene Pitney.
Pet Shop Boys & Lisa Minelli.

Fine Young Cannibals . . . The Old Beat.
Simply Red . . . No. 1 in USA.

MOVIES

Dangerous Liaisons.
Working Girl.
Rainman.
Indiana Jones and the Last Crusade.
Scandal . . . Joanne Whalley . . . from Stockport to Santa Fe . . . not bad, young lady.

Mick in the middle in a muddle in Malibu.
Karen.
Bloomers.
Hawkins.
And Batman of course.
Manchester has 5 groups in the Top 10.
Stone Roses.
Happy Mondays.
Morrisey.
Lisa Stansfield.
State 808.

New Order haven't even got a record out.

Nor could I, given my character, be satisfied with a quiet, mundane existence because something would then go wrong.

Variety is all.

I have a piece of Owen Oyston's radio stations (Red Rose/Piccadilly Radio/Miss World). A friend gave me the idea that Owen and I should meet. He thought we would get along well and brought him to the Hall. He looked around, and as he was gazing at a picture of Viv Richards, Brian Close, Ian Botham and Hudson, a brilliant painting by Tony Cooper, he said, 'I want you in.'

He thought I would be good for the station. I said: 'Great.' He did not mind what I put into the company: £5,000, £10,000, half a million. I think I surprised him, because I came up with a lot of money, and it was all done very properly through merchant bankers. I put on my new money hat. I told him that Red Rose needed a jolt, and that they should put writers and creative people in there, interesting people. Radio generally is full of boring DJs poured out of a disco cannon like some ugly sons-in-law you do not want and your silly daughters have fallen in love with.

I went to Oyston's home for dinner one night and said, 'Why don't we go for the big city? Piccadilly Radio, Manchester?' He did not think he had a hope of doing it, but the *coup* came off and I think it froze me out. Like I always do, I open my big mouth, give ideas to someone, and the ideas come off and perhaps people think, I owe the bastard. Well, we won, so I am not complaining. I have got the radio show he promised me – Hudson's Theatre of the Mind, three hours every Sunday evening on Piccadilly, the Voice of Manchester.

I tried for years to get into Piccadilly Radio and Colin Walters, managing director, never allowed me to have a show. Around four years ago we had a verbal agreement with him to go to America and do a radio show. We did one called *Hudson in Hollywood* (we still have the tapes) and it cost around 10,000 dollars. We invited about seventy of our friends and acquaintances to Oscar's, the best English restaurant on the Sunset Strip, hired the best engineers and producers, and sent out invitations to the party. We said this was being recorded for 'Piccadilly Radio – Hudson in Hollywood – sex, drugs and rock and roll'. And because we mentioned the word 'drugs' they did not run the show. Any mention of drugs could have been all gone in twenty seconds. We had some of the most famous people in Hollywood on the show plus the top good music of the time and it stayed silent on tape. Wasted.

Which is why, when Red Rose took over Piccadilly, Maxi/Hudson sent two dozen red roses to Owen Oyston to congratulate him and why Colin Walters got a wreath from me.

Then I suggested *Red Rose Presents Lancashire*, meaning the cricket club. I brought them together for a meeting. To this day I think it was a wonderful idea. What would it cost? I would put money in myself. But Owen has his own people around him; people who went to school with him. Maybe he likes me, but you can't bring in a guy you like if there are others around who don't want him in.

I would not mind buying Sunshine Radio in Antibes, South of France. I thought maybe Owen would sell me that station and I could get off on my own. I had a couple of wives who were French and am happy with the language. And I like France. So maybe we could buy a house down there.

I did a season of twenty-seven shows on Signal Radio, Stoke-on-Trent – my way. No intros, no call letters, no Hudson name in the middle of the show. I was going to America to do the big-deal, live radio show from LA to Stoke, and just when I got back the October Stock Exchange crash of 1987 happened and I was scuttling around picking up the pieces of paper dissolving and floating everywhere. I was lucky to come out all right; one of the many people having a little trouble and it wasn't that bad after all, but I could not concentrate at the time.

Times change and moods shift. The shifting of earth at my field echoes the shifting of our own minds. Maxi gets more beautiful, more real with time, and she does not like America any more. She loves England more than the English. Adores it. We are thinking of living here, not commuting, as we do, between Cheshire and California. California is a place to be young in. Once you are no longer young, run away. I am not into sun any more. That's gone ... just lying there, soaking it up, is boring now. We have a flat in London. I would like to know more about the galleries, the museums and meet old friends again.

I have my Bellany paintings, lots of those, and they tour the world now. To me it is like having The Beatles publishing. Buying a Bellany collection was a magnificent move that came out of the Botham affair and it more than covered my losses. As I stroll through my pavilion, I ponder the magnificence of our involvement with Bellany, and the story of our friendship. It began when John Bellany was asked by the National Portrait Gallery to paint a famous sportsman. They gave a couple of suggestions. I think Kevin Keegan was one, I'm not sure ... but Botham was the other. Bellany was overjoyed. He loves cricket. He loved Ian Botham. He saw Botham as this Adonis. So I met John Bellany when he came here to Birtles Old Hall to paint the Adonis ... as he called him.

John painted Botham here at Birtles ... the famous painting that hangs in the National Portrait Gallery right now. It was a very hectic day because I remember that *The Cricketer* was doing a feature story on Ian's thirtieth birthday. From this they came out with a front cover depicting Ian wearing our rugby shirt. So in one day, one fell swoop, we had him painted for the National Portrait Gallery, a picture that

hangs for eternity, and that front cover. Everything that I did in regard
to my promoting has come to pass now. People are beginning to get paid
for their worth. Especially in cricket. I *did* have an influence on the
game.

We heard that John Bellany was going to have a one-man show at
the National Portrait Gallery. The first one-man show ever. Well, I
woke up in the middle of the night, and I shook Maxi and I said, 'Why
don't we buy the collection?' I imagined that Maxi would say, 'Go to
sleep, Hudson, forget it.' But she didn't. She said, 'Why not?' So we
went out and bought the entire National Portrait Gallery collection that
hung for several months. The only one we didn't get was the actual
painting of Botham, but we have an alternative which John painted
especially. Maxi's favourite from the whole thing is a pencil drawing of
Ian. A wonderful drawing which really gives that beautiful side of him.
It is very rare to see a picture of Botham where he looks beautiful. It's
usually that beefy image. But this one drawing really captures just how
handsome he really is.

But I think that became the most valuable investment we have ever
made. I foresee that John Bellany will be spoken of in the same breath
as Picasso. A period of time down the road, I'd say that every single one
of them will be worth, let's say, a million pounds.

John had an incredible run, about that time. In February 1986 he
had the show I mentioned at the National Portrait Gallery. Then he did
the famous poster for the Edinburgh Festival. He had, again, the first
one-man show at the Scottish National Gallery of modern art. There
was another show in November '86 at the Serpentine Gallery. There
was the Royal College of Art show, at which Bellany's paintings shared
the stage with Henry Moore's sculptures. It was a tremendous year
when he was just honoured, and honoured and honoured. We bought
what is probably one of his most famous paintings at an art show in Los
Angeles, where we bought *Celtic Lovers Under The Lighthouse*.

We took Bellany to America in December 1986, one year after
Botham. Through Botham, I met Bellany. I gained a friend. The whole
family became friends of ours. We lost Botham but we gained Bellany.
Even financially, although this isn't so important, we gained. We might
have lost the Nike deal, all those contracts we were negotiating in regard

to Botham's career. All the things he has gained, which we predicted.
As I talk, Ian Botham is a television star now. He is on *A Question Of
Sport* every week. Incidentally, I've heard that more women are
watching that show than ever before and I have no doubt that is because
of Mr Botham ... and the attractive sporting friends he brings on. So
what we lost with Botham, emotionally we certainly gained with Mr
Bellany. Right now we have the finest collection, bar none, of John
Bellanys.

When I met John he was a very, very sick man. He was definitely
on the down side. Sloping out. Since that time, he has had a liver
transplant at Cambridge. In Edinburgh there was a big show of all the
paintings he painted while he was going through that experience. So
Maxi and I have travelled with John from a very black area. Right along
the spectrum to absolute vivid technicolour. His painting uses tinges,
ambers, influences of our Flower Power colours. He has immortalised
our black, yellow, red and green in art. Only recently the Museum of
Modern Art in New York and the Tate Gallery bought several of his
works.

I don't know what we are here for. Whether to leave monoliths to
ourselves, memories to ourselves or titles to ourselves ... It doesn't
matter who it is. Whether it is the artist painting the portrait, the author
writing the book, the television star leaving his TV ... on and on down
to Joe industrialist down the road who puts a stained-glass window in
the local church. Even if you leave a tombstone, you leave a memory to
yourself. So, in that sense, we have been immortalised through Bellany.

Other than that, I've really found somebody that I can talk to.
Relate to. Every time I have the slightest doubt about my ability, it is
always John who comes along with his dour Scottish way, and says,
'Hey, you mustnae talk like this, you must never let them ruin ya ...
don't you dare say that, don't you dare say you are not good.'

Sometime you want to feel humble in front of such a great man,
but he won't allow it. I love the fact that I can talk to John about the
commercialism of art, I don't mean that in a nasty way but I talk about
putting his art on sheets, on pillowcases ... and he never throws me
out. Some artists would say, 'How dare you', but he doesn't. It's all art
and the more people who can see your art, the better. That's what

Picasso did. He got his art through to lots of people.

I really like his family and John has an interesting angle. He married his first wife, Helen, had children by her, divorced his first wife, married somebody else ... and just before the showing, in 1985, John's second wife died. So John was really in a whammy, man, he was on the dark side of midnight ... and then things just seemed to buck up for him. The art world began to honour him, he re-married Helen, his transplant was successful and we were lucky enough to come along as well. Since I met him, he has painted Botham, Sean Connery, David Bowie ... River Hudson. He's enjoying himself. He is well, happy.

We have just bought a flat in London, very close to John, in an area where John used to live, many years ago. So, we are not just friends, we are neighbours. John is a major reason why we are moving to London. I've felt, for a long time, living at Birtles Old Hall, that it was marvellous as long as I was banging on the telephone, reminding people. But it's a long way from London to Cheshire. London is the capital and if one is going to be an entrepreneur then London is where you have to work from, even if it's only three days a week. You have got to be there.

Not bad, not bad, I think, as I walk my grounds on this June morning.

We have Hudson's Hardware – a complete range of leisure clothes and we are coming back strongly now. Our clothes will be in all the major stores sooner or later. I think it would work. Harrods. I would like that.

I convinced my wonderful daughter, River Hudson, to go to Millfield School and she loves it. I did not choose the school because of any reputation it has for being an upper-class establishment, but rather I gather it is my kind of school where, if you are rich, you pay for the not-so-rich. I suppose River is on top fees and that I am paying for someone else as well, so that's fine by me, a bit of Flower Power. No guilt there about private education. I am very happy she has been accepted. She has just won the Actress of the Year award in her first term.

Mother is in the family cottage in Prestbury, and all this stems from a kid in a council flat in Wythenshaw. Me.

Not bad, not bad I think, once more.

Henry Broughton Hudson, major, Prince of Wales Dragoon Guards, taught me a lot of things. Taught me how to dress, how to talk, how to charm, how to play the gentleman's game. I am always conscious of public-school boys talking to grammar-school boys. They play a game and I know the game they play, so it's OK. I cracked the code. I believe that public schools should be open to everybody so that all kids can sit side by side, whoever their parents happen to be. Otherwise the system will not work. It can only do so when everybody has an equal chance.

Privilege should be earned, and then shared, or so I believe.

It is not everyone's belief. I was talking to someone the other day. He was new to the area. I asked whether he had met any of the other landowners.

He said he acted as a beater during a shoot and one of the Cheshire gentlemen shouted, 'Open that gate, boy.'

He doubted his hearing.

'Open that gate, boy.'

'Excuse me, sir?'

The gentleman became so irate he opened the gate himself and stormed off.

'Yes,' said this newcomer, 'I've met your landowners.'

I am not too happy with some of them myself. Nor are they happy with me. Last of the English eccentrics – that is what a writer called me. The gentry are never at ease with eccentrics. There is nothing in life they admire so much as continuity so long as that continuity preserves their privilege. I have never minded upsetting the gentry and the gentry

---

1990

Mick Middles says, 'What happens in 1990? . . . Thank you . . . we can still predict . . . that's dangerous . . .

1 Old music will make a big comeback . . . old songs . . . love songs and good songs . . .
2 Fish and chip shops will hit the high street.
3 Lancashire will win the cricket County Championship.
4 The best summer ever . . . they say good summers come in twos.
5 Botham elopes with Chris Evert.
6 Ted Dexter returns to Mustique with his Harley Davidson.
7 Mike Gatting is re-elected Captain of England.
8 Lord Hudson of Birtles, Greenpeace MP, becomes manager of the England cricket team . . .
9 Hudson will button down and write the Cheshire epic . . . Birtles . . . the Dallas of the Nineties.
10 The Halle plays the Birtles Bowl with special guest New Order on the same bill . . .
11 Magic Mushroom party at the Bowl Royal Manor of Birtles. P.S. The Hudsons retire to battleship on the Manchester Ship Canal . . . The Birtles Bowl donated to the National Trust . . . Birtles Manor becomes a museum to hold the Collection of Rock and Roll . . . Cricket and Art . . . of all our friends and lovers, some who are here and some who have gone.

Flower Power.

Hudson.

Thanks . . . Maxi . . . Middles . . . Mather . . .

have never minded upsetting me.

Maxi, like me, feels that everything is going in the right direction. Is there life after Botham? There certainly is. She says the saddest thing was not losing a cricket player, but losing a friend. I'll go along with that. An empty champagne bottle and a couple of glasses left on the back doorstep; that was the last visible memory of him.

Who knows? One day...

For this is not the end of the story. It merely provides the blank page for a new beginning.

Lovers Day

The Royal Manor of Berkes ·
Cheshire
1ˢᵗ May 1990 ..

I would like to thank my Friends
Geoff Mutter and Duncan Mensae
for enjoying · — — ·
The Romance of my life · ·

P.S.
And
Mick Middles for coming to Malibu · ·

FROM THE HUDSON SCRAPBOOK

—

Surrey County Cricket Club

KENNINGTON OVAL

A Surrey XI v. Surrey Assoc. of Cricket
Thursday, June 14th, 1962 (1 Day M

A Surrey XI	First Innings
1 W. A. Smith	
†2 J. Cook	
‡3 G. Brumwell-Hudson	
4 S. J. Storey	
‡5 E. G. Noller	
‡6 R. G. Davies	
7 D. Gibson	
8 R. Harman	
*‡9 V. J. Ransom	
‡10 O. D. Kember	
11 G. Arnold	

B , l-b , n-b ,
Total

Fall of the wickets
1— 2— 3—
4— 5— 6—

Average runs per over

BOWLING ANALYSIS First Innings
O. M. R. W. Wd. N.b. O.

Surrey Association of Cricket Clubs First Innings

*1 K. Cracknell	East Molesey
2 D. Herdson	Alleyn O.B.
3 N. Heroys	Limpsfield
4 O. Lainé	Leatherh
5 G. Lucas	Guildf
6 W. Peters	Wimble
7 A. Rahaman	S. Railway-Croy
8 T. Rosier	Dulw
‡9 G. Smith	Me
10 M. Stapleton	Borough
11 D. Thompson	Su

Fall of the wickets
1— 2— 3—
1— 2— 3—

BOWLING ANALYSIS O.

*Captain ‡Wkt.-keeper ‡Am
Umpires—J. Shearlaw & F. J.
HO

NEW B
Next Match,
1962 CRICKET POOL.

TELEPHONE:
TRAFFORD PARK 0261-2

TELEGRAMS:
'PAVILION, MANCHESTER, 16'

Lancashire County Cricket Club

PATRON: H.M. THE QUEEN

C. G. HOWARD
Secretary

Old Trafford
Manchester, 16

Lancs II v Yorkshire II
2 Day...
May 22nd and 23

1. Mr. S. Miller Capt.
2. Mr. Townley Keri
3. G. T. Hudson Am.
4. K. Schof.
5. B. Booth.
6. H. Pilling
7. G. Hovilla
8. K. Goodwin — w.keeper.
9. K. Howard
10. G. Miller
11. P. Lever.
12th man S. Sullivan.

both ... Old Trafford 2.00 pm

BRIAN STATHAM BENEFIT
A Lancashire XI. v. A Cheshire & District XI.
at Chester. Sunday, May 28th, 1961
Wickets Pitched 2.30 p.m.

A Lancashire XI.

1 R. W. BARBER. Capt			
2 J. B. STATHAM			
3 K. GRIEVES			
4 B. BOOTH			
5 R. COLLINS			
6 G. CLAYTON. Wkt.			
7 E. GREENHALGH			
8 T. HUDSON			
9 J. BLIGHT			
10 P. LEVER			
11 K. HIGGS			

Extras
Total

A Cheshire & District XI.

1 F. MILLETT Ches. & Minor Counties Capt	
2 D. C. HUGHES Cheshire	
3 P. A. C. KELLY Middx. & Ches.	
4 K. CRANSTON Eng & Lancs	
5 J. R. PAGE Chester	
6 K. WAZIR Pakistan	
7 R. BURNET Yorks	
8 T. DEWHURST Chester	
9 D. SMITH Cam. Univ. & Ches	
10 C. D. R. BARKER R.A.F. & Ches.	
11 K. HOLDING Ches. Wkt.	

Extras
Total

Umpires: A. G. Snape, & T. G. Plant, both of Cheshire & Chester

BENEFIT MATCH - Lancashire v. Australians, at Old Trafford
Sat. Mon. Tues. July 1st, 3rd, & 4th.

Manager :
H. B. LISBERG,
20, Waterpark Road,
Salford, 7.
CHE. 3341.

CHARLES SILVERMAN.

HERMAN'S HERMITS

MODERN MUSIC.

Bookings :
HARVEY,
CHEetham Hill 3341.
GEOFFREY,
WHItefield 2128

June 15th. 64.

Dear Tim,

  I am writing to you re our conversation at the Clef D'Or club when you were in Manchester last re getting a disc for one of my groups submitted for Juke Box Jury and a T.V. appearance for Ready Steady Go, Thank Your Lucky Stars etc. I try to contact you by phone when I was in London last Friday but the young lady I spoke to did not know where I could contact you. I am now sole agent for a big M/C recording group called The Whirlwinds and they have on release at the moment an H.M.V. recording and will have another out by September, and they are very anxious to have some T.V. coverage which I hope you can accomodate me with, re the prices we have already discussed. I am also interested in getting my own group accomodated ditto as soon as their record is released within the next two months, and I am also interested in arrang -ing a tie-up with you in London re Publicity and bookings down South for my groups.

  I trust you will let me know as soon as possible what you can do for me because I am going very big at the moment and I am sure I can give you some big business if you are able to accomodate me at the right price. Please let me know as soon as possible what you can do because I am very busy planning ahead, and maybe we can arrange a meeting in London when I am downtown during the next few weeks, possibly if you could contact me by phone before then at CHE 2538 any time after 7pm.

  Kindest regards and hoping to hear from you in due course.

Yours sincerely,

CHARLIE.

28, Broom Lane,
Salford 7,
Lancs.

15-go up.

Show me. Girl.

A GROUP WHO SPECIALISES IN THE UP TO DATE SOUNDS

ANDES SOUND

138 IVOR COURT GLOUCESTER PLACE LONDON NW1   'PHONE AMBASSADOR 1811

Tim Hudson esq.,
Seventh Avenue at Ash,
San Diego 1,
California.

REF ALO/VW

17th June, 1965.

Dear Tim,
Thank you very much for your letter of June 8th.
I am very pleased that you like"Satisfaction"so much.
This is a quick line to let you know our address and telephone
number as I would be grateful if you could keep me informed in all
thats happening in your end of the World.
I would always be extremely grateful i f you have any records wort
covering if you could let me know at this address - as this would
a great benefit to me.
I will be on the coast on July 15th staying at Chateau Marmon,
8321 Sunset Boulevard - and I would be delighted to see you.

Yours sincerely,

Andrew Loog Oldham.

ANDREW LOOG OLDHAM LTD :
MIRAGE MUSIC LTD   :   AN

NEMS

SUTHERLAND HOUSE, 5 6 ARGYLL STREET, LONDON, W 1
TELEPHONE REGENT 3261
CABLES: NEMPEROR LONDON W1

TB/JN

20th July, 1965

Tim Hudson, Esq.,
Radio RCBQ,
Seventh Avenue at Ash,
San Diego 1,
California,
U.S.A.

Dear Tim,

THE BEATLES' TOUR OF AMERICA: AUGUST 1965

I refer to your application to travel with The Beatles while they
are in America next month. I am pleased to say that a place
has been reserved for you on the charter aircraft. I shall look
forward to meeting you in New York.

..., I enclose information which should assist you
... arrangements. May I draw your special attention
...THREE and SIX.

Yours sincerely,
for NEMS ENTERPRISES LTD.

TONY BARROW
Senior Press and Publicity Officer

OFFICIAL BEATLES PARTY
IDENTIFICATION PASS

ISSUED TO

TIM HUDSON
VALID THROUGHOUT TOUR. AUGUST 1965

AUTHORIZED SIGNATURE   NEMS/GAC

... CONSTITUTE CONTRACTS   ... ANNUALLY BY THE LONDON COUNTY COUNCIL

Lord Tim Wins "DJ of Month" Title

KFWB's Lord Tim has been voted the Number One disc jockey in Los Angeles by the thousands of readers of "It's Boss," the newspaper connected with the teenage nightclub of the same name.

Lord Tim, heard each night from 6-9 p.m. was very pleased at his selection.

"I feel this is the greatest honor I have received since being in America, and I am doubly pleased because it was voted by the Number One club, "It's Boss," said Tim.

"I think Los Angeles teenagers are the swinginest, hippiest, happiest, sloopy-doopy dollies in the 'ol wide world. I feel that the kids identify with me because I don't dress up—I live in jeans, mix with the kids, I go to their clubs—I understand what the kids want—my mother still calls me her big baby," said L.T.

Lord Tim has wanted to be a success in the U.S. for a long time and he has special feelings for Los Angeles.

"The only way I can describe my feeling for Los Angeles is by remembering how I felt as a kid in the rain, damp and gloom of the miserable climate of Manchester, England, and saying to myself that one day I was going to live in that sunny State of California. I'd like to thank the kids again for this tremendous honor."

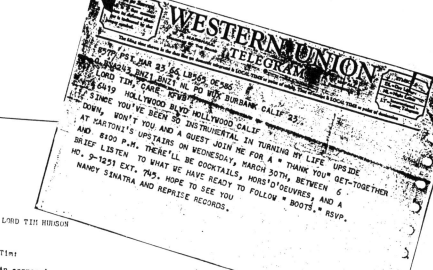

WESTERN UNION TELEGRAM

857?? PST MAR 23 66 LB565 OE586
A NA243 BNZ1 BNZ1 NL PD WUX BURBANK CALIF 23
LORD TIM, CARE KFWB
6419 HOLLYWOOD BLVD HOLLYWOOD CALIF
SINCE YOU'VE BEEN SO INSTRUMENTAL IN TURNING MY LIFE UPSIDE
DOWN, WON'T YOU, AND A GUEST JOIN ME FOR A "THANK YOU" GET-TOGETHER
AT MARTONI'S UPSTAIRS ON WEDNESDAY, MARCH 30TH, BETWEEN 6
AND 8:00 P.M. THERE'LL BE COCKTAILS, HORS D'OEUVRES, AND A
BRIEF LISTEN TO WHAT WE HAVE READY TO FOLLOW "BOOTS." RSVP.
HO 9-1251 EXT. 745. HOPE TO SEE YOU
NANCY SINATRA AND REPRISE RECORDS.

LORD TIM HUDSON

Tim:

An expression you used last night in performing a live commercial for Kodak, coupled with the use of certain words in a "Teen Topics" program with Lou Christie, lead me to believe that you are entirely too flip with the station, the management of the station, your audience, and our license.

Specifically:

On the Kodak commercial, the expression ... "...and all that crap" came out during the course of the commercial.

On the Teen Topics show, words such as "shafted" and "screwed" were both used. Because this show was pre-recorded, we did not permit these tasteless words to get on the air. However, the Kodak commercial was being performed "live", and as such could not be edited.

The Kodak commercial came less than two weeks after you were cautioned about use of words in bad taste while performing for this station.

I simply will not put up with this kind of nonsense. Mr. Bernard is out of the office today, and when he returns tomorrow I will discuss both incidents with him, and then I will talk again with you.

William J. Wheatley

CC: Mr. J. J. Bernard

★EXTRA★
Hollywood EVENING STAR

FLOWER CHILDREN
BLOOM FROM SEEDS

LYDIA AQUILAR

The Flower Generation

What gives a generation its name? What makes a generation or a movement? First of all, there has to be something happening out there. Then somebody has to see it and give it a name. If it sounds accurate and the name sums it up, a creature with a new. People talk about it. Other people want to belong to it.

There are those that flowers are the next kick, that the music is in the air and that you out there are the flower generation.

The flower terms were coined by a nonstop-talking year-old ex-DJ out in Los Angeles named Lord Tim Hudson ("When I was in school . . . well . . . I was always ready to express what I believe in so everybody called me Lord Tim. Lord Tim, who came here from England three years ago, always hated the term rock 'n' roll. "There had to be a word to replace that monotonous, terribly boring, insipid expression." So he thought of flowers as representing "feeling, color, happiness, vitality and love." He uses the term "flower children" to describe all young people who want these things. "Anyone over 30 is an old flower; anyone under is a petal child."

Lord Tim, whose talk darts abruptly from one point to another, says that he noticed a few years ago that old ladies wore flowers on their dresses. "I think old ladies were way ahead of what's happening. Maybe they're grooving being old. Did you ever think of that? Maybe on the old park bench seeing the little birds go by . . . it's really great."

"I thought that flower clothes would come in. The first time I was a DJ met this group called The Seeds."

He took over the management of The Seeds (see note into flowers, right?) and called their music flower music. A girl named Marcia Strassman, who has a record called "Flower Children," was also adopted as a representative of the movement.

Seeds Spread Flower
Power Word to N.Y.C.

NEW YORK — Seeds—and Flower Power—emissaries Lord Tim Hudson (the group's manager) and Sky Saxon (lead singer, writer and producer) visited Record World last week during the Crescendo label stars' engagement at the Electric Circus.

"We played at the Scene first for a week," said Lord Tim, "but we found that the room was just too intimate for the Seeds. We don't usually play clubs, mostly concerts, as you know, and we cater to people who have to feel the music, have to be free to mill around and not be all bunched up to just listen. This is not to put down the Scene. It just wasn't right for the Seeds."

The group, whose new Crescendo album is titled "Future," will be two weeks at the Electric Circus.

The Seeds are making their first appearance in New York, and return to their West Coast flower bed on Tuesday, July 25. "We didn't come here basically to make money or knock out the Hippies or anything like that," Lord Tim continued. "We're here mainly so that people in the business can see and hear the Seeds and learn about Flower Power. And it's been great. The Circus has been packed every night. The Monkees, Angela Lansbury, the Who and the Dave Clark Five were down to see the Seeds, along with many others. TV producer Gary Smith also came in. He says he has an idea for a television series for the Seeds."

Spreading the Word

Both Hudson and Saxon feel very strongly about spreading the West Coast music word to the still slightly reluctant East. "After all, this is a democracy.

If an American artist on the West Coast has a hit record, he has the right to have it played everywhere, not only there," opined Hudson.

Both, too, were profuse in their thanks to Coast deejays for their belief in Flower Power, which the Seeds initiated.

Then Back Home

The Seeds are returning home with several TV guest shots lined up, including Joe Bishop's 90-minuter on Friday, July 28, and promises of at least two Smothers Brothers exposures. Then tour plans, including one in England for late September-early October. "Flower Power has hit very big in England," said Saxon. "West Coast music has no trouble making it over there, for some reason."

Saxon added that he has had several offers to produce for other artists while in Manhattan, but he has turned them down. "I don't want to produce for anyone else. Timmy has turned down several offers to manage other big groups, too. I figure if he can do that, I concentrate on the Seeds I can too."

Such is the power of Flower

—Doug McClella

Sky Saxon & Lord Tim Hudson
Holding the 'Future'

'Seeds' Created Flower Music

The Seeds are a group of young men who may suddenly become the fastest rising American pop stars on the music scene. Besides having had three hit singles — "Pushin' Too Hard," "Mr. Farmer," and now "Can't Seem to Make You Mine" — they've become the spokesmen of a new revolution among America's youth: a revolution in search of that "next plateau."

The Seeds are the creators of "flower music," a musical concept that having an impact upon your radio and music industry, some teenagers now record themselves as "Flower Children," disc jockeys can be heard screaming such phrases as "Flower Power."

At a recent concert in Los Angeles' Valley Music Theatre, over 3,000 teenagers — flowers in hand — screamed frantically throughout The Seeds' entire performance. Only at appearances of The Beatles, The Stones, or Elvis Presley, has

there been such a spectacular response, complete with tears, fainting, and mass mysteria. And the pandemonium did not stop with The Seeds' last song — as the group's limousine sped away, from the theatre, cars filled with their most ardent fans followed them down the freeway for the grand finale, the Big Chase!

The Seeds are under the direction of Lord Tim Hudson, a Londoner now living in America, who has been connected with many top music personalities. He has travelled with The Beatles, been associated with Herman's Hermits, and was the discoverer of The Moody Blues. In the United States, ho has become a popular disc jockey on several top radio stations. His belief, regarding his management of The Seeds, is that the continued success of the English acts, such as The Beatles and The Stones, is due largely to "their treating rock and roll as a regimented form, like any other type of big business."

Los Angeles Times

MONDAY MORNING, MARCH 27, 1967 Part I

UP THE HIPPIES

WE'RE THE FLOWER PEOPLE

INTERLAND © 1967, LOS ANGELES TIMES

"Of course they're dangerous— they're not political—they're not violent —they're a new force—'flower-power'!"

Flower Fad Blossoms on Disks

NEW YORK—Flowers, eternal symbols of love and peace, have become the new banner of youth, with consequences blossoming strongly on the disk scene.

At various "Love Ins," "Be-Ins" and "Happenings," flora, namely the daffodil, is being worn by boys and girls alike as an expression of love, sometimes associating itself with anti-Vietnam demonstrations.

The record industry, ever on the look-out for themes to peg songs by, is at the moment flower crazy. Among the new disks featuring "flower" themes are the Ode label's "San Francisco (Wear Some Flowers In Your Hair)" by Scott McKenzie, Marcia Strassman's UNI disking of "Flower Children," the same label's "Flower Music" by the Osmond Brothers and P. F. Sloane's Dunhill recording "Sunflower, Sunflower."

The next Rolling Stones LP will be called "Flowers."

Even group names — and perhaps solo acts to come—tie-in with the idea. They include The Seeds, heard on GNP Crescendo, whose credo has been expressed as "growing into the new flower generation," and the Giant Sunflower, whose "February Sunshine" is presently involved in a legal hassle between the Ode and Take 6 labels.

Those close to the flower scene view the movement as a "friendly kind of thing" and nothing whatsoever to do with narcotics. Its origins

seem to have San Francisco as a base, where such far-out groups of youngsters like the Diggers have spread the flower gospel.

As for flower-laden "Love Ins,"

> **'A Recreation Of Happiness'**
>
> "Flower music is a recreation of happiness—early childhood memories, and also a return to nature and love," says Lord Tim Hudson, former deejay and now manager of the Seeds. "Music is going into two bags now, hard rock and beautiful things. Pretty music is basically flower music, a poetic throwback to one's early childhood, a generalization of a fairytale generation." Hudson says he started to use the phrase "Flower Child" on radio station KFWB about a year ago, and arranged to have a number of Flower Shirts sent over from England.

radio stations KRLA and KAHJ in Los Angeles will sponsor such an event, on May 28 in Los Angeles' Griffith Park. Several "Love Ins" have been previously conducted in San Francisco.

The flower idea is making further inroads into the fashion world, where dresses are beginning to sprout featuring massive floral displays. Even a feature film, called "Flower Children," is said to be in the works.

151

213B

MARTIN 2/7 HC

HOLLYWOOD (UPI)--ACTOR DEAN MARTIN'S DAUGHTER, CLAUDIA,
WAS REPORTED TO HAVE ANNOUNCED PLANS TO MARRY BRITISH-BORN DISC JOCKEY
TIM (LORD TIM) HUDSON.

"WE HAVEN'T SET THE DATE YET AND WE DON'T KNOW JUST WHERE THE
CEREMONY WILL BE PERFORMED, BUT WE WILL BE MARRIED NEXT (THIS) WEEK,"
MISS MARTIN WAS QUOTED AS SAYING LAST SATURDAY.

MISS MARTIN, WHO WILL BE 21 ON MARCH 16, WAS MARRIED BRIEFLY TO
ACTOR GAVIN MURRELL A FEW YEARS AGO, BUT THE MARRIAGE WAS ANNULED.

HUDSON ARRIVED HERE FROM LONDON ABOUT SEVEN MONTHS AGO AND APPEARS
ON A LOCAL RADIO STATION (KFWB).

JY929APS

WESTERN UNION TELEGRAM

206P PST FEB 11 66 LA250
WOJ256 0 NB041 RX CGN PD 3 EXTRA AR NEW YORK NY 11 418P
EST
LORD TIM TRY BLR
RADIO STATION KFWB HOLLYWOOD BLVD HOLLYWOOD CALIF
CONGRATULATIONS AND THE BEST OF EVERYTHING TO YOU AND
CLAUDIA. WE ARE THINKING OF YOU, LOVE
MARGARET WHITING AND TOM JONES

(30).

WESTERN UNION TELEGRAM

419A PST FEB 11 66 LA025
L CDU07 CTC792 C LGD001 PLG113 31 PD INTL FR CD LONDOLNLG
VIA ITT 11 1048
TIM HUDSON RADIO KFWB
6419 HOLLYWOODBLVD HOLLYWOOD (CALIF)
THE BEATLES BIRAN AND WENDY JOIN ME IN SENDING CONGRATULATIONS
AND ALL GOOD WISHES FOR THE FUTURE TO YOU AND TO CLUADIA
TONY BARROW

KFWB 6419

(52).

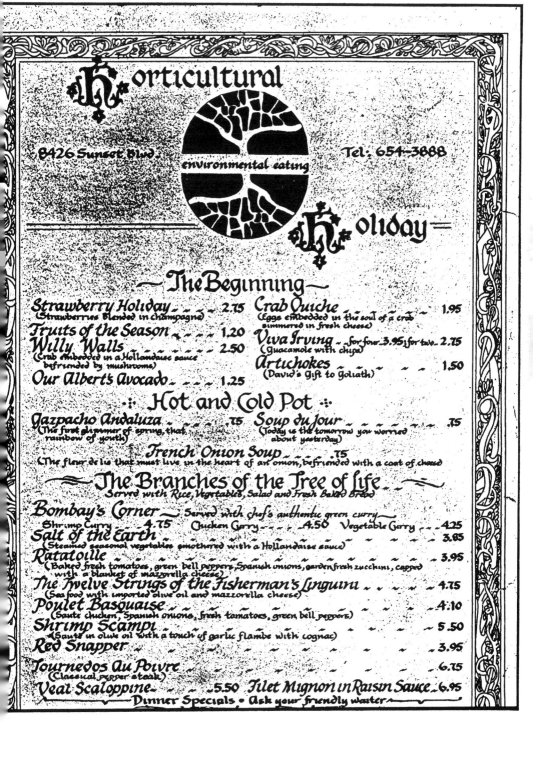

Horticultural Holiday

8426 Sunset Blvd.

environmental eating

Tel: 654-3888

~The Beginning~

Strawberry Holiday ~~~ 2.75
(Strawberries blended in champagne)

Crab Quiche ~ 1.95
(Eggs embedded in the soul of a crab simmered in fresh cheese)

Fruits of the Season ~~~ 1.20

Willy Walls ~~~ 2.50
(Crab embedded in a Hollandaise sauce befriended by mushrooms)

Viva Irving ~ for four 3.95; for two 2.75
(Guacamole with chips)

Our Albert's Avocado ~~ 1.25

Artichokes ~~ 1.50
(David's Gift to Goliath)

∴ Hot and Cold Pot ∴

Gazpacho Andaluza ~~~ .75
(The first glimmer of spring, that rainbow of youth)

Soup du Jour ~~~ .75
(Today is the tomorrow you worried about yesterday)

French Onion Soup ~ .75
(The fleur de lis that must live in the heart of an onion, befriended with a coat of cheese)

~The Branches of the Tree of Life~
Served with Rice, Vegetables, Salad and Fresh Baked Bread

Bombay's Corner ~ Served with chef's authentic green curry
Shrimp Curry ~ 4.75   Chicken Curry ~~~ 4.50   Vegetable Curry ~~ 4.25

Salt of the Earth ~~~ 3.85
(Steamed seasonal vegetables smothered with a Hollandaise sauce)

Ratatouille ~~ 3.95
(Baked fresh tomatoes, green bell peppers, Spanish onions, garden fresh zucchini, capped with a blanket of mozzarella cheese)

The Twelve Strings of the Fisherman's Linguini ~~ 4.75
(Sea food with imported olive oil and mozzarella cheese)

Poulet Basquaise ~~ 4.10
(Sauté chicken, Spanish onions, fresh tomatoes, green bell peppers)

Shrimp Scampi ~ 5.50
(Sauté in olive oil with a touch of garlic flambé with cognac)

Red Snapper ~~ 3.95

Tournedos Au Poivre ~~ 6.75
(Classical pepper steak)

Veal Scaloppine ~~~ 5.50   Filet Mignon in Raisin Sauce ~ 6.95

~Dinner Specials • Ask your friendly waiter~

LORD TIM REIGNS AGAIN

By JAMES BROWN

In 1965, with the British Invasion well under way and AM rock radio at the peak of its creative powers, a young man named Timothy Hudson arrived in Los Angeles and proceeded to set the town on its ear.

He was "Lord Tim," a disc jockey for the times—and the times were never better. He was English, he knew the Beatles personally, wore his hair fashionably long and had a wardrobe that was the image of Carnaby Street mod. The ladies adored him, the guys probably envied him and a whole lot of people listened to him, every night from 6 to 9 on KFWB. Lord Tim had it all in 1965. Yeah, those were the days . . .

"I was really the first British disc jockey in L.A., and I got the full treatment, the full media blitz," Hudson recalls. "I was also 23 years old, had all the ladies I'd ever want, was egotistical, tyrannical and probably not at all prepared for success. You have to be careful when it happens to you real fast. It can get crazy."

It was the '60s version of living in the fast lane. Lord Tim made all the parties, popped up in the gossip columns, traveled with the Beatles on their American tours and was a card-carrying man about town. In 1967, after two years at KFWB and a brief sojourn at KFRC in San Francisco, Lord Tim left radio to take over the management of the Seeds. Remember "Pushin' Too Hard"? Remember Flower Power? That was Tim, and he was now on the inside.

But the ride was coming to a close. By 1970, the Beatles were finished, Flower Power had gotten nasty and Lord Tim was nowhere to be found. He had dropped out in the other direction—leaving the scene because the scene no longer had anything to do with the effervescence, or even the relative innocence, of those days in '65.

"I just needed to fade away for a while," Hudson said. "I built a restaurant, I got involved in renovating houses—houses don't answer back when you give them a coat of paint. The music had gotten soft and there didn't seem to be a need for radio personalities anymore. It was neither the time nor the place for someone like me."

However, as you've probably figured out by now, Lord Tim is back. He's older and wiser, but he's still playing rock 'n' roll—only this time, instead of the powerhouse forum of a KFWB, Lord Tim is doing his act these days at non-commercial KXLU-FM (88.9), the radio station on the campus of Loyola Marymount.

Every Wednesday night at 11, "Hudson's Theater of the Mind" unfolds—a unique program that incorporates a multitude of musical expressions within a basic rock framework.

"It's a show that can go from Delius to Edith Piaf to Charlie Parker," Hudson says, "but it's more than simply eclectic because there's always a story line, always a thread. The whole idea is to do a 'Theater of the Mind' type of thing with music—to make people forget they're just listening to the radio."

While Hudson's "Theater" fuels his creativity, his other KXLU program, "Jukebox Saturday Night"—which airs

Timothy Hudson, in heyday as Lord Tim (1965) at left, and as himself in 1982.

on Saturdays at 9—enlivens the spirit. It's a live remote from Madame Wong's where the latest strains of the punk/new wave idiom are on display.

And Lord Tim, with co-host Michelle Meena, is right there enjoying every minute of it.

"The reason I decided to come back to the business was hearing the Sex Pistols four years ago," he said. "That turned me around. I was listening to something that was new, vital and innovative. The music was coming back to me."

With his newfound enthusiasm, Hudson first mounted a stage show, "Where Were You in '65"—which was a nostalgia piece in which he narrated the highlights of the previous era's music. He then made the rounds of radio stations. There was a show for a while at KFOX-FM in Long Beach, then later at KGOE in Thousand Oaks. But when he tried to interest Los Angeles stations in the return of Lord Tim, he discovered a lot of people had forgotten there ever was such a thing.

"I was dealing with program directors who acted like drill sergeants," Hudson said. "When my phone calls were returned, which wasn't very often, I'd hear things like, 'We don't break format.' No one would touch 'Theater of the Mind.' It was just too different."

So finally, Hudson took his ideas to public radio. "I called KCRW-FM, KPFK-FM and KXLU," he said, "and I picked KXLU because it was the only one of the three that was doing a significant amount of rock 'n' roll."

And Hudson says he isn't at all ashamed to be doing his act for a small public station, having once commanded big bucks and a lot of attention at KFWB.

"Loyola Marymount has given me a home and for that I'm always going to be grateful," he said. "And one of the joys is that I'm teaching some of the young people who're working there how to do a live radio show."

This is not to say that Lord Tim wouldn't take another shot at the Big Time. He'd like to see "Theater of the Mind" picked up by a commercial station. And he feels the time is now right.

"The era of personalities is going to come back strong," he said, "and I think Lord Tim is a pretty good trademark. I also think that if you survive in Hollywood you've also accomplished something. I've gone through wives, organic living in the mountains, living at the beach, tennis . . . you name it. I've done it and I've come out the other side. The KXLU shows have also given me a certain amount of self-respect back. I really think I'm one of the best disc jockeys in the business. And radio can use a lot more of what I have to offer." □

Ian Botham Benefit Committee

John Wainwright & Co. Limited,
Downside, Shepton Mallet,
Somerset BA4 4JF.
Tel: 0749-2366

291 Cricklewood Lane,
Childs Hill, London NW2 2JL.
Tel: 01-794 4051

19 January 1984

Dear Tim and Maxi,

Ian has phoned me from New Zealand to confirm that he will be delighted to play at Birtles Bowl on May 8th against Geoffrey Boycott's team.

Kind regards,

Cathy Botham

Cathy Botham

Geoffrey Boycott O.B.E.
YORKSHIRE and ENGLAND
Testimonial Fund 1984

Tim & Maxi

Look forward to seeing you Birtles Bowl in May

Will have a super day.

Every good wish

Geoff Boycott

THE BIRTLES BOWL
HOME OF
HUDSON'S HOLLYWOOD XI
PRESENT
THE INAUGURAL GAME
BOYCOTT v BOTHAM at BIRTLES
TUESDAY 8 MAY 1984

SOUVENIR PROGRAMME 50p

...ordinator: John Farrar, 3 Greenwood Avenue, Blackpool   Telephone Q...
...asurer: Mr. J. Surgey, 56 Yorkshire Bank, 2 New Street, Barnsley   Telepho...

HUDSON IN HOLLYWOOD

iNvites you to
AN Orgasmic Night
at **OSCARS**
on the Sunset Strip—
to be recorded live
for Piccadilly Radio
in Manchester, England, England....

Doors open at 8.30
Show begins at 9.
Supper will be served
Black tie & black underwear
Lovers, lovers, sinners & saints

on Monday
11th March
1985

A magical mystical musical tour through 50 years
of sex & drugs & rock & roll

svp Michèle
54 3457

OSCARS
8210 Sunset Blvd, 90046

Biggles Botham could be a high flyer in Hollywood

Times 6/12/86

Simon Barnes

Tonight Ian Botham dines in Hollywood with Jackie Collins and other glittering guests of his agent, Tim Hudson. How come this never happened to Colin Cowdrey? Or Peter May? Must we accept that the nature of cricket and its stars is changing? "Mr Botham is coming here to look at California, Hollywood and Beverely Hills, and so that I can introduce California to Ian Botham," Hudson said.

"Mr Botham will become one of the great bang 'em, shoot 'em up stars. We're not talking about making a film tomorrow, he is coming here to make new friends. But we will slowly break Mr Botham into Hollywood, and Hollywood will get to know this English conquering hero."

No one quite knows how to take Hudson, with his pony tail, his rock 'n roll talk, and his plans for turning Botham into a socko-boffo movie star. What is certain is that he has put a new spring into Botham's step: the new haircut, the stripy blazers, the panama hats, have all gone to make Botham more Bothamesque than ever. The disillusionment with cricket that he felt as he left Pakistan two winters back is utterly vanished. "He is very disappointed to hear people out here are making a film of Biggles, because he would love to play Biggles."

You certainly can't fault Hudson for effort. He thinks watching Botham batting is as good as watching a Bruce Springsteen concert, And wears with pride his own Ian Botham blazer, which prompted Frances Edmonds, wife of Phillip, to say on being introduced: "Hello, whatever happened to good taste?"

"But there is always Raffles," said Hudson, talking about the gentleman burglar, not the founder of Singapore. "Raffles played cricket for England, remember, and that would be perfect for Mr Botham."

Hudson always refers to the Golden Boy as Mr Botham. Doubtless the title goes with the Charley's Aunt outfits, but it reminds me of that peculiar pop singer, Tiny Tim, who always referred to his wife as Miss Vicki. Hudson, whose interest include Californian property as well as rock 'n roll, is convinced he can make Botham a megastar. There would seem to be a number of obstacles in the way. "Oh, no. I don't talk about cricket to Hollywood people. I would lose them straight away. I talk about heroes. Mr Botham is England's greatest living hero." You ask any policeman.

One might add that Botham's voice is not exactly RADA trained, and that turning a habitué of Scunthorpe dance halls into a great English gentleman would seem to be something of a challenge. "This is Hollywood, this is tinsel town. Anybody can be anbody! Cary Grant went to an elementary school in Bristol, and ended up as one of the classic gentlemen of all time. Errol Flynn, Stewart Granger, David Niven – they had presence. And Mr Botham has tremendous presence. As for his voice, talking is an art form. And one he can learn."

Hudson took Botham under his wing in belief that it was "time Botham grew up". "Mr Botham realised that he had been giving it away for 10 years: for the next ten

Hudson's plans for English cricket

years he can gain the kind of financial rewards he is capable of. He is at a crossroads. He can become Fred Trueman or Fred Perry."

And he believes that through him Botham can become an international figure financially secure – sports talk for rich – for the rest of his life. He is not talking about taking Botham away from cricket, not yet. Botham has, he says, three or four more years at the top before he need consider becoming James Bond. It is three of four years in which Hudson can do the groundwork – like getting Botham to pose as Rambo on the front page of The Sun under the heading "Rambotham!" which, as my press box colleague Matthew Engel remarked, sounds like a town in Lancashire.

And while Botham remains in cricket, so Hudson's interest in the professional game increases. Hudson has long been a cricket lover, a wicketkeeper until his knees gave out, who now bats a bit and bowls the odd floater. And he has discovered something very true about the county game.

It is unquestionably the case that many top Test match cricketers – Botham, Richards, Edmonds and others at this sort of level, get roundly fed up with revolving around the county circuit seven days a week. There is a real sense in which such players have outgrown the relentless round of the county championship. For them. Hudson has a plan.

He wants to set up a kind of festival circus, a circus of the stars playing cricket at holiday grounds like Blackpool and Scarborough, "That would attract people in the same way that they go to rock concerts".

"People over 70 will splutter into their gin and tonics and say 'Who is this fellow Hudson?' But I want to pass on what I have seen in the New World, just as Sir Walter Raleigh did 300 years ago.

Hudson sees himself as a believer, you see, in the finest traditions of the game. this is the meaning of the stripy blazer."The game is often administered by people who are out of touch. It is as if the man who used to be Mantovani's agent were to handle Duran Duran." On the other hand, putting Hudson in charge of English cricket would be like putting Duran Duran's agent in charge of the Royal Philharmonic.

Hudson has, with considerable shrewdness, put his finger on a certain restlessness on the county circuit. Many players find the championship a bind but stick to it because it is necessary.

Smart entrepreneurs have been able to exploit such rumblings of discontent in the past, Kerry Packer being the prime example. These business ventures have been for the benefit of the businessmen – not for the benefit of the sport. That's business.

It's easy to get distracted by the pony tail and Biggles and the blazers, and to write Hudson off as a clown, as a no-account. But he has a measure of support among professional cricketers, and powerful contacts in the media through which to publicize his ideas. With football in a trough, and cricket popular as never before – thanks no least to his No 1 client, Ian Botham – to say there is no market for the Duran Duran approach would be to blind oneself to the new huge drawing power of cricket, and the miniscule drawing power of the county championship. Of course, a circus might turn out to be just one of those flashes in the pan that leave lasting scars on the game. But as they say in Hollywood, thats' show business!

BOTHAM IN HOLLYWOOD

BOTHAM TO GO INTO FILMS

HE SAYS YOU TEACH HIM TO BAT AND HE'LL TEACH YOU TO ACT!

Batting for Botham

TIM HUDSON may not be such a wild man as he wants us to think he is.

Mr Hudson — he likes to be called 'Lord Tim' but that's another story — is the new agent who hopes to 'sell' Ian Botham big in the States, which is why Botham has been posing for all these pictures in a wide-brimmed hat and Jacob jacket.

But will Lord's consider Mr Hudson a fit and proper person to handle the affairs of one of England's greatest cricketers? Have they heard of the party which Mr Hudson gave at Oscars on Sunset Boulevard, Los Angeles, in March, a party which Mr Hudson described as 'an orgasmic night on the Sunset Strip.'

Short

His invitation also stipulated 'black tie and black underwear ... livers, lovers, sinners and saints' and ended by describing the evening as 'a magical, mystical musical tour through 50 years of sex and drugs and rock and roll.'

Not quite the Lord's image, is it?

Our inquiries, however, reveal that the party fell short of its promise. Only about 50 people turned up and the owner of Oscars, Michele Booth, says: 'It wasn't wild at all. It was just a few of Tim's friends. No big deal.'

The guests were served home-made bangers, steak and kidney pie and Savoy mixed grill. They even broadcast the whole thing live to Manchester.

Somehow, not quite the Ian Botham image, is it?

BOTHAM'S BOSS IS CHUCKED OUT OF PUB

SUN 13/5/86

Botham's manager Tim Hudson was thrown out of a Californian bar yesterday after a bust-up over his millionairess wife.

The cricket star's flamboyant Mr Fixit accused comedian Nathan Moore of insulting his wife Maxi by saying he "only married rich women."

Maxi looked on, he grabbed Moore by his tie and hurled a pint of beer over him. But before a fight broke out, Hudson was collared by a bouncer and dumped outside the British-style King's Head pub in Santa Monica.

Afterwards Bristol-born Moore—who works the US club circuit—growled: "All I said was that he married rich women.

Madman

"I don't think that's an insult. I'd like to do it myself if I could."

Moore, 44, added: "He was like a madman. If he had stayed I would

Tim Hudson ... insulted

From JOHN HISCOCK in Los Angeles

have hit him."

Last night 40-year-old Hudson said: "I threw the beer over him on behalf of the league of English gentlemen.

"He said nasty things about my wife. The man is a twit but I didn't want to hit him because he is such a little guy."

Bouncer Bill Lourie, a heaving 18 stone, said:

"The man was causing trouble so I wrapped my arms around him."

Maxi, Hudson's second wife, received £2 million as part of her 1984 divorce settlement from ex-husband Walter Silber, a property developer.

Hudson's previous wife Beatrice Tesdorpe was also wealthy. The couple lived in a mansion in exclusive Malibu Lake.

159

FROM THE BEATLES

TO BOTHAM

PRIL 6, 1986   BRITAIN'S BIGGEST SALE   Price 28p   No.741

EXPOSED!
TRUTH
ABOUT
CRICKET STAR

PLU
Su
da
COLO
MAGA

He snorted drugs on pitc

BOTHAM COCAINE AND SEX SCANDAL

LINDY: Had sex and snorted cocaine wit

WORLD EXCLUSIV

TODAY the News of the Wo
the lid on the real story
Botham and drugs.

For the truth is that "I
Botham—English cricket's extro'
perstar—IS heavily
into drugs, includ-
ing the jet-set
favourite, cocaine.

And he has been
for at least TWO
YEARS.

Incredibly, the world's
greatest all-rounder even
took the field at least
once with coke hidden in
the pocket of his flan-
nels.

Now we can exclu-
sively reveal his part in
cocaine-snorting and sex
frolics only TWO WEEKS
AGO, during the England
team's humiliating cur-
rent tour of the West
Indies.

Botham and former
Miss Barbados Lindy
TURN TO PAGE 3

Beau
quee
night
passi

160

SPORTSMAIL CRICKET · SPECIAL

Botham's bust-up

England star set to confront his manager

IAN BOTHAM in thoughtful mood yesterday

IAN BOTHAM is ready for a showdown with his manager, Tim Hudson.

Botham, England's best-paid and most popular cricketer but a forlorn figure on the disastrous tour of the West Indies, 'could not be more angry' about drug-taking allegations said to have been made by Hudson, according to his closest friends.

Hudson was quoted yesterday as saying of Botham: 'I'm aware that he smokes dope, but doesn't everybody? Ian does not have a serious drugs problem. Yes, he's taken pot, but that's not a drugs problem.'

Offence

Alan Herd, Botham's solicitor said yesterday. 'The allegations are absolute nonsense. They are a lot of eyewash.

'As for the drugs, what Hudson is said to be alleging is a criminal offence. My client does not wish to comment on that until he has had a chance to talk with Hudson.'

That confrontation could happen today, with Hudson now in Trinidad to watch the fourth Test

By RUTH GLEDHILL

If Hudson cannot give a satisfactory explanation for the allegations, Botham will —according to friends—sack him.

Hudson's reported comments yesterday also included 'He will quit three-day cricket after this coming season From then on it will be one-day cricket and Test matches.'

Before leaving Los Angeles for Trinidad, Hudson refused to be drawn on the statements attributed to him.

He said: 'I am going to the West Indies to sort this matter out. As far as I am aware, Ian doesn't do drugs.

'I am going to be discussing drug use with Ian and I shall be telling him to change his lifestyle, but that doesn't mean I'm saying he does drugs.

Botham himself said : 'It's the same old thing—it is the 'alleged' again As far as I am concerned, it is old hat now, and I would think the majority of people in England are getting pretty bored with it as well.

'Tim is on his way out here and when he left a message to say his flight was delayed, there was no mention of this. 'I just treat it with contempt

—as far as I am concerned, it is the usual fabrication.'

The apparent rift between the two is the climax of a year of dreams by Hudson, the 41-year-old self-styled 'Lord Tim' who was once a disc jockey in the United States, and Botham, the flamboyant 30-year-old star who thinks fame on the cricket field could make him an international celebrity.

Hudson took Botham to Hollywood last year with the words: 'Mr Botham will become one of the great hang 'em, shoot 'em up stars.' He added: 'Hollywood will get to know this English conquering hero.'

Windbag

But Botham failed to bowl over a single movie director, and screen tests and talk-show offers were absent.

Peter Laver, former England fast bowler and now Lancashire's coach, said last night: 'I was unfortunate enough to share a room with Hudson once on tour. I can't say he's changed that much.

'He's a bag of wind, an empty barrel. He lives in cloud-cuckoo land. He has some very strange ideas.

'Botham is his bread and butter. When the team and I saw this in the paper, we just could not believe it Why do such a foolish thing?'

★ □ ★

ELVIN McKenzie is soon to be succeeded ...tor of the *Sun* newspaper by Tim Hudson, ...ergetic agent of Test cricketer Ian ...botham", and a connoisseur of exotic

...ortly before Christmas Hudson arrived in ...in offices, though he seemed to be "in ...at the time. His nose streaming from a ...cold, he wandered into McKenzie's office ...roceeded to spell out what he wanted in ...aristmas stocking.

...estly, he demanded that Botham's salary ...s drivelish, ghosted *Sun* column be in-...d from £30,000 to £50,000 per annum. ...he requested space in the newspaper to ...his own celebrity column on miscellaneous ...ts. Finally, he insisted that the *Sun's* ...t correspondent, Steve Whiting, should be ...ed from his post for displaying insufficien ...ation of Botham's talents, and that he ...d be replaced by Chris Lander of the *Mirro* ...irmed "Rambotham" toady.

...esumably because it was the season of pea ...odwill, the normally aggressive and profa ...nzie immediately agreed to these absurd ...nds, and the euphoric Hudson vanished ir ...d of talcum powder.

Private Eye.

STAR

121 FLEET STREET, LONDON EC4P 4JT, ENGLAND

TERRY WILLOWS
Accredited West Coast
Correspondent & Columnist

21044 Chatsworth Street
Chatsworth, CA 91311
Phone: (818) 341-3035
Telex: 215452

April 12, 1986

Dear Tim e Naai,

I am appalled at what happened with the 'Star' and the gross error that was made in using my personal memo as copy. I know John understands the error and it obviously affected him.

I have not written a single word about yourselves or Ian since the 'Star' story appeared and do not propose to do so in the future.

I can only offer my apologies at the 'Star's' comedy of errors. I do know that steps have been taken by the Editor to ensure it can't happen again.

Once again my apologies, I did not break my word as given to you on the night.

Best Wishes,

TERRY

CRICKET

Hudson wants Botham and Richards for Lancashire

By Ivo Tennant

Tim Hudson, Ian Botham's former agent, said yesterday he has offered Botham and Vivian Richards, both of whom are to leave Somerset, £50,000 each to play for Lancashire in 1987 and 1988. Hudson is hoping to oust Cedric Rhoades, Lancashire's chairman of 22 years, in order to bring this about.

Hudson, an eccentric entrepreneur, and a Lancashire life member would want to become chairman himself. He feels he can achieve this through the backing of the club's members. Botham, he said, would give him his answer by next Friday.

Hudson, who is renowned for his unusual ideas, lifestyle, dress and dialogue, was, a year ago, intent on making Botham "the first millionaire rock n'roll cricketer in the world". It was not a dream that lasted, Botham subsequently

Vivian Richards and Joel Garner, who are not being retained by Somerset, make their final appearances for the county tomorrow at Taunton against Derbyshire in the John Player Special League (Ivo Tennant writes).

Neither will play in the county championship match, also against Derbyshire, which starts today, but Ian Botham, who has threatened to leave the county in support of the two West Indians, will play in both matches, an ankle injury permitting.

dismissing Hudson for commenting on his lifestyle.

Hudson, who lives not far from Old Trafford is reportedly a self-made millionaire, although it is sometimes to distinguish fact from fiction in his life. "I guarantee the cricketers my personal money," he said. It is time Mr Rhoades made way for a

young rebel with plans to put Lancashire back on top and bring more youngsters through the turnstiles than Old Trafford has seen for years.

"I have spoken to a senior committee member, Murray Birnie and he was excited at the prospect of both players coming to the club," Hudson said. "I am breaking no TCCB rule by offering them my own money."

Hudson will face considerable opposition to his plans from Rhoades, who has criticised Botham's lifestyle and approach to cricket in the past. Rhoades is currently on holiday and Lancashire's annual general meeting will be held in December.

"I am sure I will have hug support from fellow Lar cashire members if I stan against the chairman on th issue," Hudson said. "T chairman has grown old. It time for changes."

Tim Hudson

Tim offers to revive Lancashire

By Jimmy Armfield

SELF-STYLED entrepreneur Tim Hudson wants Lancashire to sign West Indies's skipper Viv Richards.

And he's prepared to pump £50,000 into the crisis torn club to aid the bid.

But first Hudson wants Lancashire's entire committee to follow in the footsteps of Chairman Cedric Rhoades by quitting.

The committee meet tonight to discuss Rhoades's shock decision to resign — and Hudson is waiting in the wings ready to move in.

He says: "We have a super ground, Test cricket, and every facility at Lancashire, but we need to make the game appealing to young people.

"In Australia now, they are getting terrific crowds because the game has been presented well. We haven't grasped that yet, we need some flair in the place, something that will grip the public's imagination.

Backing

"For starters, we should think about signing Viv Richards, he is the best batsman in the world and it looks as though he will be playing in the Lancashire League. The crowds would flock to Old Trafford to see him."

Hudson also believes it is time that Lancashire played more games around the county: "There is a big cricketing public in East Lancashire and they would pour in at Accrington and Oldham to watch the county game. It would make them feel part of the club. The time has come to take the game to the people."

Hudson says it is time for the autocrats to move over and make way for an impressario.

He believes he can do it: "I can put £50,000 into the club, and I have business backing that could provide Lancashire with the best players. Let's be truthful, the members feel it's time we started winning a few matches.

"I know I don't fit the M.C.C. image, but 75 per cent of the people who watch cricket don't wear the old school tie. I am prepared to work for a place on the committee and ask everyone not to judge me on the way I look.

"I am Manchester-born and love cricket and I think I have the credentials to put new life into Old Trafford."

I'll do the business for Lancs — Hudson

ny GRAHAM FISHER

TIM HUDSON last night roared out his strongest challenge yet for the leadership of Lancashire cricket.

He dismissed the claims of Murray Bernie and Mike Whelan, two men mooted to take the chair following the resignation of Cedric Rhoades.

Millionaire Hudson said: "They are terrified of me right now. Neither wants to come out and say 'Oh my God, Hudson is different from us, he wears his hair differently'.

"But that's what the club needs. It needs an impresario,

a Barnum and Bailey, someone with ideas to sell Lancashire. I could make Steve O'Shaughnessy, Graeme Fowler and Neil Fairbrother into stars.

"Murray Bernie is one of a committee that are just 'yesmen' for Rhoades. Whelan is an insurance salesman, another autocrat, another Rhoades.

"People would be crazy to ignore what I'm saying. I want to be the new chairman. I intend to be the new chairman."

MANCHESTER EVENING NEWS

DIARY — 8 FEB 1989

Piccadilly spot for Lord Tim?

☐ Hudson — cock-a-hoop

DO I sense a craving on the part of sometime DJ Tim Hudson, now basking in the Californian sun while his millionaire entrepreneur friend Owen Oyston struggles for control of Piccadilly Radio?

The flamboyant Hudson tells me that, last year, he bought a large share in Oyston's umbrella organisation, the Miss World group, which already owns three other radio stations.

Hudson has long nursed an ambition to appear on Piccadilly. As long as eight years ago, he says, he tried to invest in the station but his bid was unsuccessful.

On the line from California he tells me bitterly that Piccadilly's managing director Colin Walters blocked his bid to buy a large chunk of shares and would never have him on the air. About this, Walters has been unavailable for comment.

Now cricket-crazy millionaire Hudson, who came back from the States to buy Birtles Old Hall at Nether Alderley, is cock-a-hoop about Oyston's bid.

Ever since his own attempt to buy into the station failed, he says, he's been waiting in the wings for a white knight to come along. "Now Sir Lancelot has walked into my life in the shape of Owen Oyston."

So would "Lord" Tim get a presenter's job at Piccadilly? He will only say: "Well, I'd have a better chance with a take-over. I can only say I hope my ambition would be fulfilled."

THE BIRTLES BOWL of HUDSON'S HOLLYWOOD

'Hudson's Theatre of the Mind'

presented every
Sunday Evening on
Piccadilly Radio Manchester 11:52AM
from 8pm to 11pm

Join Hudson for a magical, mystical, musical fantasy for three hours

Livers, Lovers, Sinners and Saints enjoy radio as you remember with **'Hudson's Theatre of the Mind'** every Sunday Night on Piccadilly Radio

Maxi/Hudson Street Cinema presentation

HUDSON'S
Hollywood Eleven

Secretary: Bernard Jordan
Telephone: 061-456-2542

HUDSON'S HOLLYWOOD XI Fixtures, 1989

Sun., May 14 - YORKSHIRE GENTLEMEN, 12 noon
    ,,   ,, 21 - STAFFORDSHIRE GENTLEMEN, 2 p.m.
Sun./Mon., May 28/29 -
                CRICKET WORLD, 12 noon both days
Sun., June 4 - CHESHIRE LEAGUE ALL STARS, 12 noon
    ,,   ,, 11 - YORKSHIRE FARMERS, 2 p.m.
Wed., ,, 14 - OXFORD UNIVERSITY, at The Parks ——— AWAY
Fri., ,, 16 - SHEFFIELD CRICKET LOVERS, 2 p.m.
Sun., ,, 18 - (Over-40s) MR. PIMLOTT'S TOP 40, 2 p.m.
    ,,   ,, 25 - LIVERPOOL PIRATES, 2 p.m.
Fri., ,, 30 - CHESHIRE WAYFARERS, 1 p.m.
Sat., July 1 - (Over-40s) ROSS'S RACQUETEERS, 1 p.m.
Sun., ,, 2 - CHESHIRE CATS, 1 p.m.
Tues./Wed., July 4/5 -
                NEW YORK STATEN ISLAND C.C., 12 noon both days
Sun., July 9 - BILL FRINDALL'S MALTAMANIACS, 2 p.m.
                (Collection for Blind - Guide Dogs)
Wed., ,, 12 - BLACKPOOL, at Stanley Park ——— AWAY
Sun., ,, 16 - STRATHALLAN OCCASIONALS, 2 p.m.
    ,,   ,, 23 - WHARFEDALE RAMBLERS, 2 p.m.
            ,, 30 - DAVID FRITH'S CRICKET MEDIA XI, 2 p.m.
Wed./Thurs./Fri., Aug. 2/3/4 -
                YOUNG ZIMBABWE, 11.30 a.m. each day
Sun., Aug. 6 - BLACKPOOL, 2 p.m.
    ,,   ,, 13 - NORTHERN INVITATION XI, 1 p.m.
    ,,   ,, 20 - NORTH OF SCOTLAND XI, 12 noon
Fri., ,, 25 - ISLE OF MAN, 2 p.m.
Sun./Mon., Aug. 27/28 -
                THE VIRGIN XI, 12 noon both days
Sun., Sept.3 - NEIL O'BRIEN'S XI, 1 p.m.
    ,,   ,, 10 - WILMSLOW, 1 p.m.

Special social events:-

Tues, July 4 - ANGLO-AMERICAN REGGAE BALL - members only
Sun., Aug.27 - THE VIRGIN BALL - members only

THE BIRTLES BOWL
Birtles Lane, Birtles, Cheshire.

E INDENPENDENT

– 11 NOV 1989

Beyond the boundary

IT'S a small world (of agents). As Ian Botham concludes his tour of the halls, an interesting confluence has taken place, alerting the legend's solicitor, Alan Herd.

Botham parted from Agent 001, Tim Hudson, amid public insults, first installing Bev Walker, then the Australian Tom Byron. Byron could not secure a work permit, so Botham moved to Ron Goodyear. The iridescent Hudson retreated to write an autobiography, the title of which — *From the Beatles to Botham and all the BFs in Between* — has alarmed Herd. Odd that the man who commissioned Hudson to write this less than flattering tome is ... Ron Goodyear.

HE TIMES

IMON BARNES.

I want to go Green says 'Lord' Tim

"LORD" Tim Hudson of Birtles Hall wants to make a challenge for Westminster and become a Member of Parliament.

He says he will stand as a "Green" candidate in the next general election, flying the flag for Macclesfield environmentalists.

But his self nomination has come as a shock to the town's official Green Party who say he isn't even a member.

Backing

Spokeswoman Susan Wardell said the nomination was news to her. "He will have to join the local party and receive the backing of at least two existing members by the end of the month to be considered," says Susan.

Meanwhile "Lord" Tim is confident he would be the right choice.

He has experience of Green politics having backed a successful Green candidate in local elections in California.

One of his prime aims as M.P. will be to put Macclesfield on the airwaves. Already there has been the recent successful expansion into Macclesfield of the Stoke-based radio station Radio Signal.

"The whole idea of local radio is to put money back into the community," said Mr. Hudson, who wants to start his own community radio station in Macclesfield.

W ho is your sportsperson of the decade? Please write and tell me. He or she should be remarkable, of course, in the traditions of this column. Eddie Edwards? Zola Budd? Ian Botham's "Hollywood" agent Tim Hudson? Send me your nomination, and tell me the reason for the choice. If I find the reason suitably capricious, stylish, ludicrous, or moving, I will publish it here and reward the sender and the nominated sportsperson with a magnum of Taittinger each. There: and you thought I was joking about service to readers, didn't you?

165

We know they've done better than anyone else from the Thatcher years but what are the wealthy like? **Erlend Clouston** tracked them down in the north west

A blast from brass sectio

Tim Hudson knew exactly what wealth was. "Wealth is style," said Mr Hudson who has a pigtail, several radio stations and a Georgian hall whose curtains appear to have been run off from the remnants of psychedelic cushion covers. Mr Hudson, latterly famous as, briefly, Ian Botham's manager, could afford several Porsche 959s but he prefers a Jeep and a deep blue Rolls-Royce with a Greenpeace sticker on the bumper.

Born a Mancunian, Mr Hudson represents an extreme, and probably confused, form of entrepreneur. He has, as a former disc jockey in Los Angeles, made lots of money out of of a business that regularly pours scorn on the money ethic. He

claims to have invented the phrase "flower power".

He bought Birtles Old Hall, his Cheshire home for six months of the year, unseen, because it was adjacent to the cricket ground he had bought, unseen, a year earlier. There were rumours that the neighbours had made a last-ditch attempt to prevent the Old Hall falling into Mr Hudson's clutches, and looking at Mr Hudson's pigtail, one is inclined to believe it. People have died of heart attacks in Cheshire for much less. Mr Hudson has now painted the Old Hall's exterior woodwork black, red, green, and yellow, the colours of the West Indian cricket team.

"How rich am I? Rich enough never to have to work again if I don't want to." Hudson's office is in the vast converted stable block that he was surprised to discover came along with the Old Hall. Tea was brought in by Edie, which enabled Hudson to demonstrate his vagueness with the milk and sugar. "Which do you put in first?"

He is vague, too, with telephones. "Hopeless," he groaned. "I press a button and everything comes up wrong. That's why I need Maxie!" Maxie, his American wife, sat at a desk signing piles of business letters with a large green pen. Possibly some of these were concerned with "communication stocks", which Mr Hudson prefers to science fiction magazines as a device for amassing riches.

"I honestly believe," he said, cake crumbling in his mouth, "that the potential for making oodles more cash is there now."

There is just one thing miss-

ing from Mr Hudson's life, and that is a batman. Mr Hudson craves a batman because a batman would give Mr Hudson more opportunity to fulfill what he suddenly reveals he believes to be the historic mission of the extremely wealthy, namely the protection of the less fortunate. Mr Hudson already protects his uncle Charlie, Jeff the groundsman, his gardener John.

"If these people need £500 to pay their tax bills, I have to pay it. I might ask work for that . . . but I would offer it."

But these were people he knew. What obligation did Mr Hudson feel towards the 9.4 million fellow citizens who had an income at, or below, the supplementary benefit level?

"We DO help people. We give them money. We award them sweaters, or a rugby jersey, or a pair of socks if they play well for us" (in Mr Hudson's cricket team). "We try to share it along. We have a Virgin Ball." This, he realises, is not creating the right effect. So he makes a straightforward protestation of allegiance.

"I like a man who works with his hands. I love the men who went over the trenches and won the war for this country, not the wimps who stayed behind. I will willingly share whatever I have with the working class."

This was rather a dramatic view from the bridge. At Macclesfield Conservatives, Mrs Shooter did not appear to give it much chance of catching on.

"Don't mention Tim Hudson. He is not a Conservative. I think he would like to be, but he's far too dangerous."

THE HUDSONS IN HOLLYWOOD

by Mick Middles

Postscript

October 1988

A car, containing me, a ragged journalist in search of some kind of story, hurtles through the Cheshire countryside on this disarmingly beautiful autumn day. I'm not sure where I'm going, or why. I had received a phone call, a couple of days previously, from a highly respected retired journalist named Duncan Measer, Mr Manchester himself.

'You'll like this guy, Hudson,' he had said. 'He's right up your street.'

I wasn't sure how to take that at first. I'm still not, actually. Like many people living in the Manchester area, I'm only acquainted with Hudson via the enormous amount of local press coverage he has attracted over the years. Much of which, it must be stated, has been laced with highly partisan comments from a variety of outraged 'neighbours'. Now that *has* always intrigued me. Any man who can cause such a continuing display of hilarious pomposity *has* to be doing something right. Far better, I think, for someone who has the good fortune, or whatever it takes, to come across money, to use it in a spectacular and interesting way than to do the usual and hide themselves away behind the barriers of snobbery and aloofness. One thing is certain, Tim and Maxi Hudson, whoever they are, are not in the business of building an ivory tower. What they do, they do in public.

But what do I know? As I'm writing this, in my head, as I drive through Alderly Edge, I have never met Tim or Maxi Hudson. They could be nice, pleasantly deranged people. I do hope so and all these stories seem to indicate that this is the case. I love pleasantly deranged people. On the other hand, they could be cold and manipulative. It is always foolish to judge people directly through their public persona. Also, I'm not sure how big their story really is. Everyone, of course, remembers the Botham affair and I am aware that Tim, in a past life, was one of the most influential and innovative DJs of all time – but are they famous? Oh, what does it matter anyway? As it happens, I'm a touch jaded about the famous preferring, quite seriously, to research into the amazing story that lies behind the cameraman, rather than the dull predictable tale that surrounds the star, if you catch my drift? No? Oh well, never mind.

My car is now pulling through the gates of Tim and Maxi's home, Birtles Old Hall, and, for some bizarre reason, I feel as though I'm at the beginning of a true story. Not a frivolous piece of sycophantic newspaper gossip, but a 'real' story, of substance … containing real feelings. I hope so. To be honest, I've been getting bored with life of late. Although uncertain about the people I'm about to meet, I am sure about one thing. They are not going to be boring.

I remember the words of my editor at the *Evening News*. 'We need the Hudsons of this world … they sell newspapers … they make life interesting.'

I do hope so.

I park my silver Fiat behind their blue Bentley. I try not to be intimidated by such things. So far, I could be visiting a Conservative cabinet minister at home, or the chairman of some dreadful fast-food chain. Everything seems alarmingly conventional. But then I take heart as I notice the flag pole flying the Skull and Crossbones, the rebel Californian Republic flag and, of course, the 'freak' flag that depicts Flower Power. No, I decide, this won't be anything like visiting a Conservative cabinet minister.

Maxi greets me first ... warm, cheerful, welcoming, American.
Then Tim pounces round the corner, pony tail flapping in the wind.

'Hi maan ... how ya doin'? Good to see you, maan. C'mon ...
we'll go over to the coach-house and have a chat.'

Which is exactly what we do. Well, actually, that's not quite true.
Tim has a chat. I sit, dazed, in the armchair, and attempt to take it all
in. Tim talks and talks and talks and talks ... he spins round, his arms
fly in all directions. Within ten minutes he has thrown thirty ideas in
my direction. Many of them, I secretly admit, are rather intriguing. A
few of them are just plain bizarre.

Although I can fully understand why many people, especially in
this most reserved neighbourhood, are instantly fazed by this man's
sheer gall and energy I decide, here and now, that I like him. I love his
enthusiasm, his apparent honesty. How he throws himself, sometimes
without due consideration, into a particular line of thought ... as if just
to observe what will happen. To tempt providence. I find him inspiring,
intriguing and not at all the blank egomaniac that I had half-expected.

I pen these thoughts in a story in the *Manchester Evening News*. It's a
story that I know will ruffle a few feathers, so I immediately stand back
and wait for the flak to fly. Nothing happens. The silence is deafening,
extraordinary. I'm greeted by the same, almost paranoid silence when I
tentatively ask my contacts within the radio stations of the North-West,
how they view the Hudsons. This seems very strange. Almost as if
someone, somewhere, in a position of great but unseen power, wants to
make this provocative duo invisible. Then again, this could just be my
over-enthusiastic imagination playing tricks on me again.

As it happens, I spend a good deal of time at Birtles during the
next two months and get to know the Hudsons both as associates, and as
friends. I help Tim with his book, this book, and, together, we decide
that, when his remarkable life story is written down, it appears to be
divided into strict, deliberate, formal sections. As if meticulously
planned, if not by Tim, then by some guiding force. Of course, this
hasn't really been the case. Tim's life has been something of a
rollercoaster ride and, frankly, as the ride continues, and I seem to be on
it, it doesn't take long for the sheer speed and scope to scare and excite
me. This book, we again decide, needs to capture the feel of this

possibly-out-of-control rollercoaster.

So it is decided that I should go to Hollywood, for two months, with Tim and Maxi. The object of the exercise is to capture the feel of California, to meet many of the people who have been influential in the story and, frankly, to chronicle 'having a good time' with the Hudsons. So the forthcoming chapter, 'The Hudsons in Hollywood', is born. It remains in raw diary form. Much of it may appear trivial and irrelevant. Some of it is vital. Whether or not it succeeds in digging deep, behind the general story, I cannot say. Before we leave for California, I promise myself that I will write the truth. Not as Tim and Maxi see it, but as I see it. For better or worse, exciting or dull, important or frivolous. As it turns out, it is all of these things.

Much of our stay in Los Angeles, or Malibu to be exact, is videoed, partly for the purposes of this book. Often this involves Tim interviewing an influential face from his past. Where appropriate, during this forthcoming chapter, I allow these interviews to remain in full question-and-answer form. Tim is a skilled interviewer and it hardly seems fitting for me to bludgeon my way in, adding my thoughts, to what is generally self-explanatory.

Extract from 'Mick Middles' column, Manchester Evening News
Monday, 9 January 1989

...back to the flight. At Heathrow, I boarded the British Airways plane and a steward, upon learning of my dubious intent to send missives back from the States, remarked, 'Make sure you give us a good mention.' He would soon come to regret this remark.

We boarded the plane at 12.15 pm. Everything seemed fine. We taxied to take-off position and then ... then ... the inevitable happened. A bland, seemingly unconcerned remark seeped from the Tannoy. 'I'm sorry,' said the captain, 'there seems to be a minor fault with a tiny valve in one of the engines. It will only take a second to replace, but first, we must taxi back and have it seen to.' He was right, too. It did only take a second to replace. Once the engines had cooled down. This, unfortunately, took a little over four hours. With paranoia understandably rife and security painstakingly stringent after the Lockerbie disaster, we were not allowed to leave the aircraft. Then, at 4.15 pm, came another cheerful announcement. 'Well, the good news is that the valve has now been replaced . . .'

The sound of 256 people cheering in perfect synchronisation is a happy one. 'Unfortunately, due to regulations beyond our control, the cabin crew have now gone overtime and will have to be replaced. This means that we will now have to wait until 6 pm when the new crew arrive.' The sound of the same 256 people groaning with helpless frustration, is not so happy.

This situation, to be sat on the runway for six hours, awaiting the start of a ten-hour flight, is one of the most intensely frustrating situations that I have ever come across. Now, I'm a reasonably placid person but, I tell you, I almost crack at one poignant moment during the proceedings. I want to swear at the stewards. I want to vent my frustration on them. Then, I realise that I'm sat next to Tim Hudson. A man with an unprecedented reputation for being helplessly volatile. Surely, I think, he will explode at any given moment. But he doesn't. He submerges himself in what must be every newspaper in the western world. He reads, and absorbs, every printed word. Every classified ad. He reads everything in sight, obsessively. I try to read a Margaret Drabble novel and I find Tim reading it over my shoulder. I almost expect him to comment on the plot . . . to question the author's ability to paint a character . . . Tim Hudson, sitting next to me, helpless on this runway, has escaped from the tediousness of the situation by immersing himself in every surrounding written word. His ability to concentrate is both impressive and genuinely surprising. Until this point, I had him down as some kind of enthusiastic butterfly. Perhaps I have been wrong?

Los Angeles International Airport
Wednesday, 28 December 1988
This particular check-out area, a bland, featureless place manned by a staff who go about their duties with terrifyingly ruthless efficiency – as if to say, 'This is Los Angeles . . . it is *not* merely Tinseltown . . . we know exactly what we are doing', must be one of the most photographed

indoor areas in the world. A million forgotten press shots. We've all seen
them. Worried-looking film, rock and soap stars, pampered and
pestered, dashing through the departure lounge or arrivals area. Even
tonight, a stray from the *papparazzi* pack lurks, hoping to catch someone,
something, on the extremely late 12.45 from London Heathrow. Well,
you never know.

We are no better. There's one man, suitably scruffy, who may or
may not be Stuart Copeland from The Police. We can't decide. It could
be.

'I never forget a face,' says Tim, 'but I'm not convinced. Does
anyone really care?'

We weary arrivals drag our exhausted bodies through the various
bewildering avenues of entry. It's all right for some, Maxi included ...
as a US citizen she is allowed to waltz straight through. I notice the
photographer and possible Copeland begin to slink away when, all of a
sudden, a scorching bright light beckons them back. They turn to face a
wonderful pastiche of a Hollywood entrance. The bright light fronts a
video camera deftly controlled by the rock-biz wacky figure of Bulgarian
film-maker Juliana. (Both the camera, and Juliana, are to become silent
and omnipresent throughout our nine-week visit, the idea being for her
to capture this chapter, not just here, with me in print, but on endless
stacks of video tape.)

In the centre of the light ... Tim and Maxi Hudson. Back home
and basking in hilarious mock glory. Obviously ... perfectly, a limo
awaits. The photographer nervously eyes this spectacle. He takes a
swift, sly snap, just in case. Tim loves the camera glare. He smiles
warmly ... and falls into an instant narration.

However, such unashamed decadence doesn't come easy to me and,
once inside the limo, I slide craftily next to Juliana and her camera,
leaving the spotlight glaring towards Tim and Maxi ... and the limo
pulls smoothly away.

Thursday, 29 December
A quietish, jet-lagged day. The Hudsons have arrived in their temporary
Malibu home. Last night it was but a cute wooden beach hut filled with
packing cases and articles of furniture retrieved from their Santa Monica

home. Soon, in fact, after just eight hours' feverish unpacking, the
brown interior becomes distinctly 'Hudsonised'. Quality local paintings,
the work of Santa Monica artist, Packard, are hung with pride, and
slowly they are surrounded by layer upon layer of Hudsonia. Framed
press cuttings, resplendent in red, green, yellow and black surrounds,
cling to each corner. Old pictures of Botham, of Richards and Lord Tim
suddenly materialise. A John Bellany book lounges happily next to a
copy of *Cricket World* magazine and this little house, in Malibu, takes on
the distinctive air of a corner at Birtles. Glaring through the huge
windows ... the unmistakable panoramic expanse of the beach and, of
course, beyond that, the Pacific Ocean.

Friday, 30 December
In Santa Monica, on Hollister, two houses from the beach, amid a
cancerous spread of new flatblocks and low-rise hotels, a house screams
from the street. A wooden house. The Americans would call it 'funky'.
At first, I don't see it. Tim, driving, directs my attention.

'We used to live just off here,' he states as we slowly approach the
site.

'Which house?' I state ... and then I laugh ... I *have* to laugh. As
the house springs proudly into view, my question becomes comical ...
absurd. Which house, indeed. There it sits, empty but cheerfully
boasting the loudest colour scheme in Santa Monica. A Flower Power
house, evocative, defiant in the face of the overwhelmingly partisan
landscape, and still there, but only just.

'It's about to be knocked down, though,' reflects Tim. Even so, it
will outlast our visit and, in a more flamboyant moment, as you will see,
we will return.

Later we meet Juliana at the flat of her musician friend, Carl, just
off Sunset Boulevard. Once ensconced inside, we are forced to watch
the video of the arrival at the airport. Despite the disturbing sight of
myself wandering around in a moronic daze – my normal state, as it
happens – the video is fun, with Tim hyping it up, as only he can.

It is a rock-biz-type flat ... I'd recognise this ambience anywhere.
It is soundtracked, fittingly, by constant frenzied telephone
conversations. Today they are mainly about the piecing together of the

173

forthcoming psychedelic revival concert at The Universal Amphitheatre. This is a more than curious coincidence. The event, which comes as a complete surprise to us all, will be highlighted by the appearance of Sky Saxon And The Seeds. The first time, in fact, that the original band will have performed together for over twenty years. On the night, famed Los Angeles DJ Rodney Bingenheimer will introduce Tim on stage before Tim, in turn, will introduce The Seeds. A meeting betwen Tim and Sky, which will be historic to say the least, is being arranged.

'WHAAAT ... NO WAY, JULIANA ... I DON'T WANT TO MANAGE HIM, FOR GODSAKE ... but I'll take him to lunch.'

'Lunch!' laughs Maxi, 'Sky doesn't eat!' Which, to me, is just about the best line of the afternoon.

Nevertheless, an important lunch does follow minus, I hasten to add, the increasingly curious figure of Sky Saxon. It is important, not because of the food, which is excellent if a little cold, or the conversation, which is somewhat warmer, but because of the place itself: Butterfields. Formerly Horticultural Holiday. The very restaurant that, some sixteen years previously, had been built by Tim and his ex-wife Kathy. For Tim, walking up the steps from the car park must be an eery experience.

'I built these steps ... every single one of them ... every step ... I put these plants in ... I built this patio ...' Etc., ad infinitum.

Inside the restaurant, the mural has been submerged by a wash of white paint but Kathy's individualistic mosaic stained-glass windows remain. Now they are complemented by an exhibition of paintings that openly pay homage to the colourful fragmentation of the glasswork. The fireplace, now curiously in vogue over in England, where Victoriana reigns supreme, sits large and dominant in its natural central space.

Tim: 'I don't think they like me coming back here ... the old ghost ... they like to think they created it all by themselves.'

But we all know who really created this oasis of yuppiedom, fifteen years ahead of its time, slap bang in the centre of crazy Sunset Boulevard.

Sunday, 1 January 1989

Surely not. This *cannot* be 1st January. The temperature edges into the eighties. Two houses down the beach, around the pool in the house next to the house that belongs to John McEnroe and Tatum O'Neal, a rock band of undecided name lounge about the pool, flash V-signs at the odd passers-by, i.e. me, and generally cavort with a bizarre collection of groupies. Tim, however, is feeling less than frivolous. Still jet-lagged and attempting to recover from the obligatory bout of transatlantic flu. As such, ventures into the new-found relevance of Flower Power are hardly a priority.

An American popstar from yesteryear, named Creed Bratton, or 'Chuck' to us, calls round for a 'good old days' conversation. This is to be the first of many. Chuck used to be the leader of a Sixties bubblegum band, The Grassroots, who, as I am amazed to discover by glancing into my Billboard Chart Hits file, scored no fewer than fourteen Top-Forty hits in the US in the Sixties. The talk, perhaps predictably, is of The Doors, Steppenwolf, Three Dog Night ... old stories laced with drug references. In the Sixties, drugs were seen, however naïvely, as a vehicle of freedom, of release, and not the reverse as we see them today. But the memories are still vivid. Wild times on mescaline and acid.

Tim: 'I remember once, on acid, I was supposed to meet Kathy Fitzpatrick at Dan Tana's restaurant in Hollywood. When I went in and asked for her the maître d' led me to a table ... the lady at this table just happened to be Kathy Fitzpatrick and was dining alone. She was an executive for Mattel Toys of California but it wasn't my friend Kathy. Still we got to talking and I ended up spending three days with her. Can you believe that?'

Monday, 2 January
A hot ... hot holiday. The Tournament of Roses Parade fills the television screen and fuels the conversation.

Tim: 'This is wealthy, white America. White Christian America ... it's all on there, on the screen. Look at that. They've got Shirley Temple Black ... and Linda Gray doing the commentary. This represents wealth ... real unashamed wealth. This is the power of America, this is the ego ...'

In Pasadena, Los Angeles, The Tournament of Roses Parade sweeps through a five-mile orgy of colour. Flowing, waving banners, screaming, yelling hordes, floats the size of apartment blocks, costing up to two hundred thousand dollars and flanked, as always, by gleaming majorettes – the embodiment of American sexuality.

College football fills at least three other channels throughout the day, no let-up. Because I'm profoundly stupid in regard to such matters, these games mean little to me, at least, initially. However, as the days wear on, they begin to make a little more sense ... and a little more.

'FOOTBALL!' screams Tim, whirling and enthusing in true Hudsonian fashion – his influenza fading fast – 'more than anything else, more than any other sport, represents America today. It is loud, brash, overstated, aggressive but, you know, I have never seen a scrap of violence at a football game ... it's all out there ... on the field.'

Juliana calls round, plus camera, as ever. I spend the day, and this is the way I am to spend most days during the forthcoming nine weeks, desperately trying to stay out of camera shot. Over tea, there is a long, heated discussion over the basic nature of the demo movie.

Tim: 'Look, Juliana, I know Hollywood ... it's my town ... I've seen it all and I worry about projects such as this because I've seen so much waste. I hate waste ... there's nothing I hate so much as waste. There's more money wasted in Hollywood than in any other place on Earth, and all in the name of showbusiness. I'm worried ... I look at you and I worry. I worry about that camera you are using. (Points towards Juliana's hi-tech but simple-looking video camera.) That's a joke camera ... right?'

Juliana: 'No ... no ... not at all. It is a perfectly acceptable demo camera. It isn't broadcast quality, of course, but we are not intending to broadcast this ... are we? We are just making a demo ... a pilot, to sell the idea. Your life. It's a great movie ... it's a great idea.'

This banter, which sees Tim, Juliana and Maxi all falling into strange instantaneous roles of Devil's Advocate, revolves for an hour or so before laying to rest, more or less, where it began, with a decision to continue the filming. I'm confused but, not wishing to pull the conversation into an even tighter, more negative circle, I say nothing.

At 9.15, Sky Saxon phones. It is a welcome break ... a comedic and historic moment.

Tim: 'Hi, Sky ... listen, are you going to be together for this concert ... or what? What do you mean you haven't started rehearsing yet? You've only got three weeks. You what? You cut an album last week? Who for? Oh that's great ... Sky, listen ... where can I buy cassettes of The Seeds? I can't find them anywhere and what about CD? Are The Seeds on CD? They are ... that's great because, you know ... CD is everything nowadays. What? ... I think you are a bit late in thinking that, Sky? What? You are going to perform *L.A. Woman*, on stage, as a tribute to Jim Morrison? Oh, Sky ... listen maaan ... can you sing? ... let me hear you sing ... listen maan ... yeah, that's OK but try singing something I know. Sing *Mr Farmer* ... Hey, that's not bad ... you are improving with age, Sky, what have you got planned? A double album and it mentions me on the back ... what does it say? IRON BOTTOM? ... Who? ... You mean Ian Botham? What on Earth is Ian Botham doing on the back of the record? ... What has he got to do with The Seeds? What? It says that Ian Botham likes your music? He's never even heard your music ... Sky ... Sky... Who is in your band now? ... Oh, yeah ... all the old band plus Mars Bonfire? Didn't he use to be in Steppenwolf? ... He wrote *Born To Be Wild*, didn't he? ... Look, Sky, I'll ring you tomorrow ... we'll arrange a meeting ... OK ... Bye...'

'I can't believe it,' says Tim. 'He sounds so together. That's the first time I have ever got him to sing over the phone. He would never have done that in the old days.'

'Why don't you put a single out in Europe for him?' asks Juliana. 'It would be sure to make money ... how much is he getting paid for those shows? Oooh, that's not enough...'

As Juliana's rock manager's brain begins to kick into gear, I sense that, neatly, the stage has been set...

Tuesday, 3 January
We have a strange problem. We don't need anybody ... nobody at all, but we have to let people know that Tim is back in town. So I type a press release, to be sent, tentatively, to the most influential areas of the LA media. It reads:

HUDSON. THE UNTOLD LEGEND OF HOLLYWOOD.
LORD TIM, as he was known, was the first British disc jockey in

America, and discovered The Moody Blues. In 1965, Lord Tim came to Los Angeles and became the embodiment of the feel, the pace and the rush of the times. While managing The Seeds, one band whose influence in underground circles far eclipsed their eventual commercial success, LT and singer Sky Saxon coined the term 'Flower Power'. The initial concept was pure, poetic and prophetic. To be destroyed, as such things so often are, by the ensuing scramble of commercialism.

Since those heady days, Hudson's life has been full and, as always, spiced by outstanding radical success and innovation. He provided worldwide success for Joe South's *Games People Play*, opened the first wholefood restaurant in LA and began to organise his life around three passions: rock and roll, real estate and cricket.

Back in England, with his wife and partner, Maxi Hudson, he moved sensationally into all three areas, buying his own cricket ground, managing and grooming the greatest English cricketer of the century, Ian Botham (England's Joe Dimaggio) and forcing radical changes within English commercial radio, both as a presenter and as a shareholder ... and all along the way capturing the full glare of publicity from the, at times partisan, English national press.

But Hudson never really lost his belief in the initial stirrings of Flower Power and that history has provided an incorrect vision of those times.

Now, Hudson's back in town and back in vogue. He's here to set the record straight, researching a book for Goodyer Associates in England, to be released in Spring '90, called *From The Beatles To Botham* and for a film series based on an original play, *Where Were You In '65?*

It is one of the greatest of all rock and roll stories. Were you part of those times? If so please contact ... etc.

Thursday, 5 January
LT on Botham
'I think that year he was with me, 1985, that summer, Botham garnished more press than any other cricketer ... of all time. There were shades of Denis Compton about it. It must have been a little like that in 1947–48 ... Compton was the big golden boy, the Brylcreem boy. But it was bigger for Botham because of television ... the media is

so much more powerful now. I don't know ... maybe it was better
before. Maybe it's better to receive when it takes longer to get here ... I
remember when I was young ... I used to listen to Test matches or
heavyweight boxing matches on the radio from Australia or New York.
I found it all terribly exciting, I really did ... maybe I was just young
and hadn't been exploited by the media ... I don't know.

'I think that Botham and Hudson had a really good time in 1985
... I suppose, at times, I went a bit over the top, but not in regard to
the "smoke dope" thing. It was common knowledge that Botham smoked
the odd joint. Look ... there was this article, in the *LA Times* dated 12
December 1985. It reads, "Botham was considered both by his peers and
by the public as England's most prestigious all-rounder since W. G.
Grace. Botham today hits like Babe Ruth but pitches like Sy Young and
fields like Jackie Robinson. A distinctive and exultant winner of cricket
matches. Botham, 30, also lives like Errol Flynn ... a public fist-fight
and one fine for possession of marijuana.

'I personally feel that the Botham camp, his family, probably
wanted to get rid of me. I never thought of myself as being too popular
with his family but, during the summer of '85, Botham spent a good
deal of his spare time over at Birtles. It wasn't me, inviting him. My
home was open to him. I certainly wasn't procuring women, as I have
heard people say. I have never procured a woman ever, for Mr Botham,
that just isn't my talent. I'm certain that any lady who was seen in Mr
Both's company was there totally on his own charm. He didn't need me
to procure women for him. The amazing thing about it all is that I was
the first person he ever allowed onto the same stage as him. I was up
there to perform my part.

'It was my idea to let his hair flow like the wind, it was my idea to
let him have a pony tail ... and even earrings but it wasn't my idea for
him to bleach his hair blond ... though I thought it looked attractive ...
it was his choice. I do agree that he didn't look great in a striped blazer
but there were times when he did look good in it and could easily pull it
off. I'll put up pictures from 1985 and Mr Botham looked as good, if not
better, than he ever looked in his entire career. What's more, throughout
that season he was happy ... he told me so. He had a good time ... he
told me so.'

LT on Billy Birtles (The Hudsons' famous dark blue Bentley)
'We went for a drive, to Mere in Cheshire, to look at some cottages we were considering buying. We were in the Jensen, an old, beautiful car that unfortunately never really ran very well. We called it "Jenny" and, as Maxi says, she was in hospital a lot. We stopped because Maxi wanted to buy some Polo mints and while she was out I noticed this car, this Bentley. It was blue, my favourite colour of blue ... a kind of navy ... deep grey blue, really traditional looking. I didn't have a clue how much it was going for, I mean, I wasn't in the habit of checking out the prices of Bentleys but I just had to go over and find out. It seemed so amazingly cheap to me. Well, you expect Bentleys to cost fortunes, but it didn't. It had belonged to the chairman of Harrods and that freaked me out. What a trip. What a gimmick. When Maxi came back with her Polo mints, I told her, "I've just bought a Bentley." '

Maxi: 'That was the most expensive packet of Polo mints in history.'

Tim: 'We drove it home, there and then. We really bought it so we could take Botham and Richards out, as there just wasn't enough room in the Jensen.'

These stories are delivered to me, with typically endearing Hudson gusto, over breakfast on this strange wet, squally, Thursday morning. There had been plans to film but, as the rain intensifies to almost Mancunian proportions, we soon find ourselves, somewhat predictably, in their favourite Santa Monica bar ... The King's Head, British Pub. A remarkable place, indeed.

'It's remarkable because of the clientele. You will get the average working man, the English "brickie", at one table and, say, Dustin Hoffman at the next. And yet everyone is treated equally.'

The bar and walls are littered with photographs of the famous who have tested the rather strange bitter within these walls. George Best, Dennis Healey, Ian Botham, Billy Idol, Brit Ekland and even President Reagan ... and Tim's wrong, actually, it is remarkable not just because of the clientele but because of the very 'feel' of the place. The smell, the smoke, the darkness ... the nicotine aura, so untypical in Santa Monica and I felt, at once, at home. The restaurant area is heavily reminiscent of Berni Inns in England. Dumb waiters housing racks of sugar sachets, cheerful waitresses scribbling away at bills. But at the bar, engaged in shop talk, the tabloid journalists (stringers) lurk. More of them, later on.

The pub is the creation of a remarkable man, namely Phil Elwell. A Brummie. One of those people Alan Whicker always manages to ferret out and, indeed, this was once the case. You can always tell a 'Whicker Man' from the way he 'glows' with self-pride and Phil Elwell is definitely a glowing type. Cheerful, likeable but not without a certain business-like intensity. Every time he playfully thumps you on the shoulder, as he does continually throughout the conversation, he is really saying, 'Look at me, I did all right, didn't I?' And, of course, he did do all right. He started with a hot dog stand and is now the proud owner of a three-million-dollar Malibu home. Had I achieved that, then I would probably be going round thumping people on shoulders.

Friday, 6 January

Hell ... where am I? Oh yes ... sitting here in the back of a hired Buick ... wondering where the hell I am! We are passing through Westwood, or somewhere. Multi-million-dollar middle-class homes line the streets, each one a stunning example of domestic architectural beauty ... Beverly Hills ... and then on past Century City, the new tower-block financial capital. Tim and Maxi are just driving around, enjoying themselves, pointing out landmarks, familiar-looking corners. 'Didn't we have an accident here, once?'

And outside the car windows, the formless simmering town slides past.

Just off Sunset, once again, we pick up Juliana plus various technical boxes containing video equipment, and we head off ... deeper and deeper into the Hollywood hinterland. As we snake upwards, Tim's enthusiasm explodes from the front seat.

'I lived here,' he screams, shortly before diving out of the car and practically embracing his former abode.

'Can you imagine the view from the front of this house ... I mean, can you imagine it?'

We don't have to imagine anything. Twenty yards past the house we stop, turn, and are confronted by a panoramic expanse that could match anywhere in the world.

Tim: 'Look ... there's downtown, over there ... and Hollywood Boulevard ... and Century City. How can anyone call this an ugly city, maan? It's beautiful and, oh maan, I was the first Englishman to really experience all of this.'

On we drive, upwards, onto Wonderland Avenue. Houses are perched, precariously, on stilts. Personally, I don't understand it ... it doesn't seem feasible ... none of these would survive even a moderately large earthquake, surely? I'm going to have to halt the text here in order to concentrate on one particularly distinctive Hollywood vision. Directly above us, on enormous wavering stilts, stands a full-size tennis court. Just jutting out there, into space.

'Probably some pop star owns that,' concludes Tim. Personally, I wouldn't even walk on such a structure, let alone play tennis on it.

We discover the house at the end of Wonderland Avenue where, all those years previously, Sky Saxon and Tim had coined the phrase Flower Power. With the omnipresent silent camera of Juliana behind us, we tentatively approach. The lady of the house, an up-market girl from, oddly enough, Liverpool, is understandably sceptical.

'Look ... if you want to tell everyone that this is the house where Flower Power was invented then it's fine by me. But I'll not believe it, I hear all kinds of things up here.'

We drive out, down through Laurel Canyon, and back down to the Highland Camrose.

The Highland Camrose reminds me, weirdly, of the theme village, Porthmeirion in North Wales. Whereas the latter has been described as a 'Light opera in architecture', the Highland Camrose where, I sense, Tim spent his happiest years, is something of an acoustic rock song in architecture. It is Birtles. A small colony of houses, cute wooden houses, angled haphazardly on a hill at the back of the Hollywood Bowl. Green, blue, yellow, red houses ... sadly some are now boarded up, although the agreeable man who lives in Tim's ex-workroom/basement informs us that the area is to be turned into a California historic area, of sorts. The prevailing atmosphere is one of 'village', right here, slap bang in the centre of this extreme city. A place, created by Hudson, that possesses all the tranquillity of a quaint parochial outpost.

On a wall, just below the navy blue and grey house that was once occupied by Kathy, Tim and River, stands the mural that had once been painted to celebrate Tim's life. Amazingly, it is untouched ... still quite beautiful. The house, a sweet American abode that conjures up visions of Anne of Green Gables, sits happily in the dominant position in the village.

The history of this little colony remains, even within this locality, largely unknown. Perhaps the perfect metaphor for this story.

'In that house,' exclaims Tim, pointing to the least impressive of all the abodes, 'The Eagles were formed. Linda Ronstadt lived there. Jackson Browne lived in the house opposite and ... over there lived Tyrone Power. In that one ... Marilyn Monroe and, of course, Howard Hughes lived here.'

Afterwards, as we sit in the ghostly expanse of the Hollywood Bowl, attempting to imagine the comparable link with Birtles, a tour guide screams irritably at Juliana: 'Don't video me ... turn that camera off.'

'Why is everyone so paranoid about being filmed?' I ask.

'Because they probably have too much to hide ... they are on the run or something,' says Maxi.

They probably are, too.

The first time I see Sky Saxon, he's there, on the balcony, at the Malibu house, locked in embrace with Tim. The meeting of lost friends ... divided by time and, well, a few other things. Sky pulls away, turns to look at me. Now I've seen some strange sights during my time spent on the fringes of rock and roll, but this is one of the strangest. Red, baggy silk pants are tucked, cossack-like, into wide boots. A belt, twelve studs deep, gathers a silk shirt to a pencil-thin torso. On top of a purple velvet jacket sits his bearded face. A craggy spectacle, hiding behind dark glasses and a voodoo wand. He smiles, warmly, shakes my hand and begins to talk about peace. About John Lennon. About Elvis Presley. About The Seeds. He is shivering.

'Look I'm shivering because I'm cold ... it was freezing last night. It's so cold at this time of year.'

'It will be colder in Europe, Sky ... When are you touring?'

'Fifty-eight dates, starting in Berlin on 18 February. I'm going to enjoy England ... I'd love to stay there. I'm sick and tired of being put down by this country ... America is killing me. I hate America.'

Saxon has brought with him two albums. One is yet another compilation of Seeds songs, this time gathered together by the English Bam Caruso label, and an album of newer material. With respect, everyone would rather he just puts The Seeds on but, as it turns out, the newer stuff turns out to be a rather gutsy affair, topped by Saxon's raw rock and roll non-voice.

'I just did this stuff because they asked me. It's not what I'm really into. I have a new band called The Dragonslayers, that's what I'm really about but everyone just wants to hear The Seeds ... Still, The Seeds will open the door for The Dragonslayers who are going to be so big ... the biggest, you know.'

Sky Saxon sits down on the floor in the corner of the room, then on the sofa, then he disappears ... wanders back in ... begins to reminisce ... talks some more. Juliana circles him, as silent as ever, with the camera. Somewhere, from within his huddled frame, he finds an ounce of comic energy, a touch of showmanship and for a couple of glorious minutes he camps it up, mimicking Elvis and, well, God knows who else.

'Look Sky,' says Tim. 'How long are you going to be on stage during this gig?'

'About an hour and a half. I can do that standing on my head.'

Tim: 'I don't think you can do that, Sky, I think it would be too long. People would get bored.'

'Oh yes I can ... I may cause a riot ... a riot!'

Now, I don't know. Maybe it's me but there are odd moments in life when you just have to stand back and ask what the Hell is going on? One such moment takes place this afternoon when, back on the balcony, Sky Saxon begins to teach us an exercise. Even in a city that has, rather moronically in my opinion, spent the past seven years wiggling about in front of Jane Fonda work-out videos, we must have looked a bizarre sight. Standing there, arms outstretched, taking instruction from the most unlikely looking health guru in the history of the world. There's Saxon, facing us, with his head tilting upwards, breathing heavily ... and us attempting to do likewise. I'm not sure what the true point of this exercise is ... I don't even bother to ask. Afterwards, before lunch, Sky Saxon tells us not to eat salt. 'Salt,' he states, quite forcibly, 'is very bad for you. I've never eaten it.'

I doubt the credibility of this statement, as it flows from a man who makes Keith Richards look like Sylvester Stallone.

But Saxon is a curious mixture of fun and sad pathetic cynicism. Unfortunately, as the day wears on, the latter angle of Saxon's persona begins to emerge.

'The Seeds,' states Tim, 'were just a moment.' And that's the problem. Exactly that. They were a moment in rock history. A tremendously inspired moment, an innovative moment, but just a moment none the less. Many bands have ridden to greater success on the platform provided by The Seeds. That isn't a rip-off, that's just the way things are. The Seeds, Sky Saxon in particular, were never able to adapt and improve. That stated, it's still interesting to see the extent of their influence, the size of their cult following over in Europe. Even now, something could be salvaged. It is possible. But Saxon is bitter ... boy, is he bitter.

'I've never made a penny from my music. It has all been stolen. I never copyright anything because I know they will just steal it anyway. I don't mind. I don't need them. I don't deal with record companies ... I deal with people. Actually, I'm going to start printing my own money. That's my big game plan. People can have my money for free. They'll turn round to the government and say, "We don't need your money ... we'll use Sky's." I can write a song worth a million dollars right here and now ... I wrote one the other day called just *Imagine* ... it's a tribute to John Lennon, in fact I think I had his spirit in me when I wrote it ... Another one I wrote is called *Sexy Dancer* ... the big song last year was *Dirty Dancing* ... so why not *Sexy Dancer* this year ... it's a smash. Do you want to own the name, The Seeds? It's yours for £50,000. That's a bargain ... Do you want to make a few million? Put my record out ... you can't lose. I'll think of a title for it ...'

Tim: 'I don't want to put your record out, Sky. I'm just here making this film and ...'

Sky: 'Well, I stayed behind to come and see you because I thought you were making a full-length film ...'

Tim: 'No Sky, I never said that.'

Sky: 'Look, I'm not going to be in this movie unless you give me one hundred thousand pounds. That's what I'm worth and this film will be nothing without me ... I'm tired of letting assholes pick at my flesh ... take whatever's left, go on Tim, take my eyes ... take them.'

Tim: 'What are you talking about, Sky? This is just a pilot at the moment. It's just a home movie about my life ... I'm not ripping anyone off.'

Sky: 'Well, I don't want to be in it. I don't know. You'll be hearing from my manager. Whatever she says, I'll do. Look, I can handle it ... I really did just stay because of this movie. I really thought ... well, I haven't got any money. I can't even afford oat cakes.'

Oat cakes? Sky's departure, from this rather stunned room, is swift. Tim gives him some money and Juliana helps him into her car. After they depart, a sad, reflective air prevails.

Tim: 'The trouble is that there is no way I can bridge the divide between having money and not having it. That's why, when people make money, they move into new neighbourhoods and make new friends. There is nothing anyone can do.'

There isn't, either. Twenty minutes later the door bell rings. There stands Sky.

'I couldn't leave without giving you a hug, maan ... you can put me in your movie if you want.'

Postscript
Juliana takes Sky back to her flat where he meets Carl, a fully fledged musician complete with his own recording studio and an undeniable thirst for unusual recordings. A marriage made in heaven, perhaps. Together they cut a number of songs. Carl's music with Sky hastily scribbling accompanying lyrics. The session finishes at around 4 am.

'We recorded some really interesting stuff,' says Carl, at a later date. Maybe there really is hope, after all.

Saturday, 7 January
Tim: 'Did I ever tell you that I nearly became a rock and roll star once? It's true. It was in Prestbury and it must have been ... hang on ... I must get the year right ... 1956 or '57. It was in the village hall ... the whole village turned out. I had three guys backing me. All going "Doowap ... Doowap". It must have sounded awful, I'm sure I was off-

key all the way through. Anyway, this guy recorded it. He said he
knew these guys in London from this record company. He *did* know
them, too. Anyway, he wanted to take the tape to them. Do you know
what I said? I was so twattish in those days. I said (*adopts upper-crust
English accent*), "Do you realise that I am a public schoolboy?" What a
twattish thing to say.

'I've always been scared stiff of singing on stage. Bobby Buck
didn't help. When we did those things together he would always tell
me that my singing was off-key, so my confidence just diminished.
But I've since found out that it doesn't really matter, even if you are
off-key.'

Monday, 9 January
We walk down Hollywood Boulevard. We mix with the Japanese. For
the first time, since coming over, I feel like a tourist. Juliana films the
long, hot walk and Tim, now recovered from 'flu, is in fine form,
dragging her plus camera into every other shop along the way. Finally
we reach the ex-headquarters of KFWB Radio, now a rehearsal studios
and theatre ... I think, although no one can quite work out the nature
of the premises. Perhaps it's better not to know. But, although just the
skeleton of its former self, it still holds the air of a radio station. A
decayed reception desk, general manager's office, record store-rooms,
Tim's old studio ... all empty apart from a gaggle of workmen and a
radio, effortlessly blasting out the sound of Manchester's The Smiths,
rather fittingly, I think.

The new owner, however, is initially less than enthusiastic about
our camera-wielding intrusion. I don't blame him, we should have asked
permission but, I guess, enthusiasm gets in the way sometimes. Later,
after being warmed by Tim's stories of the old KFWB, he mellows
considerably and grants us permission to film.

As we troop out, we notice the new name, HAUNTED
STUDIOS ... again, quite fitting.

Outside, simmering away, sits Hollywood Boulevard, nowadays
little more than a typical trashy souvenir strip. Our walk, from the
Chinese Theater to Hollywood and Vine, just past Hudson Avenue, is
filmed and laced by the occasional taunt from the locals.

187

'Hey you ... don't point that camera at us ... you are narcs, aren't you ... you just want our pictures for your files...'

Tuesday, 10 January
Slow-down day ... back in Malibu, in the sun, Tim and Maxi talk excitedly about their new venture into the metal sign memorabilia exhibition with Liverpool-based colour technician Ken Mapstone.

Tuesday, 12 January
We travel up the Topanga Canyon. A beautiful gorge peppered by distinctive but wealthy rickety ranches. The road is lined, poignantly, by Mexicans, hoping to cadge a day's work. They don't look unhappy.

The canyon unfolds to reveal the San Fernando Valley. A remarkable pristine clean smattering of middle-class America, nowadays well and truly stigmatised as the home of bland but wealthy 'Valleyites'.

'They have the best delis in the world down here,' says Maxi as we cruise into this bowl that was, just fifty years ago, mere desert. Today it is carpeted by fitted greenery, designer nature.

'They could do this to the Sahara, y'know,' Tim points out. 'All this vegetation ... it's just a question of money.'

Ten minutes later I'm sitting in the reception area of an accountancy office, wondering just what I'm doing there and talking to the dottiest nine-to-five Valleyite girl imaginable. Undaunted, I pick up a copy of a local film magazine. Inside there is a lengthy article about British brat film director Julian Temple (of *Great Rock'n'roll Swindle/Absolute Beginners* notoriety). His latest film, a trouble-torn commercial comedy called *Earth Girls Are Easy*, is about this valley. Temple, himself now a resident, speaks highly of the area. Pretty soon, I sense, there will be a hyper-trendy exodus from Soho, London, to the San Fernando Valley.

Maxi and Tim's meeting over, I meet the accountant, Orville, a man once so instrumental in helping Tim restructure the course of his life by turning him on to the Highland Camrose. He takes us downstairs to show us his new car, I'm not sure why. It turns out to be an ostentatious gleaming white and gold Cadillac which reminds all of us, quite strongly, of one of Elvis Presley's suits. The Cadillac is the embodiment of the aura of flaunt which prevails in the valley.

Later, in Santa Monica, we film a walk down Main Street. An infamous, speciality yuppie shopping area, Covent Garden with palm trees. The cafés, and there are many of them, are filled with archetypal LA women. Modern, strong, business- or jogging-suited, expensive hairdos ... they nibble salads and chatter away. It is up-market and less friendly than Hollywood Boulevard. The shop assistants are cold, untrusting and just don't like the appearance of Juliana with camera.

'You are not filming in here ... get out now.'

Tim, tauntingly, 'Well, all right then, if you don't want fifty million people to see your shop on television.'

'No kiddo, I don't ... I'm telling you.'

That told us.

Around the corner we arrive, once again, at Birtles West. The Hudson's Santa Monica home, sadly now just days away from demolition. We sneak round the back, past the Botham Suite and onto the idyllic veranda.

Tim: 'I built this ... this veranda ... I was annoyed at living so close to the sea and not be able to see it, so I built this roof patio. I would just sit and work here ... this was my heaven. I wasn't interested in business ... I just wanted to be a gardener, stay out of all the hassle. Beautiful, isn't it. And look at this, the Botham Suite. The newspapers had to find the lowest angle, so they called it a shack ... But it's really beautiful.'

Saturday, 14 January
We drive to Palm Springs. A fascinating drive, showcasing a near-perfect cross-section of Southern Californian life, from the grace and financial prosperity of downtown LA to enticing desert wilderness and all the motels, diners, billboards and ranches in between. Our arrival in Palm Springs, however, is somewhat less than majestic. I fax a report to my newspaper, the *Manchester Evening News* which, I think, explains everything.

PALM SPRINGS
This is, I think, what is known as an embarrassing situation. We

have been in Palm Springs for less than half a day and already we have attained legendary status. Forget Bob Hope, it is our party. Tim and Maxi Hudson, myself and bemused Bulgarian film-maker Juliana who are now the talk of this town. We stand around our vehicle, in hysterics. For there it sits, hissing away at us, all four of its tyres ripped to shreds. We have just driven the wrong way over a spiked 'sleeping policeman'. The residents of the housing estate, a sleepy, middle-class, ageing reservation, have already begun to talk about us. They are kind, but, I guess, this is the most exciting thing to have happened in their district for years.

This is Palm Springs. Heaven's reception area. A beautiful retirement town situated slap bang in the centre of a desert.

'It's not as good as it used to be,' says one ex-native, on a New Year visit from Stockholm. 'In the old days we would find all manner of scorpions and snakes in the bedrooms ... but they have all been driven away.'

Oh, what a shame ... never mind. Perhaps such creatures can't stand the slick, dreamy sophistication that prevails today. I can though, I can handle it.

Palm Springs is the land of fifty golf courses. Lush, green, spectacularly landscaped ... this is the true heart of white, Slazenger jumper-wearing, Frank Sinatra-listening, unashamed comfort. Smug, showbizzy, successful ... and old.

We are here, in Palm Springs, to celebrate River Hudson's sixteenth birthday. We stay with Kathy (Tim's first wife), River and Kathy's boy friend, Ben, in their elegantly modern home on the aforementioned estate. It is, in a sense, the ultimate Californian dream. Tennis, golf, swimming pools ... grapefruits growing in the garden, ready to be picked and squeezed for breakfast. A glimpse of heaven maybe, but, on the other hand, it is very much a plastic fantasy land. Escapism via the credit-card buffer. You take your choice ... the scorpions went one way ... but there are certainly worse places on Earth.

Tim and Maxi though, I note, don't appear to be too comfortable within the lush cocoon that is Palm Springs. Maybe it is just too safe for them. That said, a year prior to our visit, they nearly bought a radio station in the vicinity.

'I still say that you could operate a great radio station from this area,' states Tim.

In the evening, the entire place is bathed in soft lighting. Every palm tree is beautifully highlighted ... landscaped ... perfectly in position. We are taken, in Ben's Rolls-Royce (registration 'FLAUNT') to Sonny Bono's restaurant. Outside it is like The Ritz ... inside, more like a Sheffield steel works. Empty of character, clumsily shaped ... ugly.

Twenty-four hours later we travel back. For 130 miles we are entertained by Tim's monologue. A sprightly, entertaining speech, highlighted by one important question:

'But I can't understand ... I mean, I really can't understand just why someone in American radio doesn't say, "Hey, what a great idea ... let's put Lord Tim back on." It doesn't bother me, I mean, I don't need to do anything. I don't need to play anyone else's game any more. When I walked out that day and said, "I'm going to play tennis for the rest of my life," I meant it, and that's just what I have done, basically. But after saying that ... I still can't understand why someone within radio doesn't respond in a positive way ... WHY?'

Tuesday, 17 January
Roger
Tim's old friend, from the Sixties. A fast-talking ex-hedonist, nowadays happy to bask in yuppie Bohemia. Charming, eloquent, intelligent. The first person I've met who can talk faster than Tim. Roger comes to the house in Malibu. His conversation is filmed by Juliana. Watching this is rather like observing a free-form television chat show. Here are a few important snippets:

Tim: 'I remember Michael Caine's very first night in Hollywood. I took him out to dinner at that restaurant next door to The Whisky. I got him a date with this actress. He was very polite, very gentleman-like. I knew him from the King's Road days ... anyway, she didn't fancy him.'

'Do you remember Mary Hughes ... she used to be the pin-up of the Sunset Strip?'

Roger: 'Yeah ... that old Sunset ... it was a very special time in California.'

Tim: 'It was a time of innocence. It hadn't been totally bastardised and corrupted. It was a Californian love generation ... although I don't feel that people were doing much more than drinking beer and having a good time. I never felt that it was a drug culture.'

Roger: 'Oh, I don't know ... drugs became a way of life, in many ways.'

Tim: 'What do you think is the biggest difference between California then and California now?'

Roger: 'I don't know ... I mean, that's what I meant about drugs ... in the Sixties they became a whole way of life and people came out of that and had to survive the Seventies, which were very bland ... nothing happened really ... today people's whole consciousness has changed ... in some ways people have woken up ... at last.'

Wednesday, 18 January
On a day that provides us with the first earthquake of the visit, and quite a large one it is, we seem to travel the entire spectrum of human activity ... well, almost.

The day begins in earnest at 1 pm outside Sir Rehearsal Rooms at Santa Monica and Vine. A large station wagon, registration plate DRMMR, pulls onto the forecourt. It contains The Seeds minus Sky Saxon. Three guys, all American nice guys, short beards, clean jeans, looking for all the world like the reformed hippy father in *Family Ties*. They are Daryl Hooper, Jan Savage and Rick Andridge, and they carry in organ, guitar and drums respectively. It is the first time they have set eyes on Tim for twenty years ... the reunion is light-hearted. Another car sweeps to a halt. Out step Sky Saxon and bass guitarist Mars Bonfire – a well-dressed, unassuming, disarmingly courteous chap who, when pressed, will admit to being the writer of Steppenwolf's *Born To Be Wild*. Without doubt, one of the truly great anthems of the Sixties. That this charming, neat, silent character has continually provided the laced soundtrack for generations of bikers seems to be truly amazing. Mars is to play bass for The Seeds.

The difference between Saxon and the rest of the band, including Bonfire, is startling. Whereas the collective seedlets have drifted into comparatively happy and profoundly ordinary lifestyles, Saxon is still

A dream come true.

Lord and Lady of the Manor.

'Why do you want to buy a cricket ground, Mr Hudson?'

Bellany and clar
sporting the HH
colours.

The family at
home.

Maxi in Malibu.

River Hudson in
1988.

The River Hudson,
by John Bellany,
A.R.A.

A view from the
Hollywood Hill,
Birtles.

Boycott v. Botham.
1984. Maxi
captioned this
picture, 'What the
Hell am I doing
here?'

Tim Hudson flanked by the men who have put his own name on the map in England. Who needs whom most?

...will
...two
...heir
...iam
...han

...nole
...eters
...efore
...hough
...have
...t years
...hand
...should
...rative
...in the

...Vivian
...Judson
...d Ivory
...fered a
...ed for a
...ers can
...be shot
...xpands
...a place
...al good
...in of the
...nd three
..."goodie"

...ill be a
...out his
...life is
...ng in
...nore

...not
...in't
...out
...nd

...ing
...ians
...the
...ccord
...and
...Robin
...rt of

and, given the cavalier style which has
become his hallmark, there is no reason
...lieve he won't do so
...he inevitable.

there and just hit the ball.
The man who has thrilled crowds the
world over is adamant that he will retire
...ricket while he is on to...

Blazers will be
worn.

The Botham Bar at Birtles on a summer's day.

A Mountain Of Men, by Tony Cooper. Both., L.T., B. Close, V. Richards.

Birtles Old Hall . . . by John Hurst.

Geoff Foley,
the Birtles
Professional 1989
('The Digger'). A
member of the
Birtles family,
forever. He broke
the record for the
Cheshire County
League by scoring
over 1,000 runs
and taking 50
wickets. We
predict that he
will play for
Australia.
(After this caption
was written Geoff
Foley celebrated his
debut for
Queensland by
scoring a century
against the Pakistani
tourists.)

The 'Big Bird' at
Birtles.

Robert Haynes,
the 'senior pro' at
Birtles in 1989.
"More juice, Lord
Tim" played for
the West Indies in
India that
autumn.

Hudson's
Hollywood XI at
Blackpool: Foley,

Haynes, Callahan,
Hookey, Dublin,
Jones – all future

international
players – and not
to be forgotten,

the Birtles umpire,
Lawrence.

L.T. with Moody,
Veletta and
Hookey.

David Hughes and
Graeme Fowler,
Lancashire's best.

Rock 'n roll Harry
with Peter Taylor
and Geoff
Lawson, 1988,
Birtles.

Sexy Sadie – livers,
lovers, sinners and
saints, emperors,
lords and kings all
come to play at
Birtles.

there ... fighting for his rock and roll. Whether the world will ever be ready to listen or not, is another matter.

Tickets for the series of eight psychedelic gigs have not been selling too well. The promoter, a continually morose young man named Stephen, lurks in the corner, looking worried. Hardly an inspiring sight for such a rusty band attempting a comeback. Already the San Francisco date has been pulled, although I'm told that the advance ticket sales for the LA Universal Amphitheater bash are moving respectably.

The band, on one side, pick up their highly polished, well-loved instruments as Saxon, on the other side of the room, seems to feel the need to remain aloof. Content to gargle indecipherable noises into his tape mike.

For the first time in twenty years, The Seeds blast into a performance of *Pushin' Too Hard*. Saxon, as if by magic, leaves his cynical normal persona and kicks into performance. The transformation is impressive. His voice, still raw, shows the ability to fall into apparently instant hard-edged pop, as the band, improved by twenty years of garage musicianship, provide a solid backing.

I'm not a fan of practice sessions, insular and tedious as they so often are, and I know that Tim and Maxi feel the same, but the set run-through proves to be not merely entertaining, but enthralling. *Pushin' Too Hard*, *Mr Farmer*, *It's A Hard Life*, nuggets indeed. To glance at this band, in truth, is to see a vision that is mildy pathetic. Middle-aged men playing at being popstars but, unlike many of their more successful peers, The Seeds still manage to convey a certain naïvety, if not purity. They remind me, and fairly strongly, of the embryonic 1977 version of The Fall, one English band who have never been afraid to list Sky Saxon And The Seeds as a major influence.

'Can I make a suggestion,' says Tim, rather forcibly. 'Why don't you begin your set with *Pushin' Too Hard*, it would get people in the mood.'

'Yes, but the trouble is, we want to save it till the end ... keep people waiting.'

We watch the practice. The divide between Saxon and the band, seemingly unbridgeable, melts a little during the performance. Saxon is far more palatable when on stage, happy and singing. But when the music's over ... he reverts to his rather lonely god-like persona.

'Will you help me carry a box from the car?' he asks me and then, on the way back when I am laden with said box, and he isn't, I regret my willingness.

'Artistes shouldn't have to carry things.'

As it happens, I don't drop the machine right there and then, although I really should. When I tell Tim and Maxi about this incident they are appalled but hardly surprised.

'I have to say it,' states Tim, 'but I really feel sorry for the guys in that band ... there they are, willing to work hard and all he can do is swan around like that. That's why they never made it, in my opinion.'

But the practice is a good one, historic even, and I know a few enthusiasts back in England who would have gladly donated a limb in order to sit in that room. The music gels and Saxon, in a moment of reckless camaraderie, even lets Tim, Maxi, Juliana and myself make appalling tuneless noises into his microphone. Only later do we realise that this, minus our intrusions, is probably the best footage ever taken of The Seeds.

That evening Tim and Maxi invite the entire band to a Mexican restaurant. The band are eager, expectant nice guys who realise that someone, somewhere, has made a good deal of money from the many re-releases and compilations of Seeds material. In England, I tell them, many student record collections contain something by them, if only as part of the 'Nuggets' Psychedelic compilation album. I tell them that, over in England, John Peel – once a San Bernadino, or was it Bakersfield, DJ who followed in the wake of Lord Tim – has been playing The Seeds for twenty years. They don't believe me.

There is another odd twist to the day's proceedings. In the space between The Seeds' practice and the meal, Michael Blumberg, editor of *Cricket World*, arrives from London. A straight upright classic Englishman whose passion for cricket and women filters into his every conversation. Unfortunately, as Sky is two hours late for the meal, the chemistry didn't really get a chance to mix. A pity, I doubt that there are two more different people on the face of this planet, such are the rich and diverse avenues of personalities that make up the Hudsonian social world.

'You are social anarchists,' states Blumberg.

Tim: 'That's true, but people, especially over in England, are
under the impression that I am some kind of wild partygoer. I'm not.
I'm a real stay-at-home person. A recluse. I don't think I've ever been
out as much as I have on this trip. It's the same with business ... I
spent all that time in Hollywood, just renovating my houses, playing
tennis, gardening and generally having a good time. That's the one thing
I'm missing on this trip, my garden ... I long to just water the garden
... and relax.'

Thursday, 19 January

Tim is back in Hollywood ... driving through the hills ... in ecstasy. I
think it's fair to say that this has been a good day. Earlier we met, and
filmed, an interview between Tim and seriously successful record
producer Keith Olson. Nowadays famed for his production of The
Eagles, Pat Benatar, Foreigner, Ozzy Osborne and the like, he once, as
a member of Music Machine in the Sixties, helped to achieve one hit,
Talk Talk. For that short moment in time, they became a small but
important part of the Los Angeles Flower Power scene.

We meet at Olson's home studios in Van Nuys. A remarkable
place. The understated exterior houses the most delicious hi-tech décor.
Like most studios, it is littered with videos, magazines ... stray LPs,
half-empty coffee cups ... and PR people. But this is big-league débris.
We are led by a friendly studio engineer into what is lovingly known as
'the intimidation room'. Naturally, it is lined with gold discs,
interesting-looking awards and the odd guitar.

'That's the guitar that The Eagles used to write *Hotel California*,'
states the engineer. 'If Keith has an idea, and the band don't agree, he
just brings them in here. They soon change their mind ... Mind you
... he's usually right. He *is* the best, y'know.'

Friday, 20 January

We browse throught the splendid shops that fill the handsome Santa
Monica shopping mall. There is more than a touch of tension in the air.
Negotiations between Tim and Maxi and *Cricket World* seem to have met
one huge, unlovable obstruction, whatever it is. An intense meeting is

195

held between Tim and Michael Blumberg, right here, right now, in the middle of a sports shop. Casual shoppers, no doubt searching for the perfect LA jog gear, glance cautiously in their direction as the meeting drags on ... and on.

Sunday, 22 January
America drowns in Superbowl. Tim is no exception. His rhetoric, throughout the game – a fiercely contested affair between the Cincinnati Bengals and the San Francisco 49ers – proves to be far more interesting than the TV commentary, which is mainly an endless supply of meaningless statistics:

'Oh, look at that, maaan ... that is America. THAT IS AMERICA. Even the hippies couldn't give up football ... they refused to give it up. This military, capitalist game ... but they couldn't give it up ... oh maan, what a game, what a game.'

Later, after dinner, in a more reflective mood:

'Sometimes I feel like closing the Birtles Bowl down and letting nobody play there at all ... I could just go away ... just like that. All these people would say, "Where's he gone?" I would just piss off and leave. I would get more publicity, more write-ups. That would stimulate my adrenalin probably more than playing. It's hard to get the adrenalin going, sometimes. There are times when I've been really bored. I was really bored as a DJ. I'd realise that I had a marvellous job, getting all that money just for talking, but I was still bored.'

On Sunday evening we tune in to Rodney Bingenheimer's famous *Rodney On The Rocks* show on KROQ. Something of an institution. Tonight's entire show seems to be a promotion for the forthcoming Psychedelic Summer Of Love concert. The Seeds, in particular, are featured throughout the three-hour slot, punctuated neatly by Tim's promo advert.

'That's one of the best trailers I've ever heard', states Bingenheimer, a touch too sycophantically for my ears, but never mind. The highlight of the evening, at least in theory, is to be a phone interview with Sky Saxon and The Seeds. Perhaps predictably, this turns out to be something of an embarrassment. Interesting, intelligent comments from the surrounding band are brushed aside by Saxon's

rampant megalomania, which is either charismatic or pathetic,
depending on your point of view.

Saxon: 'We feel that, you know, that John [Lennon] is no longer
with The Beatles and The Seeds can carry on with his legacy. In
America we have produced the group that I know are gonna rock the
world with peace and love because, God knows, now we need Flower
Power. That's what we are about ... peace and love. I understand The
Cult are going to be at the gig, and The Bangles. I'd like to say Hi to
them because they are our friends ... We wanna thank you Rodney
because, you know, you have been great, playing the music, and to me
Rodney is the Prince of this area, Rodney is actually the sixth Seed...'

Rodney Bingenheimer: 'What bands, that are cred, do you like
now?'

Saxon: 'I like all the bands ... all I can say is that there are a lot of
bands out there, including bands like Poison and Guns And Roses, as
far as we are concerned, they are like The Rolling Stones ... just warm-
up acts.'

Bingenheimer: 'What about bands like The Pandoras and The
Bangles and The Fuzztones who are really into you ... do you like them
too?'

Saxon: 'I love them but they are all warm-up acts ... The Seeds
are probably, right now, I'd say that The Seeds are the second greatest
band in the world...'

To me, an outsider, this seems to be an appalling thing to say.

'Yeah, but, that's just Sky you know,' says Tim. 'That's just the
way he is. In a sense he is a great publicist ... but he just goes on for
too long and people say ... "Ahhh, fuck off, Sky".'

Monday, 23 January
Raining. The plentiful colours of Los Angeles are dulled considerably by
rain. We travel to the tennis courts where Tim, in his previous existence
as swashbuckling restaurateur, would spend every morning.

Tim: 'I came here because I had to get myself out of drugs. I had
to get myself out of feeling sorry for myself. I knew I had to get healthy
again and also, basically, that I didn't really want to work. The people I
met down here became really good social friends. I'd lost out on rock

people. On DJs, on promoters, on record company men. I stopped
going to restaurants ... Down here I met a businessman's wife, a
professor, a shrink, people from all different walks of life ... and they
all became my friends. All that was a saving grace in my life. This
tennis court saved my life. If I hadn't found them I probably would
have ended up on drugs. I discovered vegetarianism down here. I gave
up junk food ... down here showed me a new way.'

Tuesday, 24 January
In the evening we travel to an impressive wooden bar named Ocean
Seafood in Santa Monica. The place is alarmingly beautiful, and Tim
and Maxi are in a buoyant mood. Michael Blumberg searches frantically
for members of the opposite sex. For some reason, and nobody is sure
why, an argument breaks out between myself and Juliana. It is
intensified, not by debate, but by a spiral of misunderstandings on both
sides. This is not irrelevant, as Tim points out.

'I had this problem with two of my wives. Because they were from
France and Switzerland, there were subtle differences in the way we
spoke. In our sense of humour. We used to have the most terrific
arguments, all over nothing ... simply because of misunderstandings ...
Mancunian humour doesn't travel well.'

Thursday, 26 January
Eddie Garner
The phone calls, prior to the meeting with Tim's old friend Eddie
Garner, were less than encouraging. Eddie, once the archetypal
Californian beach boy, a Beverly Hills kid with a film career and a
contacts book bigger than a phone directory, a boy whose very lifestyle
typified 'freedom', is now a member of the corporate structure. Tied to a
desk. Pulling the line.

'We could talk in the conference room,' he suggests.

So we travel to his place of work. The smart, angular hi-tech
offices of Jerry Weintraub. Once again, we see walls lined with success
symbols. This isn't an intimidation room, it's an intimidation building.

Eddie seems shy, extremely polite but, nevertheless, his
conversation doesn't appear to be affected by Juliana's camera or, for

that matter, my tape machine. The interview is, I instantly decide, the finest of our little adventure so far. Together, Tim and Eddie fall into the past.

Where did they meet?

Tim: 'When I first came to LA, I was the only English guy here of my particular age group. I went to a club called The Trip. Remember it, Eddie?'

Eddie: 'On Sunset ... yeah, of course.'

Tim: 'We went down this night and I was dancing with Mary Hughes, The Lovin' Spoonful were playing. I had long hair, I mean, it wasn't really long but people called it long, in those days. Because of this hair, a guy wanted to punch me. I met Eddie Garner when he stopped this guy from bashing me. You, Eddie, were the first Californian, blond hair, six foot, you were part of an era that made some movies. Beach-blanket bingo movies I call them. You were under contract to make those movies?'

Eddie: 'We were all part of an established programme that they were trying to bring back called Contract Players. We were doing Frankie Avalon and Annette Funicello movies, we were just the backing people, really.'

Tim: 'Later we had a group called The Seeds. What do you remember about them?'

Eddie: 'Acid ... speed ... they always had it on them in those days ... everybody did. Everyone was very free in those days. They wanted other people to succeed, not like today. The whole English market came and took over, including you. I thought it was very exciting. You were one of the biggest personalities on the Hollywood scene, you went out and got publicity for yourself. You were a madman, no doubt about it. That's why a lot of people resented you, because you were so outgoing and people took it as an insult. Most people didn't have goals, didn't want to be on top, but you always did. You do now, there's no change.'

Tim: 'So you say that, at the time there was a very much laid-back attitude and for someone like me to come along, caused offence?'

Eddie: 'You would go in and you would mow people down and they weren't able to deal with that. You were very direct, very honest, not pompous but very sure of yourself when a lot of people weren't. Most of the business at that time was done in New York ... and New York people were not coming to California. Now we have people from all over the world here.'

Tim: 'There were no clubs in Beverly Hills. There were no black people in Hollywood, y'know, the Watts riots happened the week before I arrived.'

Eddie: 'I remember the night of the Watts riots. We had been notified that the Beverly Hills police department had apparently put blockades on the entrances, to stop people from getting in.'

Tim: 'The cops were nice to you in those days. They stopped and asked if you were OK. It was all very nice. Beverly Hills was a family.

'Out of all the people you grew up with, who do you think has been the most successful?'

Eddie: 'I don't know. I have been fortunate in that a lot of my friends have had success. At this point I would say Terry Melcher. He just had that Number One with The Beach Boys, *Kokomo*, and has been nominated for an Academy Award.'

Tim: 'What about Lou Adler?'

Eddie: 'Lou has just gone back into business with A & M, after twenty years, with Herb Alpert. A lot of people are coming back. That's why it is so interesting to see you again. All of us have the opportunity to do it all again ... now more than ever.'

Tim: 'Y'know, I remember being told that you needed a special pass to get through the gates into Bel Air. I didn't go for two years.'

Eddie: 'Someone was bullshitting you.'

Tim: 'I know people would always bullshit and I would believe them because, coming from England, I never dreamt that I would meet all these people ... all these movie stars.'

Eddie: 'Yeah, it was very impressive for you, at that time, to meet those people. Peter Fonda ... there's an example ... I remember going to a health food store for the first time and I told you that Peter Fonda and I were putting acid into the vegetable soup and then sitting back and watching them all fall over. There was one night when you were with us, there was Peter Fonda, Terry Melcher, Dennis Wilson ... we took motorcycles out with girls on the back and drove right into and through this club. We got thrown out, but you were going, "What are you doing?" I don't think anyone could get away with doing those things today ... but we were the élite of the élite...'

Tim: 'I was a kid, really lucky. I moved into Eddie's group who were all the children of movie stars ... Peter Fonda, Dean Martin, Desi Arnaz...'

Eddie: 'Drinking was the thing. I think that most of us drank about a quart of liquor a day when we were seventeen or eighteen. Everyone I know now has stopped drinking.'

Tim: 'I was impressed though.'

Eddie: 'But, conversely, people were impressed by you because as far as we were concerned, you brought over The Beatles.'

Tim: 'Yeah, you used to tell me to not show that I was impressed, to let people be impressed by me ... but it was hard. You introduced me to all those people. Claudia Martin ... I remember being at a party once and I heard this voice, "Hi, Lord Tim." It was Frank Sinatra. I thought, "How does he know me?" This was my downfall in a way because I was no longer hanging out with the other DJs in their silly version of Hollywood. They became very angry with me.'

Eddie: 'They were angry at you because they thought you were trying to get involved with Claudia to further your own career.'

Tim: 'But I wasn't.'

Eddie: 'Well, in a way, maybe you were.'

Tim: 'No, not in any way.'

Maxi: 'Yeah, but don't you think you can like somebody and think to yourself, it's much better to like this person because maybe they will help me get somewhere?'

Eddie: 'What is interesting about your experience in this town is that you were left a broken person in a way. Now you are trying to pick up the pieces of why it happened. I don't have an answer for that. I know that this city, and the people in it are generally not very loyal... You got hurt because you trusted people but they didn't trust you. They all closed ranks, got on with their own lives.'

Tim: 'Every other DJ in the city got work, except me. It seemed that a door closed every time the name Lord Tim cropped up.'

Eddie: 'There is a way in which you challenge people ... they were always offended. (*Turns to me.*) Tim was the biggest DJ in LA. No doubt about that ... he had all the best interviews ... everything.'

Tim: 'It was as though they eradicated me from the history books. There is no mention in rock history when, all of a sudden in LA there was this English guy on radio burning up a storm. It was the beginning of a whole change in LA.'

Eddie: 'Some people would say that when you had the ball you were a tyrant. That you were too abusive, too demanding. I don't think this is true because, basically, you just worked very hard. You meant well.'

Tim: 'I always do a job to the best of my ability, be it painting a wall or whatever. In fact I survived and now I'm a really rich guy but the one thing I came to this town to do, was radio.

'I wanted your life, Eddie. To me ... I was envious, I was never jealous, but I was envious. You had everything. I could have hung around with you all my life ... you had a nice house ... swimming pool ... credit cards ... you were six foot two, blond, good looking...'

Eddie: 'And now it's all gone ... haha.'

Friday, 27 January

UNIVERSAL AMPHITHEATER
THE PSYCHEDELIC SUMMER OF LOVE
starring
THE SEEDS ... Featuring Sky Saxon
ARTHUR LEE AND LOVE
STRAWBERRY ALARM CLOCK
BIG BROTHER AND THE HOLDING COMPANY
THE MUSIC MACHINE
Plus The Original Kaleidoscope Light Show

7pm. We stand, freezing as it happens, outside the gates of the Universal Amphitheater, people watching. An interesting pastime on the bus or train, or football match. But at a Psychedelic Revival bash, it is thoroughly enthralling, a profound experience. There are psychedelic mothers, resplendent in twenty-year-old suede mini-skirts, dragging their 'hip-hop' offspring through the ticket barriers. There are haircuts, boy are there haircuts. Are they wigs? If not, where would an afro-topped forty-five-year-old flower child hide, when not attending Psychedelic Revival concerts?

Interestingly enough, the major percentage of this crowd are youngsters, dressed in parodoxic Sixties clothes of varying quality.

'You guys, wanna buy some magic mushrooms,' asks a voice that belongs to an Afghan-clad bearded relic of yesteryear ... but he seems friendly enough, even when we refuse.

Backstage the scene is relaxed ... verging on the profoundly dull, as are most backstage areas, despite myths to the contrary. Saxon seems in good form. We watch him as he chats away to Debbie Harry ... to Rodney Bingenheimer ... to The Bangles ... to The Cult.

We have brought with us Cordula, the blonde, Germanic lady who, back in the Sixties, entered Tim's life, as in a vision. As she, enrobed in white, floated down Sunset Boulevard.

'In those days, girls would kiss the hem of my gown,' she states, and without a hint of boastfulness. Still serene, she has wandered deep into the mysterious corridors of natural healing.

'Please don't call me a masseuse, it has such shady connotations,' she pleads. Tonight, after many years, she is reunited with her old, extremely close friend, Sky Saxon.

There had been a review, in the *Los Angeles Times*, of the previous evening's gig in San Juan Capistrano. It had been less than complimentary. This didn't really matter. What did matter, however, was the line, 'Sky "Sunlight" Saxon's main contribution was his look – pure Charles Manson madness'.

Nobody, absolutely nobody, not even Sky Saxon, wants to be compared to Charles Manson. For the first time in twenty years, Saxon has shaved his beard off. This may not seem like such an awesome move, but for Saxon it represents a whole new attitude, if not religion. Rather like a Rasta dispensing with his dreadlocks, not something to be taken lightly.

Seeds guitarist Jan Savage: 'I stayed up all night with Sky, all night discussing not just the review but the whole situation regarding The Seeds. Things are going to change from now on. We are going to work

203

together as a four-piece with no ego problems ... I told Sky, we are all grown men, with our own lives. We are not kids any more but there is a lot of ground to cover. A lot of money to be made ... but we must do it together. I know he's going off to Europe with his band, The Dragonslayers, but it's The Seeds who must take preference ... Sky agrees and shaving his beard off is indicative of a whole new attitude.'

'Aw, maaan, I feel so naked, so stupid without the beard,' says Sky, rubbing his chin.

Outside in the overwhelmingly comfortable auditorium, the latterday children of the Flower Generation are responding warmly to a rather feeble, but feeling set by the Strawberry Alarm Clock. The usual things are happening. The twin promoters run around, worried, hassled, rushed ... 'Are you gonna introduce all the other bands, Tim?'

'No way ... I'll introduce The Seeds but not the rest of them ... no way.'

There are a few memories being punched from the stage, with more spirit than precision, but who cares. The Strawberry Alarm Clock's *Incense And Peppermints* and, with arrival of Big Brother And The Holding Company, a set full of Joplinesque soul. In front of me, a girl in a Mary Quant mini-skirt, calf-length boots and a beehive haircut – surely pre-Flower Generation fashion – breaks out into a full-blown arm-swinging freak-out.

The Arthur Lee and Love set is disjointed and hardly helped by the fact that Lee seemed to be living in a separate universe most of the time. Nevertheless, the sheer force of those timeless classics makes it easily the most intriguing half-hour of the evening.

'Arthur Lee was the first black hippy,' says Tim. 'It wasn't Hendrix at all ... in fact Hendrix stole so much from Lee.'

Despite Arthur Lee's comically untogether announcements, in fact he made exactly the same speech twice, and his influenza, he managed to fall in with the flow of the songs.

'I wonder if he'll make it to the end of the set,' stated a cruel voice from behind which, later, boasted of being Lee's best friend.

Rodney Bingenheimer, an alarmingly feeble figure armed with a radio voice that threatens to peter out any moment, introduces Lord Tim.

'Who out there remembers KFWB?' asks Tim and, perhaps
surprisingly, the reaction is overwhelmingly positive, although how
these kids know about such things is beyond me.

It strikes me, as Tim tells the audience about how he began playing
You Push Me Too Hard endlessly on his radio show, that I have never
seen him looking so comfortable. Out there, in the spotlight.

'...AND THAT BAND WAS ... THE SEEDS.'

Blink once. I can see The Seeds recapturing former glories, falling into a
set packed with raw energy ... granite, uncompromising rock and roll.
A glorious celebration. On the other hand ... blink again ... and I see
five old men desperately trying to produce the kind of youthful zest
which, naturally, has been diluted with the passing of twenty years. A
wonderful sight or a pathetic sight? Both visions are equally valid but, as
it is encouraging to see such on-stage enthusiasm, I'll give them the
benefit of the doubt. The set, in response to the *Los Angeles Times* critic
who made savage use of the word 'tedious', is deliberately short. It
finishes with a sixty-person strong rendition of *Give Peace A Chance*.
Quite touching actually, and just a bit ... magic.

The Flower Generation ... the hippies ... scoffed at by, perhaps,
every fad of the past twenty years, did at least *attempt* to convey a spirit
of goodness. As *Give Peace A Chance* thumps to a halt, I see the
aforementioned mini-skirted girl throw herself at the fragile figure of
Saxon. He doesn't snap. In fact, it all makes great theatre.

Backstage, of course, there is an incredibly dull party to attend.
One hundred people stand around, make idle chatter, search for an
interesting subject and then an interesting face to talk about it to.
Bingenheimer promises to put Tim on his show, which may be fun ...
but we don't stay. We make our escape before the sycophancy becomes
too overwhelming.

Sunday, 29 January
There has been, in Malibu, an appalling shark attack. Two UCLA
graduates had set off from Carbon Beach, on Thursday morning, on a
kayak trip to Paradise Cove, just one and a half miles down the
coastline. Tragically, they never reached this destination and the Los

205

Angeles media is filled with 'Jaws'-fever stories on the subject of Great White Sharks, once so rare in these parts but now, in response to a vast increase in the sea mammal population, their numbers are increasing.

As we read these stories, sitting on the Malibu veranda, it slowly dawns on us that we actually saw these unfortunate people setting off ... five days previously.

Tim is stunned. 'Hey ... I remember those dudes, maaan ... they paddled past. I remember them because they made such a change from those water scooter things that are usually out there...'

Maxi: 'Y'know, that is so rare ... so rare ... you don't usually get shark attacks at all round here. I can hardly believe it.'

Sadly, it is true. The girl's body is discovered, on Zuma Beach, and all day, and for the next three days local helicopters engage in a morbid search for the other body, combing our beach with frightening nearness. Malibu, such an unassuming community, seems to have become a veritable hotbed of disaster since we arrived. We've had an earthquake, two hundred yards away the executive producer of *Dallas* had his house burned to the ground, right there on the Colony. A horrific shark attack and, today, a suicide siege which kept the Pacific Coast Highway closed for two hours. Quaint little village, this.

Venice Beach
Venice Beach ... LA's famous hotbed of Bohemia, and all that entails.

Tim: 'It's amazing to see all the yuppiness in Santa Monica, all those prosperous homes, suddenly stop, right here ... where Venice begins. Venice is a poor neighbourhood but, I think, a good place to invest ... It's on the up now, people are moving in, restaurants are opening ... that's always a sign of prosperity.'

A turban-attired man on roller skates ... a saxophonist with a paper bag on his head ... a one-man band who plays bass with his toes ... two comedians who juggle bowling balls over the head of a ten-year-old ... two miles of joggers ... skaters ... painters ... religious con men ... and stalls, stalls, stalls ... the reggae stall is of most interest, especially to the Hudsons who share their colours with the Rastafarians.

'Mine are not the Rastafarian colours,' says Tim, addressing the Rasta behind the stall. 'Mine are the colours of the Hudson Bay

Company, the oldest company in the world. The colours are the same but the sequence is different.'

The Rasta, incidentally, is perfectly charming, in a way that only Rastas can be, but I guess you have to lock yourself in conversation with a particularly exuberant one to understand what I mean. Anyway, back to Tim.

'They are also the colours of Flower Power. We have a common interest with Rastafarians ... there are many similarities ... and Bob Marley noticed this...'

But the Rasta has a stern warning for Juliana's camera.

'Look, I'm a little more cool than most Rastas. I believe in one love ... and all that. I don't mind but you should never, ever film a Rasta before asking if it is all right. He believes that photographs are stealing from him, and in a way he is right. I see myself on postcards ... someone is making money from me ... I don't mind ... but some of them do, and they get very heavy...'

Thursday, 2 February
Pete Kameron
Pete Kameron is something of a reclusive music business legend. In the early Fifties he helped pioneer the strange art of record promotion. From his involvement with early black blues and jazz artists in America, he went on to achieve status as the prime mover behind the likes of The Who in the Sixties.

Pete Kameron first met Tim Hudson at Alfie's flat, back in Chelsea, in the early Sixties. He was one of the men sitting on the couch when James Coburn suggested that Hudson should go and become a DJ in America.

Kameron lives in an exquisite house in Laurel Canyon. Today, although happy to be adrift from the main artery of the music industry, his involvements are many. Ranging from films to the phenomenally successful *LA Weekly*, in my opinion the greatest free newspaper in the world.

Pete Kameron didn't have to agree to talk to us but the fact that he politely allowed us to walk effortlessly into his living room is, itself, significant of his respect for Tim. This is the first time, *ever*, that Pete

Kameron has agreed to talk about himself and his business, however succinctly, in the presence of a tape recorder.

Tim: 'Pete, when we first met in London, where were you working out of?'

Pete: 'New York. I was involved with a whole bunch of guys who, in 1950–51, made up a whole network of breaking records. We changed the face of the entire music business by what we did. We used to take an acetate (pre-release demo) round to the disc jockeys on radio stations all over America before the record had even been released. We could break any record. In those days, if you had so many record plays you would finally make the hit parade. That's how you launched a song. So we took the acetate and beat everyone to it. It took the rest of the music business three years to catch up with us.'

Tim: 'You were the first independent promoters, then?'

Peter: 'Yes, we learnt our craft from the speciality days because you used to have a whole network of black DJs who would cater to a black audience, and we would service them. So we just applied this logic to music in general.'

Tim: 'How did you first get involved with English artists?'

Pete: 'It was the English artists who were able to pick up and romanticise on the black music. All those Larry Parnes acts ... There was a certain charm about the British artists ... I think it was the British acts that really kicked black music off on an international basis. Mind you, Bob Dylan wouldn't have happened if it wasn't for The Weavers, who I managed. I always find it interesting, the older I get, to see how young artists react to the older stuff. I remember, for Stevie Wonder's birthday, I sent him a couple of Leadbelly albums and they really freaked him out...'

Tim: 'What were you doing, back in the Sixties, when I met you in London?'

Pete: 'Business ... originally I went over in '52 because we were being screwed by all those foreign publishers over this complex sub-publishing business and we decided to set up our own publishing system. So we started Essex Music. That's what I would have been doing when I met you. Essex Music published The Moody Blues, The Stones ... Deep Purple ... Black Sabbath...'

Tim: 'And what do you think of today's music?'

Pete: 'Well, I never really listen. I'm more interested in wine tasting or travelling around the world. Some of the British artists, Dire Straits ... Sting ... the more sophisticated stuff I like ... but it's all a foreign market to me now. I'm more into film, I suppose.'

Juliana: 'What do you think of video ... pop video?'

Pete: 'I think it's great. I think that whole new directors are going to come out of it. They have a fantastic eye but they have yet to get it together in terms of story. It's just a matter of time. I remember when I worked at Decca there was, in the studio, a huge picture of an Indian with his arms stretched out saying, "Where's The Melody?" I'll never forget that. So, whenever I get involved with movies, I always ask, "Where's The Story?" '

Tim: 'Why do you think that radio is so bland today?'

Pete: 'Well ... you have certain personalities but it just became formula. Everything has escalated in price. Once you could buy a television station for a few million dollars. It's three hundred million now. A simple FM radio station is 18 million so you just *have* to get ratings. If you discover a format and you transmit that format to a hundred radio stations, you don't need personalities ... that's economics.'

Tim: 'A pity. I'd like to see a radio station where you just throw a guy a pile of records and say, "Hey, there you go ... I don't mind what you do, what you play ... but do it well. You have three hours ... make it interesting." '

Pete: 'Well, unfortunately we are in a profit-motive world. I gave up fighting. I don't even bother with it any more. But economics serves a very big purpose. Everything is bottom line. Once, radio stations were run by guys who loved music, films were made by people who loved films, but now it's all conglomerates and they are only concerned with the bottom line.'

Tim: 'I went to a radio station the other day. KLSX. I had a meeting there with this guy but, you know what? He was so hassled. So tense, the atmosphere was horrible. I don't need that. I felt relieved when I walked out. How can anybody work in an atmosphere like that? It's horrible.'

Pete: 'It *is* horrible, but that's the way the world is now ... there's no going back.'

Now there's one thing about the Hudsons that one must remember at all times. They are social anarchists. They have this harmless but intriguing habit of throwing situations together, standing back, and observing the chemical reaction. After leaving Pete Kameron's house, I had assumed we would be heading back to Malibu, but this was not to be. Instead, the car pulls to a halt outside a typical Hollywood bungalow.

'Oh, I forgot to tell you, Mick,' says Tim. 'We are visiting my old friend and colleague Niki. We used to be partners in the Sixties. We had a kind of management agency. Now, I must warn you, he is a little bit eccentric.'

Niki, as it turns out, isn't a little bit eccentric. He's *wildly* eccentric. An artist. He is the only man, this decade, that I've seen wearing bell-bottom jeans. His speech is fast and his paintings, which literally line this residence, are generally surrealist. Each one containing some kind of UFO.

'Have you ever seen a UFO, Niki?'

'Oh yes, many times. In the desert ... you see many UFOs in the desert, they are there all the time.'

In the back room sits the bulk of Niki's art collection. Layer upon layer of heavy surrealism. Why doesn't he sell them?

Niki: 'What, why should I sell them? They exist ... that's enough.'

On the table, in the living room, sits a small sign saying, 'WHO CARES?' This appears to be Niki's current catchphrase. At times, in the past, this odd-looking Dr Who character has thrown himself into the fury of business ... he has thrived on the hassle ... but now, his work seems confined to his art. Outside, the garden is his work room. Behind a virgin canvas lies a huge built-in concrete bowl full of cigarette dimps.

'Ahh ... that's my ashtray,' he says, before adding, 'Cuppa tea ... you wanna cuppa tea? You English are all the same ... always wanting a cuppa tea ... there's the tea bags ... make one ... make one.'

The banter, mainly between Tim and Niki, smashes around like a pinball ... a million tales of past business ... past hedonism.

Niki: 'Tim here used to have one of my paintings behind his chair in the office. It was a picture of a huge rock surrounded by small pebbles and when some hopeful band would walk in, Tim would direct their attention to this painting. "See that rock," he would say. "That's me ... I'm that rock ... and these little pebbles here ... they are you ... you are just insignificant little pebbles..." Hey, Tim ... remember that time we turned down the chance of managing The Doors?'

Tim: 'No Niki ... we didn't turn The Doors down ... where did you get that idea from?'

Niki: 'Yes, my friend, we did.'

Tim: 'No ... no, I'm sure we didn't.'

Niki: 'Yes ... yes ... you forget ... you forget a lot.'

Tim: 'That's true.'

Tuesday, 7 February
Jonathon Moore
We are with Jonathon Moore, a stand-up comedian ... and a few other things. He's small, cute, very 'Dudley'. Tends to colour his humour blue but, that aside, a great wit!

Tim: 'Was there a conspiracy?'

Jonathon: 'Ermm ... a conspiracy? I don't know. Was it anything to do with Dean Martin? That's the only thing I can think of because Tim, you were the biggest DJ and the only English DJ here. (*Turns to me.*) He was, you know ... Tim was a massive star in Hollywood. But it was unusual because people wouldn't normally hire an Englishman even though England was popular, because they thought nobody would understand you.'

Maxi: 'Kids wouldn't relate?'

Jonathon: 'Yeah ... or some dogshit like that ... but anyway ... they *did* relate and you started a whole new trend and there will always be a conspiracy about that ... There was a conspiracy to stop me from working because I was English. They resented us being here. But I don't know why you vanished. Unless you said something like "Fuck off" on air or something, because in those days you would be immediately fired.'

Maxi: 'Yes, but you would be allowed to come back ... nowadays

211

people say all kinds of things on air. No ... there's more to it than that. There's a whole undercurrent ... there's a mystery. Mick, you noticed it in Manchester when you wrote that article. WHY? It's the same over there ... isn't it?'

Tim: 'Look, Jonathon ... was there a conspiracy to get Lord Tim off the air?'

Jonathon: 'Yeah ... yes there was, but you can't put it directly to the people you feel might be responsible.'

Maxi: 'It's too dangerous ... I'm sorry ... some of the people we are presently contacting ... there is so much fear ... people are terrified of talking ... terrified.'

Jonathon: 'I wish I knew why because I never knew such a disappearance. Suddenly, you were gone.'

Maxi: 'There was one guy we asked if we could interview and he said, "No ... if I talk to you I'll be out of here within twenty-four hours." And this wasn't isolated ... people just clam up.'

Mary Hughes

Mary Hughes, blonde, dressed in chic black leather, walks into the Malibu house looking every bit the LA woman of the Eighties. Although still on the fringe of the film industry – she had a screen test two days prior to this meeting – she now dabbles in real estate and runs a gymnasium, which, frankly, is just about as Californian as you can get. She speaks softly, politely, warmly.

Mary: 'You came, Tim, as part of the British invasion. You took over with enormous popularity. You were in for a long time.'

Tim: 'The only excuse anyone gave me was, one guy said, "The British invasion is over."'

Mary: 'I think that was B. Mitchell Reed. He didn't like your popularity.'

Tim: 'None of the other DJs really liked me. They were all wearing suits and ties ... They were very conservative people.'

Mary: 'It's just that listening to you was magnetic ... it was like, it wired you out. What can I say? You had everybody going ... you could feel your energy through the radio and the bandwagon just followed you.'

Tim: I didn't play shit. I didn't play Herman's Hermits or any of that stuff...'

Mary: 'No, because that wasn't your style ... Y'know, I never thought there were conspiracies to get you off, I just thought it was B. Mitchell Reed. Jealousy. Simple.'

Tim: 'But why would he kill me? I was his natural successor, you see. I really felt that I wanted to wear the Mitchell Reed mantle ... and I did. Maybe I was un-Californian. I always thought that yourself, and Eddie, were typically Californian ... very nice in the true sense of the word. Californian people are very nice.'

Mary: 'We are nice, there are some nasty ones, but we were the generation of the love child ... flowers...'

Tim: 'You weren't corrupted by the big city ... the big city had not got, then, into California...'

Mary: 'We are different ... in California you don't wear many clothes. The climate allows you all that freedom. You are really suppressed when you wear a lot of clothes ... like today, it's really cold but, normally, when you are in shorts and T-shirts you feel more open. We just feel free because we are so used to being undressed, that's really what makes us different.'

Tim: 'Mary, when was the first time you saw a psychedelic light show?'

Mary: 'The same one that you saw. At The Trip. The Trip was the place that was the hippest club. It was new, exciting. I used to go to The Trip and The Whisky, and back and forth. When I was working on all those beach movies I'd go out, all dressed up ... go home at midnight and start work at 5 am again. In those days you didn't sleep or eat. The Trip was the first place where you could get up and dance ... you could not do that before the English invasion ... then you could walk into those places alone.'

Tim: 'How did you get into movies?'

Mary: 'Michael Nadar ... He now plays Dex in *Dynasty*. Now he is a bona fide actor, a big star but in those days he was struggling. I knew him because we went to the same beach. Michael had done the first beach picture and basically he asked me to be a contract player. I did fifteen or sixteen films and an Elvis Presley movie. I did a lot of work.'

Tim: 'Who do you think was the best LA group?'

Mary: 'That has to be Love. As you suggested, I was not a Doors fan. I saw them at so many private parties. I think, by the time they made it, I was sick of them. I always preferred British music anyway.'

Tim: 'You knew Jeff Beck probably better than anyone. I always wondered if he was ever worried that he never really made it on a massive level.'

Mary: 'He could have gone very big but he was just too sensitive. If you said one little thing to him he would just go away and sulk. Just too sensitive. The reason he left The Yardbirds is that he was so wrapped up in something else that he couldn't show up for a gig. Then he started the Jeff Beck Group who were the best ... Jimmy Page, Jeff Beck, Rod Stewart, Jan Hammer ... the best musicians ever ... Jeff's guitar playing, even today, is supreme.'

Big Al

Big Al was in the mailroom at KFWB in the days of Lord Tim. Then he became owner of the Seventies punk venue The Relic House, where *Where Were You In '65* was performed. Latterly, he has been a highly qualified lighting technician working mainly in television. Al, from Tennessee, is something of a gentle giant, a reformed ex-biker with a thirst for Budweiser.

Tim: 'What position did you hold in the KFWB mailroom?'

Al: 'I was in charge of the mailroom.'

Tim: 'No ... don't give yourself titles. You were the mailroom clerk.'

Al: 'I was the mailroom supervisor. I had two people that worked for me. At the time I had to get all the credit I could get. There were several things involved with that job. Sorting out mail, fan mail. Remember *The Hit Line*, the KFWB newspaper? We had to deliver it to all the liquor stores around town. Handling all the prize stuff.'

Tim: 'How did you get into the mailroom?'

Al: 'I don't remember. It was a job. I applied for it.'

Tim: 'How did you get to LA? From where?'

Al: 'I came from Knoxville, Tennessee. Originally a couple of friends of mine came out from college. We were gonna dig beans in summer ... run around ... have a good time in '62.'

Tim: 'You told me a funny story. You were in Cuba the day the revolution broke, or something...'

Al: 'Oh yeah, that was a couple of years before I came to LA. I was in college and some friends of mine were invited out there. I said, haven't they got problems or something, but they said, "Ahh, don't worry about that, it's no big deal." So they talked me into it. After I got there the rebels started coming out of the hills and before I knew it we were in the middle of a civil war. We were so scared all we could do was laugh. Bullets flying all around, plaster falling down, gunfire outside our hotel room.'

Tim: 'How did you get out?'

Al: 'We had to get permission ... we were supposed to fly out on New Year's Day and on New Year's Eve there was a general strike. We were really stuck. We couldn't get anything to eat for three days but tuna fish and cookies. I have never got so tired of tuna fish in all my life and I would have paid good money for a good old American sandwich. It was rough.'

Tim: 'Then in LA. I never talked to you at the radio station ... you were one of the guys I'd bump into every now and then.'

Al: 'Yeah ... I was stuck in the mailroom ... the mailroom was where everyone came to complain. Everyone who had a complaint took it to the mailroom. I remember one day, you were playing this song on the radio, continuously. It played, and it played, and it played, and it played, and it played and it played...'

Tim: 'Come on, Al.'

Al: 'Wait a minute ... I was listening to this song and this secretary came running into the room screaming, "THAT IDIOT HAS BEEN PLAYING THIS SONG OVER AND OVER AGAIN AND HE IS GONNA GET FIRED." What was that song?'

Tim: 'I don't know, I did that a lot. *These Boots Were Made For Walking? River Deep Mountain High?*'

Al: 'I can see B. Mitchell Reed, God love him, I can see him now coming into that mailroom with his hands up in the air, looking at the ceiling, walking round in circles and going, "WHY ME." When you were on prime time people were coming in saying, "Look at this man,

215

Lord Tim ... look at the state of him," because you were on a better contract than anyone else, and at that station even a little dude like me had to wear a suit and tie, everybody had to. But you came to work in jeans and T-shirts and everyone went, "WOW". It was different, really different.'

Tim: 'It never happened in America, did it? That some guy like me would just walk in and be a disc jockey.'

Al: 'It never happened anywhere that I heard.'

Tim: 'We feel that there was a conspiracy to get me off the radio. The name B. Mitchell Reed has cropped up a few times now. Is this another example? This guy coming into your office, pulling his hair out and saying, "Oh gawd, this guy has taken my gig?"'

Al: 'There was a general complaint that you weren't even a DJ, and that you were reading magazine articles over the air ... but so what? What difference did it make? The thing is, and this tripped everyone out, you had the ratings. It didn't matter if it was just magazine articles. It didn't matter if you were just reading classified ads, because you had a delivery that none of them had. They couldn't cope with that. They couldn't understand because they were all suits and ties.'

Tim: 'And the average DJ on that station was at least ten years older than me. It wasn't just age ... they all looked like they had made it. That they had arrived ... they had made it to the top in their profession an' me, maaan, I wasn't even a DJ. Yet here I was in Hollywood. I was warned by my manager, actually. He told me not to speak to anyone, to just go in, do my gig, and get out because I was an intruder in their private domain ... Al, do you remember going out on that little promotion scooter?'

Al: 'Yeah, I'm glad you brought that up, actually. There was this promo going one, I'll never forget. Part of my duties was to drive round on this motorbike with this gold sportscoat and on the back it had the name of a DJ. I had one with Lord Tim on the back ... and it wasn't even a real motorbike, it was more like a girl's motorbike ... and I was oversize for it in the first place. So there was I, putting around town on this thing, on Sunset Boulevard, Beverly Hills. I didn't know you had to mix oil with gasoline and the engine overheated ... So it broke down and I was sitting on the kerb in this Lord Tim jacket. People were driving up and down waving at me ... and there was not a thing that I could do but wave back ... and wait for the engine to cool down.'

Tim: 'Then at the end of 1979 you turned up at my place. Now tell me how you got to my place. I last saw you in 1966 ... and then the next time was 1979 and you owned a club, The Relic House.'

Al: 'Bobby Buck came to see me at The Relic House...'

Tim: 'Hang on ... yes, I performed *Egomania* with Bobby Buck at The Troubadour. It was awful. The first twenty minutes were mine, the audience loved it, they were applauding and whistling, then all of a sudden, WAAANG. In comes Bobby Buck with (sings slowly) "Here at last, America" ... Oh God, we died a death. I was so angry, my wife (Lady B) was angry but this guy from Venice came along and offered to put *Egomania* on at his club. Bob begged me to do it but I said, "No way am I ever getting on stage with you again in my life." So we broke up and he came to see you with his show, called *Wish Wash*, or something. He took his own slides, made his own show and you were the first dude he saw. You had a club. One of the very first punk, intimate, different-type beer bars. Entertainment seven nights a week. I had never seen such a place. Comedians with rock groups. Normally they would be playing toilets. Well, Al's wasn't a toilet. It was a club in the Valley called The Relic House and Bobby Buck came to sell you his show.'

Al: 'Yeah, so he had this show and I asked him if he could draw a crowd. He said that his friend, Lord Tim, could. I said, "LORD TIM? There's only one Lord Tim in the world. I used to work with him." But I thought he was jivin'. I didn't think he could get you on there. I'd heard you on KRLA, I knew you were still around. I knew Lord Tim but Lord Tim didn't know me. First you came to my club then, after that I came up to Gable's Lodge, Clark Gable's old house, to talk about putting you on as a one-man show. There had been a few one-man shows that had been quite successful. I had never tried that in a club but the story was there, I knew the history was there, the classic Beatles interview, the whole works. It's a great story.'

Thursday, 9 February
Oscar's Restaurant, Sunset Strip
Oscar's Restaurant, on Sunset Strip, is a famous hang-out for many film

stars, especially visiting British ones. It is owned by Michelle, a girl who
first met Tim in Chelsea in the early Sixties. Upon opening Oscar's, in
1975, she brought a touch of delightful English sycophancy – I use this
word in its nicest possible context – to the otherwise rather brash Sunset
Strip. This little interview is conducted in the back room, a cosy affair
guarded by painted tigers and frequented by the odd passing movie star.

Tim: 'Michelle here has this marvellous restaurant, called Oscar's,
right in the centre of the Sunset Strip, as I call it. You can't be any
more Sunset Strip than down from Carlos And Charlie's, down below
the Château Marmont and next to the biggest billboard on Sunset, the
Marlboro man. Michelle here has brought the Englishness here ... not
lager-lout Britishness, it has been done here with a certain Noel
Cowardish feel. This restaurant has his ambience, where people want to
dress up ... exciting ... attractive.'

Michelle: 'Oh yes ... especially with the music room ... we have
Forties- and Fifties-type sounds. There aren't really any other English
restaurants, there are fish'n'chip places.'

Tim: 'Like me, Michelle, you came out of the Chelsea set in the
early Sixties. Why do you think that whole thing exploded?'

Michelle: 'Well, I think when it was the Chelsea set it was just
artists ... and interesting people too ... artists, heiresses, actors,
designers like Mary Quant used to have her little shop and sell her
clothes upstairs.'

Tim: 'And there weren't that many restaurants around then...'

Michelle: 'No, in the early days they were very stiff, the
restaurants then. In the late Fifties you went and ate at the Caprice ...
all dinner jackets. There were no casual restaurants, except the odd
bistro in the West End. Are you leading me up to how The Casserole
started? Yes? I think The Casserole, apart from Alexanders, owned by
Mary Quant, was the first restaurant of its kind to do a casual-style
restaurant. Everyone was young and it suddenly really took on. That
was my first day in the restaurant business, that day The Casserole
opened. It was very exciting.'

Tim: 'There's a movie just come out in London, about that scene,
the Profumo affair.'

Michelle: 'Yes, I was reading about that. Christine Keeler, Mandy

Rice Davies, they all used to come into The Casserole. They lived just round the corner.'

Tim: 'Now, you opened Oscar's in ... 1975? Why did you come here? How did it happen?'

Michelle: 'I came for a holiday at first. I did all the things you do when you come to LA. I went to the beach, went to Hollywood. It was a couple of months before myself and one other person decided to open Oscar's.'

Tim: 'What has been the most interesting aspect of the Oscar's years? We've gone from 1975 to, well, nearly 1990 now ... what have been the most interesting people you have met through this restaurant?'

Michelle: 'Well ... I was most excited when I knew that Billy Wilder was coming here for dinner, he was a great hero of mine. Some of the wonderful old directors ... and, of course, all the actors ... De Niro, Richard Gere ... I don't know where to begin ... they all came in here. But the best was to meet some of the people in the movie industry I had really admired ... writers ... Christopher Isherwood used to hang around here ... screenplay writers, script writers ... all the English people who have been in here have been very interesting ... David Puttnam ... even Laurence Olivier ate here. Unfortunately, that was one of the days that I wasn't here. Anyway, he recognised my bartender who had done a small part in a play at the National Theatre ... He even remembered his name...'

Saturday, 11 February
It is Tim's birthday. There is a party at the Malibu house. A cumulative bash, attended by many of the people we have met during the past few weeks ... and more. The entire kaboodle, captured by the camera of Juliana, which is just as well as I, somewhat unprofessionally, sink steadily into a Tequila-induced haze and much of the proceedings are subsequently erased from my memory. Such is life.

Monday, 13 February
Cordula calls round to tell us that she is leaving for Europe, apparently looking after Sky Saxon on his European tour with the SSS Dragonslayers. Hardly the easiest of tasks but, if it gets her back into

219

Europe after all these years, then surely it will be a good thing.

'I'd love to see England again,' she states and this thought seems to be shared in the Malibu house.

Tim: 'Yeah ... I'd like to get back now ... It's great out here but I'm missing my garden. Just standing there, watering the plants, I'd be happy doing that for the rest of my life. I hate business.'

Maxi: 'You don't hate business ... you love it ... Really.'

Tim: 'Well, sometimes ... but I don't love the hassle. Like, when we get back ... well ... Maxi has got to go to court to fight for our drinks licence back for the Pavilion. That's a problem that has come about just because of people, neighbours being deliberately obstructive. It's really stupid ... dumb ... narrow-minded ... pointless.'

But there are, it seems, a few positive things happening over in Manchester. Tim and Maxi's friend, millionaire cavalier entrepreneur Owen Oyston, is locked in battle for the control of the Manchester-based IBA radio station, Piccadilly Radio. A station that, in its present, rather confused state of hierarchy, has never really seen eye to eye with Tim. 'Things are about to change,' he says. 'It's going to be a good year.'

July 1989
Postscript

It goes on, you know ... it just goes on and on and on. Malibu is now a treasured memory and it is my intention, here, to put the chapter to rest with a little retrospective thinking. But that's impossible ... every time I put the pen down (or, as is the modern equivalent, every time I switch the word processor off), the phone rings. On the line is Hudson ... enthusing wildly ... a new scam has been born ... a new idea ... a new chapter. Today, for instance, Tim Hudson bid £60,000 to become Lord of the Cheshire manor of Birtles. So he really is a Lord now ... and Maxi a Lady of the Manor.

This London auction has been filmed by *Granada Reports*, Manchester's local current affairs television programme. It is a fun story ... indeed, it is a 'money' story but money *can* be fun. The people of Manchester do realise this. They will watch this broadcast, perhaps from Whalley Range or Hulme ... and will they be appalled? Will they take offence? I don't think so because this man Hudson doesn't flaunt his wealth in a cold, cynical manner, he parodies it, so skilfully, so joyously. The irony of this auction will not, I feel, be lost on the ordinary people of Manchester. On the other hand, as usual, there is certain to be the odd indignant squeal, no doubt emanating from somebody who sees Hudson as a major threat. Personally, I don't think he seriously threatens, or harms, anyone.

They are in a celebratory mood down at Birtles ... the whole gang ... Tim, Maxi, Suzi the secretary, Harry the chauffeur ... Cordula, cricketer Geoff Foley and, quite possibly, some young journalist who has driven down for an interview. But we just have to stop here ... we have to draw a line ... quickly ... before something else happens ... and it will. And as soon as this book goes to print, we will all regret that we couldn't wait another week longer, just to capture the most recent, totally unexpected developments. But, of course, we would just go on forever. So it's good, at least as far as 'The Hudsons in Hollywood' chapter is concerned, to let it snap here, and float away into recent history.

INDEX